Women, Culture, and International Relations

Critical Perspectives
on World Politics
◇
R. B. J. Walker, Series Editor

Women, Culture, and International Relations

◇

edited by

Vivienne Jabri
Eleanor O'Gorman

LYNNE
RIENNER
PUBLISHERS

BOULDER
LONDON

Published in the United States of America in 1999 by
Lynne Rienner Publishers, Inc.
1800 30th Street, Boulder, Colorado 80301

and in the United Kingdom by
Lynne Rienner Publishers, Inc.
3 Henrietta Street, Covent Garden, London WC2E 8LU

Library of Congress Cataloging-in-Publication Data
Women, culture, and international relations /   edited by Vivienne Jabri
    and Eleanor O'Gorman.
        p.   cm.
    Includes bibliographical references and index.
    ISBN 1-55587-701-X (hc.   :   alk. paper)
    1. International relations.   2. Feminist theory.   3. International
relations and culture.   I. Jabri, Vivienne, 1958–   .
II. O'Gorman, Eleanor, 1968–   .
JZ1253.2.W66   1999
327.1'01—dc21   99-19295
                                                                       CIP

British Cataloguing in Publication Data
A Cataloguing in Publication record for this book
is available from the British Library.

Printed and bound in the United States of America

⊗   The paper used in this publication meets the requirements
      of the American National Standard for Permanence of
      Paper for Printed Library Materials Z39.48-1984.

    5 4 3 2 1

Contents

v

Acknowledgments

We express our gratitude to our contributors for their participation in this project and for their support. We are grateful to the Feminist Theory and Gender Studies Section of the International Studies Association (ISA) for their sponsorship of our panel, "Women, Culture, and International Relations," at the 1996 ISA conference in San Diego. We thank our discussants at that panel, Mark Hoffman and Marysia Zalewski, for their helpful comments. Richard Purslow of Lynne Rienner Publishers is, as always, a source of solid support; our thanks also go to Gia Hamilton of Lynne Rienner Publishers for her assistance in producing the book. For computing advice, we are most grateful to Peter Mandaville and Rafal Rohozinski.

Eleanor O'Gorman thanks staff and students of the School of Development Studies at the University of East Anglia for fruitful discussions around gender, conflict, and development.

Vivienne Jabri expresses her thanks to all colleagues in the Department of Politics and International Relations at the University of Kent who stood in for her while she was on sabbatical. She is especially grateful to Mervyn Frost and Jef Huysmans and to all members of the Critical Theory Reading Group, who are her intellectual lifeline.

—The Editors

1

Locating Difference in Feminist International Relations

Eleanor O'Gorman & Vivienne Jabri

Feminist international relations (IR) has emerged in the past decade as a key critique within the discipline of international relations. The initial impetus of this critique was to challenge the fundamental bases of the discipline in highlighting the ways in which women were excluded from analyses of the state, international political economy, and international security. These traditional concerns were revealed to be male biased in resting upon Enlightenment tenets of the acting male subject in a state-centric world. Writers such as Cynthia Enloe helped to forge a feminist agenda that claimed the international as personal and questioned the primacy of the state as an international actor.

This first wave of feminist international relations has sought to reclaim women's hidden voices. The focus of research and publications has been directed at deconstructing major discipline-defining texts and uncovering gender biases in the paradigmatic discourses that have dominated the field since its inception in 1919. This has served to unravel the negation of the role of women in global politics and the exclusion of specifically feminist contributions to the analysis of such central themes as war, economic inequality, human rights, and the state. The efforts of major feminist voices in the discipline have undoubtedly had an impact, both in terms of research and in the teaching of IR theory.

The rise of feminism in international relations has been central to the critical turn in the discipline. Part of this postpositivist challenge is to write the discipline beyond the conventional triad of IR theory, namely, realism, liberalism, and structuralism. In common with other reformers, feminists have sought to question the boundaries of the discipline in terms of understanding the international and in terms of problematizing the nature and effect of relations at the level of the international.

In place of the universalizing tendencies of a discourse built upon the

1

Westphalian legacy, the critical turn has sought to move the intellectual project of our discipline so that the givens are no longer so, so that the certainties that naturalized the state and sovereignty are recognized for the reifications that they are rather than necessary conditions of ordered human interaction. Thus opening a space for interrogations of our knowledge claims, we begin to ask questions relating to who we are as subjects and how we relate to others in our societies and to those "outside."

Just as the state as the primary location of the political is questioned,[1] so too the positionality of the self as citizen comes under scrutiny where the private comes into direct confrontation with the public—where that which constitutes agency is placed in the context of the structural continuities that surround and constitute the life-world of the individual. Issues relating to global inequality and distributive justice, human rights, cultural diversity, and democratic practice come to acquire a pivotal position in a critical and normative discourse that seeks not only understanding of the forces of differential constraint and enablement but also a form of transformation of the present order.

The objective of this book is to contribute to the expansion of the agenda of feminist international relations by considering the heterogeneity of women's voices in the realm of world politics and the epistemological and ethical challenges this poses for feminist international relations. The book is concerned with developing a theoretical discourse that incorporates the combined notions of difference, culture, and subjectivity and their implications for how we conceive the agency of women and their transformative capacities. In seeking to theorize the multiple subjectivities of women and the plurality of their experiential locations, the chapters in the book draw upon major critical voices in philosophy, cultural studies, postcolonial studies, feminist ethics, and development studies. If we were to characterize the commonalities between the chapters, these would center on the question of subjectivity and its construction. Rather than pretending to include "other" voices, we engage with the question of how the theories *we* draw upon—from postcolonial discourses, Foucauldian genealogy, the ethic of care to Habermasian thought and Rortian pragmatism—contribute to the incorporation of difference within a discourse that seeks to transform practices of exclusion. The book is therefore theoretical in orientation and focuses on constructs of culture, the ontologies of "self" and "other," gendered positionality, and difference.

The aim of this collection is to contribute to the feminist discourse in international relations by investigating the place of difference and its impact on developing a feminist approach to normative and epistemological questions in international relations. In addressing the question of difference, and specifically cultural difference, the book situates feminism within the critical agenda of the discipline and in so doing makes a significant contribution to normative concerns around questions of rights, identity, and the transformation of the public sphere.

FEMINISM, FEMINIST IR, AND DIFFERENCE

Understandings of difference have been at the heart of the feminist critique in IR. The first wave of feminist IR challenged the epistemological bases of international relations and revealed the systematic exclusion of women's experiences as central to the established concerns of knowledge-creation in the discipline. These early works sought to deconstruct the gendered oppositions that excluded women from the core concepts of state, security, and the economy and to explore gender relations as power relations focused on the binary opposition between men and women and the relative values assigned to them. The main focus of difference was therefore on assumptions of masculinity and femininity in defining men and women as subjects of IR. The use of a gender lens exposed the methodological blind spots that created particular understandings of "men" and "women" in IR. V. Spike Peterson and Anne Runyan's elaboration of the "presence/absence" dynamic of gender power relations exemplifies this lens:

> Through a gender-sensitive lens, we can see how constructions of masculinity are not independent, but dependent upon, opposing constructions of femininity. In a sense, the presence of men depends on the absence of women. Because of this interdependence, a gender analysis of women's lives and experiences does not simply "add something" about women but transforms what we know about men and the activities they undertake.[2]

Situating the exclusion of gender within the context of the realist dominance of the discipline, Jill Steans highlights how "methodological individualism" has shaped the male-centered concepts and categories of international relations:

> Gender has been denied salience as an issue in International Relations because the discipline has been seen as constituted by a system of states which relate to one another in a context of anarchy. . . . The invisibility or marginalisation of gender issues in the study of International Relations is a consequence of methodological individualism which begins with a high level of abstraction, taking the state to be the key actor. The realist conception of the state as actor has been built upon the supposedly unproblematic figure of "sovereign man."[3]

The epistemological consequence that arises from such ontological certainty is that "sovereign man is in some sense held to embody the 'truth' about international relations."[4]

Cynthia Enloe was a pioneer in unmasking the silent workings of women in the myriad structures of international relations. The factory worker, chamber maid, tourist, and consumer were faces that we could recognize and that we now claim as legitimate subjects of international relations.[5] In claiming the international as personal, such gender critiques succeeded in shattering fundamental tenets of western thought, primary among which were the constitutive dichotomies built upon the separation of the public from the private and mind from body. The exclusions operative within this discourse were shown to be so deeply embedded that a reconception of the personal as political disrupted the core features of international relations thought. The discipline was challenged to rethink conceptions of sovereignty, bounded territory, and state relations based variously on the distribution of capabilities or rule following within a "society" of states. Rebecca Grant and Kathleen Newland set the challenge of developing a feminist epistemology in IR to effect this deconstruction. "A feminist epistemology means most simply that gender becomes a prime element in understanding the theory and practice of international relations."[6] What has emerged in the subsequent development of feminist international relations is a rich tapestry of works that reaffirm the continued contestation about meanings and representations of gender, feminism, "women," and "woman." The development of feminist epistemology has proved a contested exercise in the reworkings of gender power, identities, and the significance of other tropes of difference in defining social relations.

This development of feminist theory has not taken place in isolation but has drawn on wider debates in feminist social theory and tailored them to specific issues and deconstructions in international relations. Feminism as social movement and as theory emerged as a discourse of dissent. Its remit as social and political theory combines a critique of the present order with a desire to transform practices that inscribe woman as other. Its content is at the same time normative and political. As a normative discourse, it seeks to locate the moral and ethical implications of gendered social relations and the inclusions and exclusions that arise from the transformation of such relations. As a critical discourse, it seeks to relate a critique of knowledge with practical concerns around questions of equality, recognition, and freedom from oppressive social practices. The substantive content of such critique and the advocacy of a transformative discourse, however, immediately point to the troubled relationship that feminism has with the subject of "woman" and her agency. Since it emerged from a western context, feminism as a social movement and as theory has had to confront a critique from within its own constructed boundaries. In attempting to deal with the question of difference, feminism has historically varied its responses in terms of, on the one hand, a belief in the universal emancipation of women and, on the other hand, a wish to recognize the contingent daily lives of situated women. Whether we talk of a single universalism or a number of different universalisms, feminism as a primarily western discourse is daily confronted by images of both direct and structural violence perpetrated against women. These women are, however, differently located along axes of domination and therefore have differential access to rights and resources; and they have different security concerns and widely divergent capacities for dissent and transformation.

International relations are inscribed with subjectivities of race and class as well as gender in shaping international agendas and the operation of power at the level of the international. Therefore, the question becomes how men and women—and women among themselves—are differentiated and placed in different situations of risk, powerlessness, power, and security at the international level. Such understandings can be forged only through an apprehension of the interconnectedness of the international with regional, national, local, and personal relations in producing what we claim as the international.

A second wave of feminists in the discipline are now turning to confront the tensions and opportunities posed by difference among "women" and within "woman" as subject. This development mirrors the crisis perceived in the wider field of feminist theory where controversy exists over the place of collective feminist action in a postmodern context of differentiated and multiple subjectivities. The fractures of universal feminism arose from the challenge to the western, white, heterosexual, and middle-class center of the women's movement. Criticisms by "Third World" and "black" feminists prompted the exploration of differences within the movement.[7] The continued reflections on difference take place in a context where the impetus to act to transform gender power relations remains; poverty, war, and exploitation continue to claim their human costs.

There has emerged a caution against creating unreflexive categories of subjectivity that reinforce the separation of public/private and domestic/international. If women's nonpolitical identities in traditional IR were the result of constructed stereotypes, then so too must men have been constructed in nonrepresentative ways. Indeed, Jean Elshtain's early deconstructions of the "brave warrior" signaled such generalizations. Deconstructions of masculinity have consequently become a contested issue for feminist IR.[8] The sublimation of differences among women through the acceptance of a dichotomous gendered critique has also emerged, as in the continued development of a feminist critique in IR.

Jan Pettman and Christine Sylvester, taking very different approaches, have sought to redraw the territory of IR and place people and subjectivity at its center. Pettman, in ways similar to Enloe, offers us insights into the pluralities of difference that define, silence, and articulate women's positions and experiences of the international, through reworkings of sites of the "international" such as war, international institution building, coloniza-tion/decolonization, and international political economy.[9] Pettman, like Enloe, uses a rich resource of case examples to reveal the hidden world of IR beyond the western center and the elite understandings of markets, states, and militaries. The personal and the international merge as she explores the daily impact of international politics on the lives of women living very different lives across the globe. Pettman talks of "worlding women" to take account of worlds beyond an ethnocentric western center. In this way, differences among women are seen to be as important as differ-ences between women and men and are themselves drawn from under-standings of race, culture, and class as much as gender.

Writings about women from beyond the discipline form part of Pettman's project, which is explored in contexts of international trade and the conduct of war. Arguing that women's experience of the international is radically different from that of men, Pettman at the same time looks to western and nonwestern sources to stress that women and men are posi-tioned in multiple ways along highly complex intersections of power based on race, class, and sexuality. The challenge of placing relations between differently located people is not underestimated by Pettman. "Peopling IR is especially difficult, for traditionally IR takes states as its central unit. As IR makes states into international persons, most men and women are erased from its view."[10] A shared theme within the normative and political work of feminist IR has been the inclusion of women as subjects; in this way it has challenged the discipline to take cognizance of relations between people ("women" and "men"), between people and states, and between organiza-tions and economies as the dynamic of international politics and society. The challenge is nothing less than the redefinition of the constituency of IR. If people and relations, rather than states and militaries, are the primary subjects of IR, then what are the ethics, politics, and prescriptions of knowledge in the discipline?

Sylvester's normative treatise on feminist IR in a postmodern era also seeks to explore the "women" who are properly the inclusive concern of IR. She provides a devastating critique of the discipline's "great debates" while exploring the implications of feminist epistemologies for how we reconceive the international as political space. Recognizing the place of difference in any critical feminist discourse, she advocates a theoretical approach of "postmodernist feminism" that allows for a deconstruction of gendered absences and assumptions in the knowledge claims of IR while still holding on to the meaningful and multiple subjectivities of women as "subjects" of IR. In defining such a position, Sylvester develops "empathet-ic cooperation" as a feminist method that challenges the parameters of the discipline through conversation with the established theories of IR and through a reaching out to those who have been evacuated from the space of the international.

As Sylvester's arguments suggest, an important feature of such cooperation is the need to engage in "mutual recognition," not from unipolar subject positions but through the "insecuring embrace of mobile subjectivities." However, an important feature of discourses of difference is power. How difference inscribes women's experiences and voices, or silences them, is of tremendous import to the forging of feminist politics as the practice of resistance and dissent. The reclamation of voices and subjects "evacuated" from the territory of IR is the challenge posed by Sylvester in placing relations of difference at the center of a feminist critique of the discipline.

Of particular significance to such inclusiveness is Sylvester's exploration of the term *relations international,* when she challenges the imagination of the discipline to go beyond the sterile boundaries of international relations as relations among states and institutions and beyond contested assumptions about the inherency of cooperation or anarchy as the bases of such relations.[11] What emerges from this critique is a sense in which gender, culture, difference, and emancipation pose a rich tapestry of possibilities for feminist international relations. If we focus on the "international" as a contested area of many actors, issues, and processes and recognize that it builds upon, rather than separately from, other levels of social and political being, we can then concern ourselves with the mapping of "relations." Such a focus reveals that relations may be highly racialized and gendered, as well as being based on differential access to power resources. Furthermore, relations may be among peoples, states and peoples, states and organizations, and peoples and organizations. These relations are not exclusive, and indeed international relations is about the simultaneous living of such relations. It is not simply then about states in relation to each other or women in relation to the state, but the very essence of the international being is understood as relational.

These projects challenge the givens of international relations so that these can no longer be treated as gender-neutral discursive spaces but as highly contested issues that are steeped in relations of power. Despite wide differences in style and epistemological orientation, Sylvester and Pettman share the view that although women's lived experience is multiply located, it is still subject to the gendered discursive and institutional practices that typify woman as "other." Within feminist IR the fragmentation of subjectivity remains critical if we are not to replicate the oppressive categorizations and exclusions of the metanarrative. Put simply, we cannot aspire to a feminist metanarrative of history in aping the modernist discourses that have built the discipline of IR thus far. It is this realization that has created anxiety, not just within feminist IR but within wider areas of feminist theory as well.

Accusations of discursive colonialism have also prompted western feminists to be more reflexive about difference and its constructions in feminist theory and politics. Chandra Mohanty is critical of western feminism, which she sees as creating the homogenizing effects of a discursive colonialism by making assumptions about the inclusion of "third world women" and, in so doing, erasing the different experiences of such women.[12] Mohanty's criticism highlights the need to recognize difference and the power relations that inscribe difference if we are not to perpetuate cultural stereotypes in understanding "others'" experiences. The trend of categorizing "third world women" in this way is described by Mohanty as the operation of power through a "process of discursive homogenization and systemization of the oppression of women in the third world."[13] Mohanty's concern of "discursive colonialism" is well placed. Geographical location, urbanization, poverty, education, class, caste, and sex all intermesh differently to define the struggles of a differentiated category of agents often subsumed as "Third World Women." Some women will be better positioned than others to resist and survive. However, discursive colonialism is not only geographically bounded in representing "other" women of the "Third World," but it also suppresses differences within the category of the "West." The many struggles of women enacted through various sites of oppression and resistance differentially locate "women" in the "West." Poverty, exclusion, racism, homophobia, and sexism, together and separately, map the places where difference is contested and mobilized. In deconstructing the monoliths of West/Third World, the "voices beyond" can find a place to speak and be listened to: young girls and women in rural areas of sub-Saharan Africa, exiles in the migrant farmworker camps of the United States, and homeless people on the streets of Britain.

Pettman also refers to the project of decolonizing feminism. A key task she identifies is the recognition of the power inscribed in "whiteness." The ethnic constructions of power that leave white unreflected contain the assumptions of power and difference that underpin the distancing, denigration, and silencing of the "other." The political understanding of the construct "white" is now being understood in its unspoken nonracialized assumptions of self. The white self is viewed as the norm, whereas nonwhite "others" are seen to have "race" and "ethnicity."[14] We can speak of an organizational culture of states and international organizations that replicates this. The western cultural bias of international relations is problematic, with an assumed core political identity around the sovereign state or around organizational actors who know the rules of the game. We can also see the international as ignoring the cultural subjectivity of "self" in presuming major western states as the core of international power; "culture" is then exoticized to refer to those other countries beyond the center.

Within feminist international relations, the decolonization of feminism thus demands recognition of the ways in which "we" are implicated in reproducing oppressions through particular representations of "others" we claim to see as equal and seek to support through emancipatory ideas and practices. Shifting from feminist standpoint to multiple feminist standpoints finds meaningful expression through the acknowledgment that highlighting unequal relations of power, even in a field of multiple subjectivities for women and men, will involve points of conflict as well as cooperation. Confronting the uncomfortable "truths" that sometimes we (qua women in particular subject positions) can act to oppress as well as emancipate is a necessary part of building a political dialogue of difference. The activity of writing about women, gender, and change is a political act requiring writers to reflect on the effects of their representations of women. The challenge posed is to elucidate difference in a way that holds on to the importance of power and resistance.

Embracing difference to affect more inclusive theories and politics of a globalized international space should not erase the workings of power that highlight the tensions of equality and difference in feminist epistemology. Mutual recognition among subjects does not imply equality between subjects. Multiple subjectivities give meaning to mobile relations that are inscribed with power. Embracing difference, therefore, involves understanding the relative power struggles that take place within the self and intersubjectively through the meanings given to particular subject positions. The location of struggle comes to be recognized as a significant material condition that differentiates those engaged in the struggle against racism in the West from those elsewhere engaged in confrontations against both local and global structures of domination and control.

WOMEN, CULTURE, AND INTERNATIONAL RELATIONS

The title of any text immediately points to assumptions contained therein. The use of *women* rather than *gender* or *feminism* highlights the difficulties that have emerged within feminist IR in representing "woman" as subject and "women" as a category of subjects with shared experiences of discrimination and emancipation. The focus on women marks the return to normative questions concerning women's subjectivity and moral and political agency. What this volume of essays demonstrates is that the understanding of "women" as situated political agents is extended through explorations of cultural difference in the forging of women's many subjectivities as "women." Through a variety of locales of difference, the richness, diversity, and struggle of identity for women in forging subjectivity is revealed.

The term *culture* may be considered brave by some who see the contestations of identity politics, racial and ethnic categories, and definitions of culture as rendering it in crisis even to the anthropologists! However, the theme of culture in this collection of essays highlights the ways in which assumptions of sameness and difference remain in the worldview of international relations, particularly in the understandings of what Seyla Benhabib refers to as the "generalized other," set against the western norm of "self."[15] Culture is also taken on proactively to underscore the contexts and cultures of "creative subjectivity" featured in the chapters. This "creative subjectivity" refers to the experience of difference in the claiming and rejection of preinscribed subject positions.

From the title, readers should also be warned of what to expect from "international relations." Our starting point is not the system of states, the straw man to burn; rather, it is situated in the more recent critical turn in the discipline. All the essays engage with "critical" theories and seek to demonstrate their usefulness to the normative development of feminist international relations.

Women, Culture, and International Relations seeks to consolidate and extend the normative reach of feminist IR through a series of theoretical dialogues that explore the workings of gender subjectivities through discourses of culture and difference. To do so, the essays in this collection draw upon the works of critical social and political theorists such as Seyla Benhabib, Michel Foucault, Judith Butler, Homi Bhabha, Nancy Fraser, Richard Rorty, and Gayatry Spivak to introduce and elaborate the problem that difference poses for international relations theory within the specific context of gender and cultural diversity.

The overall critique of this book is situated against the "generalized other" that is found throughout international relations theory in its ethnocentric assumptions of the western center as "self." This generalized notion of otherness was challenged by the gendered critique of the first wave of feminism that revealed the construction of woman as "other" within the binary opposition of male/female understandings of international relations. However, this important critique still contained assumptions of sameness *within* the categories of "women" and "men." More recent feminist contestations have called for a more nuanced sense of these binary categories by developing a conception of political space as being multiply located within discursive settings that intersect local as well as global power relations. These power relations are inscribed by difference arising from subjectivities beyond gender, such as race, class, and sexuality.

The explorations of subjectivity collected in this volume extend this gradual shift in the core concerns of international relations away from the inviolability of state sovereignty toward a clearer focus on the relations among people and between people and states and people and organizations. In so doing, this collection also extends the dialogue about difference *within* feminist IR by elaborating upon feminist postcolonial and poststructural critiques that recast IR subjectivities in a number of locations: ethics, art, exile, knowledge creation, revolution, development policy, and postcolonial reclamations of the subaltern. In its own way, each chapter challenges the notion of a transcendental category of woman while exploring the question of subjectivity, as well as the ethical and political implications of different theoretical discourses. Our goal is to advocate a meaningful engagement with difference to effect a more inclusive approach to building theory and researching the international.

This volume's focus on difference is important because the multitudinous workings of difference—the ways in which subjectivities are conceived, challenged, and transformed—affect all aspects of international relations: from the questions we ask, to the theories of understanding we construct, to the people and agendas we claim to represent. Exploration of difference requires the deconstruction of self/other understandings of cultural difference and reveals the contradictory processes of subject creation by collapsing binary oppositions, cutting across the self/other, us/them, West/Third World categories of subjectivity. The essays collected here challenge the ethnocentric tendencies of western IR by asking how the "other" constructs him/herself. In so doing, they reveal that the categories of "self" and "other" are not separate or pure categories of being but are implicated in the discursive strategies of subjects in the form of resisting, claiming, denying, and complying with subject positions. More specifically these critiques offer particular insights into the production of "otherness," namely, the understandings of power and difference in self/other constructions and in self-understandings; how discourses of difference can emerge to oppress as well as to resist; and strategies to reclaim subjectivity through voice, agency, and representation.

The theme of representation is an important one: It underlines the need for feminist researchers and analysts to be conscious of their epistemological and methodological assumptions when developing theories and practices of dissent. Epistemological claims and methodological approaches affect the representations of "women" and "woman" as moral and political agents and are themselves sites of power and difference. Interpreting and representing the experiences of "others" and defining means of change, resistance, or escape are intricately bound up in the context of knowledge creation and the self who writes. The essays demonstrate that the building of critical knowledge through understandings of difference is not simply a concern of mapping out the self/other axis. To settle here is to leave the power-inscribed epistemic context in place. By problematizing the understanding of how the self and other are created (across different locales), these essays reject the axis of external knower-liberator and internal unconscious-native and so invite a rethinking of political strategies of dissent and transformation. The question is no longer who emancipates whom, as in earlier feminist liberation projects, but becomes one of how women and men, and women among themselves, are differentiated and placed in different situations of risk, power, and security and how that positionality sets the limits and opportunities for agency.

Kimberly Hutchings is specifically concerned with Benhabib's attempt to synthesize the universalism of critical theory with recognition of the "concrete other" as a basis for moral and political theorizing. What we see in Hutchings's chapter is Benhabib's use of insights from both Carol Gilligan's feminist "ethic of care" and Hannah Arendt's account of judgment to temper the abstractions of Habermasian discourse ethics. Hutchings argues that Benhabib's theory still runs into difficulties when confronted by issues of normative judgment that transcend deep cultural divisions. This is because the concrete other is able to take part in meaningful dialogue only if she or he already shares some of the presuppositions common to liberal political culture. The result is that the dialogue that grounds moral and political judgment and action in Benhabib's work is exclusive rather than inclusive. This poses particular difficulties for feminists dealing with normative questions in an international context. The question is raised as to whether there can be feminist dialogue across the boundaries of states and cultures without the prior exclusion of some participants. In direct challenge to universalist discourses on emancipation, Hutchings ultimately asks, Is a genuine universalism possible in international feminist normative theory?

In seeking to place the question of difference within the domain of normative discourses in international relations, Vivienne Jabri moves the terms of the debate beyond the dualism of the feminist ethic of care and the ethic of justice. In exploring the notion of difference through a problematization of subjectivity, Jabri argues for an ethical position that takes account of the multiple sites and styles of responsibility within the present globalized context. The chapter articulates a position, therefore, that centers on questions of self-constitution and self-transformation as the formative moments of a late modern subjectivity that is responsive to its constitutive other. Specifically drawing on the works of Homi Bhabha, Michel Foucault, and Judith Butler, Jabri questions originary conceptions of identity and subjectivity, suggesting in place of such certainties the view that ethical subjectivity is an elaboration of strategies of self that come to constitute a form of aesthetic ethics.

That feminist discourse may be conceptualized as a linguistic tool, giving voice to the previously silenced, brings to the forefront of concern questions relating to how we conceive of the silenced subject, how we name her, and how she names us. Feminism's tensions emerge here as we relate a politics of representation with a view that such representation negates alterity, silencing the already silenced. Gayatri Chakravorty Spivak is a foremost feminist and postcolonial theorist, whose works have made a highly significant contribution to poststructuralist perspectives and how these may be related to thought on the international division of labor, race, feminism, and the condition of postcoloniality. Nalini Persram addresses the concerns of this highly complex thinker, bringing to international relations a theorist whose works are rarely used in the discipline and yet are of tremendous value to our conceptions of race, class, identity, and subjectivity and how these relate to the global condition. Persram's chapter is of specific value to this collection in that it addresses Spivak's concern with the intersection of feminism, difference, and the global international division of labor. Interested specifically with the figure of the subaltern woman and engaging with Spivak's claim that representations of the "other," in their failure to grasp the heterogeneities that exist therein, constitute a form of "epistemic violence," Persram concentrates on Spivak's reaction to the Subaltern Studies group and its remit to recover the lost subjectivity of the subaltern.

Eleanor O'Gorman addresses the question of women's agency in the context of revolutionary struggle and examines the emergence of subjectivity through gendered forms of local resistance. Women's participation in revolutionary struggles has provided a powerful emancipatory appeal for feminist efforts to transform the public/international space. O'Gorman questions the inevitability of such a transformative potential through an exploration of difference, subjectivity, and resistance as these emerge within the context of women's experiences of revolution. Using Foucault's elaborations on power and resistance, O'Gorman argues against the universalist assumptions that an emancipatory political project may hold. She suggests instead that Foucault's thought on resistance provides a challenge to the fixity of revolutionary subjectivity and opens a space for addressing the ambiguities involved in giving women a revolutionary voice that is inclusive of their daily struggles in living through violent conflict. The epistemological question that emerges relates to how we construct knowledge claims of the local and the degree to which we remain in dialogue with situated understandings.

Sarah White evaluates the subjectivity of women in the discourses of difference inscribed in both colonial and development policy contexts. She explores the influence of feminism on development thinking and policy, suggesting that initial concerns centered on the concern to overcome the "invisibility" of women by highlighting the role of women in the well-being of households and communities. White suggests that these early endeavors concentrated on a small number of issue areas—namely, domestic labor, divisions within households, and distinctions between access and control of resources—with the implication that the lives of women in Africa, Asia, and Latin America were dissected and repackaged to enable "their" inclusion in "our" programs. In critically evaluating the impact of feminism on development theory and policy, White points to gender and development as a site of conflict between metropolitan and local cultures. She suggests that gender may serve as the bearer of other meanings besides the subordination or emancipation of women, sounding a cautious note against the rendering of either "development" or the "local culture" in monolithic terms.

As we indicated earlier, the dominant discourse in international relations has centered on the sovereign subject, assumed as masculine and white. This is the position of normalcy against which all others come to be inscribed. It is precisely this conception of the subject that underpins the triumphalism of western discourse on the course of change and that Nicholas Higgins addresses in his chapter. In evaluating the dialogue between Nancy Fraser and Richard Rorty on the place of feminism in social critique, Higgins seeks to challenge the dominant international political project that is increasingly modeled on the North Atlantic liberal democratic framework, which Rorty celebrates and Fraser questions. The dialogical setting of the chapter provides an insight into the relationship between philosophical pragmatism and feminism and the ways in which each may be constitutively built upon an antiessentialist and antifoundational conception of the self that takes account of difference. In a highly nuanced discussion between the two authors of the relationship between freedom and difference and in the disagreements they express specifically over public/private dualism, Higgins opens a space for self-reflexivity in western discourses that tend toward an untrammeled complacency in their negations of multiplicity and the figurations of gendered subjectivity.

Stephen Chan also takes up the challenge to western thought through a concern with the negation of the heterogeneities of the "other" in dominant discourses. He argues that even where room is permitted for the "other," it is rendered as a presence that is undifferentiated and essentially unchallenging of the western academy's notions of what emancipation involves and assumes. This emerges as a hegemony of defaults, and the default is accomplished by the permission of the other and the simultaneous silence imposed upon it. In a move that is shared throughout this collection, Chan suggests that when attempts are made to render the other as a speaker in terms of discourse, it is by means of typecastings, control of the academic media and publication, and assumptions that epistemologies and languages are compatible in their ontological origins. In typically proceeding by both story and essay, Chan outlines a gap in international relations thought, the major impediment to the closure of which is a sense of rationality that is universalist in its claims but partial and contingent outside of our essentially western discipline.

The challenge to set a ten-year agenda for feminist international relations is an ambitious one that is shared collectively by the community of feminist scholars. This book seeks to contribute to the setting of normative debates on that agenda. In the strong and exemplary traditions of feminist IR, this collection seeks to stimulate debate and extend the critical work of disturbing the boundaries of IR and transforming its constituencies. The editors return to this challenge in the concluding chapter.

NOTES

1. See, for example, Walker, *Inside/Outside: International Relations as Political Theory.*
2. Peterson and Runyan, *Global Gender Issues,* pp. 7–8.
3. Steans, *Gender and International Relations,* p. 46.
4. Ibid., p. 53.
5. Enloe, *Bananas, Beaches, and Bases in Making Feminist Sense of International Politics.*
6. Grant and Newland, *Gender and International Relations,* p. 2
7. See Mohanty, Russo, and Torres, *Third World Women and the Politics of Feminism;* Hooks, *Ain't I a Woman: Black Women and Feminism; Talking Back: Thinking Feminist, Thinking Black.*
8. Such deconstructions are drawing upon a growing literature on masculinities in social theory more broadly. Elshtain, *Women and War;* Connell, *Masculinities;* Hearn and Morgan, *Men, Masculinities, and Social Theory;* Pettman, *Worlding Women,* pp. 87–95; Zalewski and Parpart, *The 'Man' Question in International Relations.*
9. See Pettman, *Worlding Women.*
10. Ibid., p. viii.
11. Sylvester, *Feminist Theory and International Relations in a Postmodern Era,* pp. 219–222.
12. See, for example, Mohanty, Russo, and Torres, *Third World Women and the Politics of Feminism;* Alexander and Mohanty, *Feminist Genealogies, Colonial Legacies, Democratic Futures.*
13. Mohanty, "Under Western Eyes: Feminist Scholarship and Colonial Discourses," p. 63.
14. See Pettman, *Worlding Women,* pp. 41–44; Frankenberg, *White Women, Race Matters.*
15. This is a term coined by Seyla Benhabib. Her understanding of the "generalized other" receives fuller treatment by Kimberly Hutchings in Chapter 2 of this book.

2

Feminism, Universalism, and the Ethics of International Politics

Kimberly Hutchings

The argument of this chapter centers on the question of whether a feminist universalist account of moral judgment, which could be used to enable debate and justify critique and intervention across boundaries of state and culture, can be theoretically viable. This question has been of particular importance in feminist ethical theory because of the perceived difficulties of squaring the circle of a feminist politics that claims to speak for all women yet is faced with a global plurality of hierarchically ordered (in terms of wealth and power) cultures and value systems. It is important to note that the perception of difficulty here is principally located in the hearts and minds of white western feminists, who find themselves torn between a commitment to the universal scope of certain moral values on the one hand and the consciousness of an imperialist and slave-owning past and privileged present on the other. My argument begins with a brief summary of the dominant moral theoretical paradigms in debates over normative questions in the international context. I then move on to consider feminist critiques of those paradigms and the nature of much existing work in feminist ethical theory that relates to international political issues (work that relies on the notion of an "ethic of care" as a feminist standpoint for moral judgment). In particular, I focus on Sarah Ruddick's work to exemplify a feminist ethics of war and politics of peace.[1]

Within the literature on feminist moral and political theory there are certain standard criticisms of the kind of work exemplified by Ruddick, which I will summarize under the headings "moral imperialism" and "inadequate generalizability." In the central section of the chapter, I turn to explore the work of a feminist ethical and political theorist, Seyla Benhabib, who claims to have found a way through the inadequacies of both mainstream accounts of moral judgment and the kind of feminist account we find in Ruddick.[2] Benhabib is concerned both to give adequate recognition to "concrete others" in her moral theory and to retain a universal basis as a condition of moral judgment. She argues strongly that there is a theoretically viable universalist account of moral and political judgment that does not fall into the traps of either moral imperialism or parochial particularity. She terms this account "interactive universalism." By examining Benhabib's claims, I argue, it becomes apparent that there are difficulties in sustaining the argument that interactive universalism evades the substitutionalism involved in Kantian accounts of moral judgment or the consequences of identifying right with one particular type of state and way of life. This fact draws attention to difficulties that are endemic in the problem/question that Benhabib sees herself as addressing and resolving, which is also the question with which this chapter opened. In the concluding section I argue that in order to take the notion of a feminist international ethics any further, it is necessary to return to question the question that sets up the debate on which this chapter is based and around which so much moral and political debate revolves. I suggest that the posing of the question reflects a concern with the epistemological status of moral claims, which in turn is grounded in a set of claims about truth, belief, power, and critique that turns out to be unsustainable. Instead, I argue that we would be better occupied in turning from the epistemology of moral claims, which has its modern roots in Kantian and utilitarian sources, to the phenomenology of those claims. In conclusion, I argue that there is a phenomenological promise in aspects of the moral theory of both Ruddick and Benhabib and that it is this promise that a feminist international ethics should concentrate on redeeming.

FEMINIST CHALLENGES
TO MAINSTREAM MORAL THEORY

There are three primary traditions of thinking about ethics and interstate relations/international politics in the modern (post-Wesphalian) era. The first of these, the Hobbesian positivist position that reflects the location of right and justice at the political level of the sovereign state, takes it as axiomatic that interstate relations are essentially amoral. According to this realist tradition, there are no grounds for effective moral judgment beyond the boundaries of states, and no state (nor, by implication, citizens of any state) has a right to pronounce on moral or political rights or obligations in relation to another state. The other two traditions are the Kantian tradition, which takes on the mantle of the older paradigm of Christian natural law and claims that there are universal, transcendentally legislative moral laws that precede and have priority over any account of the grounds of particular political authorities; and the utilitarian tradition, which argues that basic facts about the human condition and human motivation underwrite moral judgments regardless of their scope, whether intra- or interstate.[3] Both Kantians and utilitarians are willing to refer to universal principles (provided by the categorical imperative on the one hand and the utility principle on the other) to validate moral judgments in the international context. In recent years, the realist tradition has been reinforced by a communitarian turn in moral theory, which locates the grounds of moral judgment not in the state as a legal entity with sovereign power, but in the state as a nation-state, the representative of a particular "culture" or "way of life." This leads in the case of theorists such as Michael Walzer to a stress on rights to self-determination of sovereign peoples and a predisposition to nonintervention as the appropriate stance of one state and its citizens in relation to other states and their citizens.[4]

Crudely speaking, contemporary moral theory in international relations engages in a complex, highly sophisticated but repetitive set of dances between Kantian, utilitarian, and communitarian positions. Dances in the plural, because we have the war dance—discussions of just war theory—*jus ad bellum* and *jus in bello*; the rights dance—discussions of the plausibility, basis, and nature of human rights; and the justice dance—discussions of international distributive justice and the morality of aid.[5] For each of these dances, all the nuances offered by realist/communitarian, Kantian, and utilitarian moral paradigms have been and are being essayed. In essence, what preoccupies all of the dancers involved is a set of claims about the grounds of moral judgment and the practical political prescriptions to be derived from those grounds. If it is known that the source of moral value is the nation-state, then killing to defend it becomes a moral duty; if it is known that respect for individual human life is a categorical imperative, then it appears that there must be moral limits on killing in defense of the state. If it is known that all human beings have an inalienable right to bodily integrity, then both torture and female circumcision should be stopped; if values are derived from culture, then tradition determines the validity of such practices. If what counts is the greatest happiness of the greatest number, then there should be a massive transfer of resources North to South; if justice refers to entitlement, then you have a right to hang on to what you have. In each case, what powers the preoccupation with accounts of moral judgment is an equal preoccupation with how to prescribe for the state of the world; it is presumed that there is a deep and necessary connection between the validity of the former and the health of the latter.

Kantian and utilitarian moral theoretical paradigms construct debates in moral theory across the range of what are accounted to be moral issues in contemporary "applied" philosophy. They also continue to be reference points for metatheoretical debates as to the nature and status of moral claims as such. Not surprisingly, therefore, these accounts of moral judgment have been the subject of feminist scrutiny in philosophy and moral and political theory. It is not possible to do justice to the range of feminist work on moral theory here; instead, I point to the most common criticism of the Kantian and utilitarian paradigms, which is subscribed to by feminist theorists as different as Ruddick and Benhabib and which turns up repeatedly in feminist readings of the moral theory canon. I then look briefly at the rather more ambivalent relation of feminist moral theory to communitarianism.

Benhabib has usefully summed up the problem with the predominant universalist moral theories as the problem of reliance on the "generalized other." Essentially, Benhabib's argument is that the predominant paradigms in moral theory rely on an account of human individuals as separate but fundamentally alike. On the basis of assuming human beings to be like Hobbesian mushrooms or Rawlsian individuals in the original position, claims about human motivation, rationality, and justice are asserted to be generalizable to all human beings regardless of context. Morality is seen to be based in what is shared, and what is shared is a set of abstract qualities or capacities, given in advance prior to and legislating for individual interrelation. Moreover, these abstract qualities or capacities turn out to characterize only certain, specific individuals (e.g., male, white, middle-class property owners). Thus, these approaches not only assume the fundamental separateness of individuals and falsify concrete differences between individuals but also universalize the value of certain qualities and the denigration of others on the basis of that falsification.[6]

Benhabib cites Carol Gilligan as the feminist theorist who has done much to draw attention to both abstract individualism and the falsification of concrete difference in mainstream moral theory and accounts of moral reasoning.[7] It is certainly the case that Gilligan's work in her seminal study, *In a Different Voice,* has provided the strongest inspiration for feminist moral theory in the 1980s and 1990s, both critical and constructive, as will be seen in relation to Ruddick's work in this chapter.[8] Before we move on to look at Ruddick, however, it is important to note how the feminist critique of Kantian and utilitarian moral thought relates to that other dominant strand in moral theory, communitarianism. What immediately strikes the reader of standard feminist critiques of moral universalism is the family resemblance between such critiques and the arguments of communitarian thinkers such as A. MacIntyre and Walzer, who claim that moral judgment must be located in concrete practices, traditions, or communities.[9] The communitarian approach avoids the universalism of the other two dominant paradigms, allows for the essential importance of concrete difference, and recognizes the fundamental relationality of individual human existence. The problem for feminist critics with communitarianism is that it can be held to repeat the imperialist moves of Kantianism and utilitarianism at the level of the group, nation, or community as opposed to that of the human race as such. Such communitarian approaches essentialize the value of community, including the power relations between men and women institutionalized within the community, and are, it is argued, just as likely to silence the voice of women as concrete others as the universalist paradigms.[10] For feminist critics in the context of moral theory, difference within community has been a much stronger concern than difference between communities.

CARE, MATERNAL THINKING, AND THE ETHICS OF WAR

In the preceding section, I provided a brief sketch of the concerns of mainstream moral theory and the ways in which it has been criticized by feminist theorists. In this section, I flesh out one example of a feminist ethics of war, which, I would argue, exemplifies the dominant feminist turn in the ethics of international politics: Ruddick's *Maternal Thinking*. Ruddick's argument in *Maternal Thinking* can be seen as following through the implications of what Gilligan refers to as an "ethic of care." It involves a critique of traditional just war thinking—in both utilitarian and Kantian variants—as well as a positive characterization of how a different kind of moral judgment and political practice is possible in relation to war. There are essentially two stages to Ruddick's argument. In the first stage she offers a phenomenology of what she terms "maternal thinking"; in the second stage she adapts Nancy Hartsock's notion of "feminist standpoint" and reads off the implications of using maternal thinking as the feminist standpoint for making judgments about the ethics of war and the appropriate feminist response to war.

Maternal thinking, according to Ruddick, "is a discipline in attentive love," a discipline that is rooted in the demands of a particular relation of care—that between mother and child—and that reflects a particular range of metaphysical attitudes, cognitive capacities, and virtues.[11] Ruddick is careful to insist that she is neither equating mothers with biological mothers nor presuming that actual mothers are all good at maternal thinking. In addition, although Ruddick's examples of maternal practice are largely drawn from the United States, she implies that the demands of preservation, nurturance, and training, although they take culturally specific forms, are not culturally specific as such, so that there is a relevance in what she is discussing to that which transcends her own social and political context. This implication is confirmed by Ruddick's use of the notion of "feminist standpoint" when she comes to apply the consequences of maternal thinking to the consideration of intra- and interstate violence.[12] The idea of a feminist standpoint derives from Hartsock's appropriation of Marx's analysis of capitalism as being based on the standpoint of the oppressed class.

According to Hartsock, the exploitative character of capitalist relations of production becomes clear when understood from the vantage point of the proletariat. Similarly, the patriarchal character of relations of reproduction as well as production under capitalism is revealed from the standpoint of the women who bear the brunt of those relations.[13] Building on this notion, Ruddick argues that maternal thinking, located as it is in the marginalized and denigrated sphere of caring labor, provides a standpoint from which the absurdity of both strategic military and just war thinking becomes evident. Although Ruddick does not follow Hartsock in maintaining that the feminist standpoint provides a demonstrably universally valid ground for truth, she is making a claim for the potential of maternal thinking to illuminate the meaning of war from a critical perspective.[14]

When maternal thinking takes upon itself the critical perspective of a feminist standpoint, it reveals a contradiction between mothering and war. Mothering begins in birth and promises life; military thinking justifies organized, deliberate deaths. A mother preserves the bodies, nurtures the psychic growth, and disciplines the conscience of children; although the military trains its soldiers to survive the situations it puts them in, it also deliberately endangers their bodies, minds, and consciences in the name of victory and abstract causes.[15]

> The analytic fictions of just war theory require a closure of moral issues final enough to justify killing and "enemies" abstract enough to be killable. In learning to welcome their own and their children's changes, mothers become accustomed to open-ended, concrete reflection on intricate and unpredictable spirits. Maternal attentive love, restrained and clear sighted, is ill adapted to intrusive, let alone murderous judgments of others' lives.[16]

Looking at these quotations, it is clear that Ruddick's argument involves the rejection of abstract universalism and the embracing of concrete particularity as the proper ground for moral judgment. For Ruddick, both militarism and universalist moral theory share a commitment to the expendability of concrete lives in abstract causes, which maternal thinking is inherently opposed to. Ruddick claims that this means that the implication of maternal thinking is not just the rejection of war but the active embracing of peace politics, a fight against war that draws on the acknowledgment of responsibility and relationship and the specificity of need and obligations that are inherent in a proper understanding of the labor of caring.[17]

Ruddick's work provides one particularly influential example of feminist thinking about war and typifies an argument common in feminist literature in the 1980s: that women and/or feminists had a particular and peculiar relation to the moral assessment of war and to peace politics.[18] From the beginning, however, the work of Ruddick and of feminist theorists such as Gilligan and Hartsock, who privilege the ethic of care or the labor of care as a starting point for moral judgment, has come under criticism from other feminist theorists. Two related criticisms have been particularly common: first, the criticism that such work essentializes the standpoint of women, assuming sameness among women according to a particular model of the kind of work women are held, typically, to do; second, the criticism that the emphasis on concrete, particular relations and responsibilities as the context for moral judgment provides a ground for judgment that is inadequately generalizable and prevents the possibility of critical engagement beyond narrow, parochial levels of social interaction. The first objection is parallel to the charge of moral imperialism, which, as we saw earlier, feminists laid against both universalist and communitarian dominant moral paradigms. It is an objection with particularly acute resonances in the context of feminist politics both within multicultural states (for instance, the charges of white and middle-class dominance in the feminist movement in the United States) and among states (for example, in arguments between western and Third World feminists about the ethics and politics of indigenous cultural practices, nationalism, population control, and aid policy).[19] This criticism is one to which thinkers like Ruddick are sensitive and to which they have attempted to respond, generally by arguing for the strategic usefulness of the idea of a feminist standpoint as opposed to making claims for its absolute status. In becoming more tentative in the claims made for a feminist standpoint, however, theorists such as Ruddick who argue for the contextualist location of maternal thinking in a specific practice appear to fall into the hands of the other side of the coin of criticism, which is that an ethic of care offers only a parochial account of the conditions of judgment and therefore disables the possibility of critique across different particular contexts. This is a criticism made particularly powerfully by Benhabib in relation to Gilligan's work:

> The Mafia is an organization based on care and mutual responsibility toward members of one's own clan or extended family, yet this morality of care is accompanied by a morality of injustice and contempt towards the lives, dignity and property of non-group members. Theorists of care must specify the criteria according to which such clans as the Mafia are to be considered "immoral" from the standpoint of a morality of care.[20]

We saw earlier that Benhabib shared the common feminist critique of the generalized other of mainstream moral theory for reasons that echo the concern with concrete difference that can be seen to underlie objections to universalist moral theory and to feminist essentialism. Here, however, she turns against the notion that this implies a turn to a particularist feminist ethic of care. In the next section, I explore the extent to which Benhabib succeeds in articulating an alternative feminist moral theory that is neither imperialistic nor uncritically particularistic in its implications.

INTERACTIVE UNIVERSALISM

Benhabib is a feminist theorist working, broadly speaking, within the tradition of contemporary Frankfurt School critical theory. As such she is preoccupied with the articulation of a theoretical position that enables and empowers critique of existing power relations—understood as the systematic exclusions of certain people from power for reasons of class, gender, or race. Benhabib's concerns are located within the boundaries of the contemporary, liberal, democratic, multicultural state exemplified, as in Ruddick's case, by the United States. Benhabib criticizes mainstream moral theory on the grounds that it universalizes a notion of the self (the generalized other), which is false or misleading on several counts. First, it assumes selves are separate and nonrelational; second, it assumes that selves are all essentially alike and excludes consideration of concrete difference; third, it identifies characteristics and capacities that are particular with universal truths. According to Benhabib, the kind of universalism involved here is "substitutionalist"; what is presented in the work of people like Rawls as a procedure in which the interests of others are central is in fact the generalization of one particular type of self-interest.[21] In Benhabib's view, however, the ethic of care does not in itself present a viable way forward for thinking about moral judgment: to the extent that the ethic of care essentializes a particular account of care, it repeats the move of generalizing one pattern for all women; to the extent that care is seen as bounded by narrower contexts, it self-consciously restricts judgment to a concern with what is best for those who are like me or those with whom I have a direct, concrete interrelation/interaction.[22] Benhabib makes a related case against versions of communitarian theory that are essentially integrationist, that is, that emphasize the necessity of value consensus for the revival and perpetuation of community (she suggests that this applies to MacIntyre and Sandel but not to Walzer and Taylor).[23] Ultimately for Benhabib, traditional moral theory, integrationist communitarianism, and the feminist ethic of care are all inherently "substitutionalist" in the sense that they all rest moral judgment on commonality of identity and are incapable of taking radical otherness into account. This is a bad thing, Benhabib argues, both because it fails to reflect the inherent plurality of concrete others in the modern condition and because it risks preserving existing patterns of inequality of power, setting them in theoretical aspic rather than opening them to critical challenge.

In *Critique, Norm, and Utopia; Situating the Self;* and her most recent book on Arendt's work, *The Reluctant Modernism of Hannah Arendt,*

Benhabib displays a consistent commitment to formulating an account of moral and political judgment that is genuinely and universally inclusive of the others disingenuously excluded by substitutionalist moral universalisms and explicitly excluded by integrationist communitarianism and the ethic of care. The theory Benhabib has developed relies upon a procedural dialogical approach to accounting for the proper conditions of moral and political judgment. In constructing her theory of such judgment, Benhabib is philosophically most indebted to Habermas's discourse ethics.[24] However, Benhabib is also critical of Habermas and uses the work of both Gilligan and Arendt as a corrective to what she sees as his mistaken assumption that certain questions remain outside of the scope of morality—a mistake, she argues, that derives from an overreliance on the notion of the generalized other in Jürgen Habermas's account of what belongs to the sphere of morality per se. Let us go on to explore Benhabib's adaptation of Habermas.

Two key Habermasian insights are crucial to Benhabib's account of the nature and conditions of moral and political judgment: First, Habermas claims that such judgments rest not on unitary, substantive identity but on the logic of communicative reason, which is essentially dialogical; second, Habermas claims that morality is a matter of establishing procedural principles for dialogue rather than one of determining specific outcomes.[25] For Habermas, the categorical imperative of morality is that what counts as moral principles are or would be the outcome of a free and fair discussion/ argument by all those who would be affected by the institutionalization of those principles; essentially what these principles institutionalize are the conditions for free and fair discussion that are implicit in the logic of communication itself.[26] This, argues Habermas, is a Kantian universalism that need not rely on transcendental reference points and is intrinsically democratic. For Benhabib, the centrality of the notion of dialogue promises a recognition of difference in moral judgment that is precluded by the theoretical paradigms she has rejected. At the same time, the emphasis on the procedural conditions for dialogue offers a universalist commitment to the right of all voices to be heard, which cuts against the exclusiveness that also characterizes the rejected paradigms.[27] But there are, Benhabib argues, problems with the ways in which Habermas thinks through the implications of his discourse ethics, largely because there remains a legacy of the "generalized other" at the level of Habermas's account of actual moral discourse, which needs to be located purely at the level of the conditions for moral discourse.[28] This needs to be addressed if Habermas's discourse ethics are to be genuinely interactive as opposed to substitutionalist in character.

Benhabib addresses the legacy of the generalized other in Habermas's work when considering the debate between Gilligan and Kohlberg. In relation to this debate, Habermas had supported Kohlberg's contention that the ethic of care dealt with evaluative issues that were not properly speaking moral issues, since they concerned particularistic and solidaristic questions about the quality of the good life rather than truly moral issues, which must pertain to establishing the parameters within which such debates may be conducted.[29] Morality involves essentially procedural principles of universal applicability; questions of the good life (which Habermas terms "ethics") may be essentially and permanently contested but are irresolvable at the level of universal morality. According to Benhabib, in siding with Kohlberg in this debate, Habermas is misconceiving the nature of morality and eliding the distinction between conditions for moral discourse and the concerns of moral discourse. This elision is due to an unthinking identification of the moral subject with a set of interests and concerns that have characterized the generalized other in the tradition of moral theory. In this sense, Habermas is not doing justice to his own theory. My thesis is that Habermas and Kohlberg conflate the standpoint of a universalist morality with a narrow definition of the moral domain as being centered on "issues of justice." These, however, are different matters. How we define the *domain of the moral* is a separate matter from the kinds of *justificatory constraints* we think moral judgments, principles, and maxims should be subject to. Universalism in moral theory operates at the level of specifying acceptable forms of the justification of moral principles, judgments, and maxims.[30]

In essence, Benhabib accepts Habermas's account of the procedural conditions on moral debate. However, in rethinking the question of what actual moral debate may entail, Benhabib is led to the conclusion that Habermas has paid insufficient attention to what those conditions mean for actual moral discourse, both in terms of who may be involved in it and how it may be conducted as well as what it may concern. Habermas has provided a way of theorizing moral universalism, but he has not fulfilled the promise of discourse ethics as "interactive" universalism. In making her argument for a genuinely interactive universalism, Benhabib makes some use of Gilligan's work but considerably more of Arendt's. Gilligan's work, Benhabib argues, provides a corrective to the misconception of selves as generalized others (abstract, rational, individual beings) that is presumed even in Habermas's account of the concerns of moral discourse. Gilligan insists on an account of the self as, in Benhabib's words, "embodied and embedded," inseparable from a whole range of contextual relations and particularities. This draws attention to the exclusivity of accounts of morality that do not include reference to issues of care and solidarity; more generally, however, what Gilligan reminds moral theorists of is that human beings are diverse and that those engaged in moral deliberation do not start from the same place but as concretely other from all others.[31] For interactive universalism, concrete difference is a starting point for "reflection and action." It is in exploring how difference can be a starting point for reflection and action that Benhabib comes to use Arendt to flesh out her account of the nature of concrete others, of moral discourse, and of the conditions of moral judgment.

At first sight, it seems odd that Benhabib uses Arendt to help think through the characteristics of an interactive discourse ethics. In reflecting on the Eichmann trial, Arendt identified the capacity for moral judgment with a capacity for internal dialogue, nourished by thinking and located within the individual self-consciousness.[32] Indeed, Benhabib is explicitly critical of Arendt's claim that moral deliberation is an essentially individual matter.[33] However, it is not on Arendt's meditations on morality as such that Benhabib relies; instead it is on Arendt's account of politics. Benhabib rejects some elements of Arendt's agonistic conception of the political sphere and what she terms the "phenomenological essentialism" of Arendt's separation of the political from the natural and social spheres.[34] However, Benhabib finds a more fruitful aspect of Arendt's theory in her late work on Kant's notion of reflective judgment. According to Benhabib, this work suggests a way in which moral reflection and action may be possible in the context of the irreducible plurality of selves. This involves Benhabib in adopting Arendt's idea of an *enlarged mentality* in political judgment and extending it to the domain of morality as well as politics. For Arendt, political judgment involves judging without a determining principle in such a way that the standpoint of plural others is taken into account; it means "to think from the standpoint of every one else." Arendt's own account of the conditions of political judgment is complex and obscure, but for Benhabib it rests primarily on an imaginative, creative capacity for listening, which will be cultivated by encounters with difference in a discursive public sphere. The phenomenology of this capacity is explicated by Benhabib as involving the categories of natality, plurality, and narrativity, which are central to Arendt's notions of political action and judgment.[35] Benhabib argues that this notion of *enlarged mentality*, a capacity to put oneself in the place of concrete others, is necessary to the idea of interactive universalism, in which respect for others is encapsulated in the simultaneous presence of universal procedural constraints on dialogue that ensure that everyone can speak on a free and equal basis (i.e., acknowledgment as a generalized other) and acknowledgment of concrete otherness (an embodied and embedded diversity and multiplicity of perspectives) that ensures that everyone can be heard.[36] Benhabib's point is that moral judgment relies on a culture of commitment to understanding difference as well as universal principle. What distinguishes this notion of moral judgment from others of which she is critical, according to Benhabib, is that it does not presume sameness of identity as its condition.

To what extent has Benhabib's account of interactive universalism addressed the dilemma of how to give an account of moral judgment that evades the charges of both imperialism and parochialism? There are two principal ways in which it may be argued that Benhabib has not satisfactorily dealt with this dilemma. The first way focuses on a charge of idealism, in which it could be argued that the conditions required for moral judgment by Benhabib are simply not available, and any attempt to institutionalize them in the world as it stands would involve a corruption of what a genuinely interactive universalism demands. In itself, this line of criticism does not imply that Benhabib's account is theoretically unviable, only that it has a utopian dimension, a charge to which Benhabib would happily plead guilty.[37] The second line of criticism of Benhabib argues that her theory fails to live up to its own pretensions to be a genuinely interactive universalism. This is a more fundamental problem than that of utopianism, since it suggests that in addition to being unrealizable, interactive universalism is theoretically unsustainable. On what grounds can it be argued that Benhabib's claims fail at the level of the theory itself? The answer to this lies in the nature of the procedural conditions on moral discourse that provide the context within which *enlarged mentality*—"thinking from the standpoint of everyone else"—operates.

For the defender of communicative ethics, even more than for the liberal theorist, Benhabib's ethical position involves a strong commitment to the norms of universal moral respect and egalitarian reciprocity. Is such a commitment also compatible with the consequences of pluralism, tolerance, and experimentation advocated above? Not always, and in instances where there is a clash between the metanorms of communicative ethics and the specific norms of a moral way of life, the latter must be subordinated to the former.[38]

Although interactive universalism claims to start from difference, this is only partly true, as Benhabib acknowledges. There are in fact clear constraints on the range of differences that Benhabib's enlarged mentality is capable of encompassing in the process of judgment. Some things are always already judged to be wrong on the grounds of "the meta-norms of communicative ethics," fundamentalist religious convictions being the example Benhabib herself cites.[39] In certain cases procedural conditions clash with possible substantive outcomes of debate; in these cases the generalized other takes priority over the concrete other. This casts doubt on Benhabib's claim to be able to avoid substitutionalism altogether in her theory. In practice it appears that selves must be understood as essentially the same in some respects for moral judgment to be possible. The procedure puts constraints on the range of plural selves that may be encountered in moral discourse. This poses a distinct problem for any feminist ethics that is looking, if only in principle, for a nonexclusivist approach to moral issues in the context of international politics. More important, however, it draws attention to the way in which in Benhabib's argument, as more explicitly in Ruddick's, an account of the conditions of moral judgment is inseparable from certain substantive moral claims. Benhabib's emphasis on procedure, following that of Habermas, is not dictated by uncertainties about moral fundamentals but by a conviction that these fundamentals must be in some way universally and rationally demonstrable. To castigate Benhabib for failing to sustain her own claims for theoretical inclusiveness misses a more interesting question: Why is the grounding of theoretical inclusiveness so important in Benhabib's moral theory? Why is it that Benhabib focuses so much not just on what she has to say about moral fundamentals and the nature of moral judgment but on the question of the right to make these claims in the first place?

FROM MORAL EPISTEMOLOGY
TO MORAL PHENOMENOLOGY

The task of moral theory since Kant has been one of articulating and then applying the grounds of moral certainty. The point of application is understood as the point of prescription in which the moral doctor needs to rely on moral science to diagnose and provide the cure for moral complaints. Insofar as feminist ethics has become caught up in the issue of whether there are universal grounds for moral judgment, it shares the assumption that the epistemological status of moral claims makes a difference to the possibility of diagnosis, prescription, and therefore cure. It is rarely the substantive nature of the moral judgments that is in doubt; the question is not about what moral theorists think but about whether they have the right to think it—whether, as it were, they have the authority to practice as moral doctors. I now go on to argue that the reasons feminist ethicists remain preoccupied with issues of moral epistemology to the extent that they are reflect a nexus of questionable assumptions about truth, power, belief, and critique. Once these assumptions are put into question, there emerges the possibility of thinking more clearly about the conditions of both moral judgment and moral dialogue. This new approach, which is already present in some feminist and communitarian work, abandons the theoretical ambition to establish the "right" or "authority" to moral practice. In place of this ambition, it puts the more modest goal of a moral phenomenology. In the light of this, I argue in conclusion that it is possible to work with the phenomenological aspects of both Ruddick's and Benhabib's moral theory while leaving aside questions of epistemological justification associated with both the idea of a "feminist standpoint" and communicative rationality.

In his Oxford Amnesty Lecture "Human Rights, Rationality, and

Sentimentality," Rorty puts forward a critique of the idea, which has been central to modern moral theory, that it is possible to "claim to know something which, though not itself a moral intuition, can *correct* moral intuitions."[40] Rorty's purpose is to argue against the notion that there is any point in the pursuit of true grounds for moral claims. He suggests instead that the cultivation of particular kinds of moral sentiment is a more productive road for those wanting to establish a culture of international human rights.[41] Although both Ruddick and Benhabib are critical of the bold claims of mainstream moral theory, it is clear nevertheless from the characterization of their arguments that they are both still engaged, to some extent at least, in playing the game of moral metatheory, that is, that of providing validation at a metalevel of specific claims. When Ruddick invokes the idea of a feminist standpoint and Benhabib invokes the notion of communicative rationality as a condition for moral judgment and moral prescription, they are establishing these grounds as guarantees of the critical power of what they have to say. The purpose of the argument is to provide an additional rationale in order to secure the status of specific outcomes of the argument. It is no surprise to Ruddick that the labor of care underwrites a feminist peace politics, or to Benhabib that the logic of communicative rationality stands in the way of dialogue with religious fundamentalists. But these claims are more than the articulation of a set of moral intuitions; they are understood as giving their conclusions a necessity they would not otherwise have. According to Rorty, both Ruddick and Benhabib are on a wild goose chase both because there are no guarantees of the validity of moral judgments that are discoverable (all such guarantees are essentially contestable and the arguments can never be settled by reason but only by reference to shared cultural norms) and because, even if such guarantees could be discovered, there can be no guarantee of their practical effects.[42] I am less concerned with the question of whether or not it is possible to make claims about either a feminist standpoint or communicative rationality as a ground for a feminist ethics and more concerned with the question of why for Ruddick and Benhabib moral theory remains entangled with an essentially epistemological project. It is in relation to this question that we encounter the nexus of assumptions about truth, power, belief, and critique referred to at the beginning of this section.

What is the reason for the connection made between morality and epistemological validation in the work of both Ruddick and Benhabib? In my view, the reason for this connection is that in moral theory there remains a commitment to the notion that truth (that which can be known with certainty) is characterized by a particular set of features: First, truth is understood to be inherently nonoppressive; second, truth is understood to be inherently persuasive; and third, truth is understood to be essential to critique. The appeal of pursuing the goal of establishing true grounds for moral claims is immediately apparent. If truth does not exclude or oppress and I can identify the conditions for moral truth, then my claims are both benign and universal in scope. If truth is persuasive and I can identify the conditions of moral truth, then all people will come to affirm my claims from their own points of view. If truth is necessary to critique and I can identify the conditions of moral truth, then critique of other moral values and practices becomes possible. All of these concerns relate to the concerns of feminist ethics identified at the beginning of this chapter as underlying the debate about feminist universalism in ethics. It is clear that the value given to truth in relation to morality is not in any sense for its own sake but for the implications that truth is seen to have. It seems to me, however, that none of the implications I have outlined necessarily follows, regardless of whether there actually are true grounds for moral claims.

In the case of the relationship of truth to power, as Foucault has demonstrated, the truth value of a claim has no necessary connection to its effects; it may sustain domination or reinforce resistance, depending on the play of forces within a specific context. However, one does not have to adopt a Foucauldian emphasis on disciplinary power to recognize that truth, exclusion, and oppression may go together. Benhabib may be right to exclude fundamentalists as participants in moral discourse, but this is nevertheless an exercise of power in the crudest juridical sense, one that marks the limits of liberal toleration and is straightforwardly exclusive. Truth cannot be divorced from politics, and yet this is precisely what is maintained in the bid to establish the parameters of moral dialogue. Ruddick's argument is obviously rather different; she makes claims for maternal thinking as a subjugated knowledge and acknowledges the feminist standpoint as a perspective that cannot be given an absolute status. Nevertheless, she does claim that this perspective provides a privileged insight into the immorality and absurdity of militarism and that its divorce from power is precisely what grounds the significance of its insights. Maternal thinking is argued to be inherently nonoppressive because it is the standpoint of the oppressed; yet it is quite clear that maternal thinking generates effects of power, in the sense that it sets up a standard of consistency with maternal thinking that privileges some actions and ways of life and condemns others. In addition, as noted above, the practice of care on which maternal thinking is based is drawn from a culturally specific context that as a site of oppression is only one among others and that may itself be argued to depend on oppressive relations. This lays the claims for maternal thinking open to the charge that it essentializes one experience of mothering as the standard for all and fails to draw attention to conditions of oppression that have made mothering in Ruddick's sense possible.[43]

The argument that truth is inherently persuasive is particularly dubious in the context of moral claims—partly because the lack of agreed moral truths makes it difficult to test—but also, as Rorty points out, because moral commitment appears to be more closely linked to the guts of moral sentiment and prejudice than to the capacity for rational analysis.[44] At the very least, it appears that rational argument from true premises radically underdetermines moral values and principles. If the point of Ruddick's and Benhabib's characterizations of the grounds for moral judgment was to add persuasive force to a particular understanding of the ethics of war or the fundamental principles of morality, then it is not clear that this has succeeded. In fact, by claiming the epistemological high ground, both thinkers might be seen as having distracted attention from their substantive claims by drawing critics into the game of contesting that ground.

The relation of truth to critique is a complex one; it is crucial to both Ruddick and Benhabib that critique comes from somewhere, a somewhere that is itself secured. However, as is evident in the case of both thinkers, the ground from which they criticize is not secure; it is profoundly vulnerable and contestable. What is not clear is whether this necessarily invalidates the critical work being done. I have argued elsewhere that theoretical critique in the Kantian tradition (in which I would include both standpoint theory and interactive universalism), in spite of its commitment to securing the ground of critique, is in fact characterized by the difficulties involved in securing that ground.[45] This means that critics claiming a secure ground for critique are misconceiving the logic of the critical theoretical practice in which they are engaged. This logic, I would argue, depends on the vulnerability rather than the certainty of claims to authority, since critique involves perpetually putting the grounds of right into question. However, even if the link between secure ground and critique were established, it is clear that the link between theoretical critique and practical critique can also be questioned. Ruddick links the theoretical standpoint of maternal thinking to a practice of peace politics; Benhabib links the theory of communicative rationality to the practice of liberal discursive democracy. Yet there is no evidence that those engaged in peace politics or democratic politics have felt the necessity to ground that practice in epistemological security.

The implication of the above argument is that moral theory's preoccupation with metatheoretical epistemological questions is a mistake and that feminist moral theory that shares these preoccupations is also mistaken. This is not because there are no such things as moral truths or because rational argument has no place in moral discussion, but because the epistemological focus of such moral theory sets up a chain of red herrings that fuels an irresolvable philosophical debate but does little to enhance an understanding of what is at stake in the realm of moral judgment and prescription. As long as claims are made to a truth that works against power, persuades, and enables critique, there will be a permanent set of counterclaims that point out the interrelation of truth and power, the lack of subjective agreement, and the uncertainty of the grounds of critique. The dance identified above as characteristic of Kantian, utilitarian, and communitarian moral theory will simply be indefinitely repeated. The question with which this chapter began was the "question of whether a feminist universalist account of moral judgment, which could be used to enable debate and justify critique and intervention across boundaries of state and culture, can be theoretically viable." What I have tried to demonstrate is that this is an unhelpful question because it keeps feminist moral theory trapped in the same patterns as much mainstream moral theory, with little progress made in relation to the reasons why the question of moral universalism was of interest to feminists in the first place. What then would be a more helpful question?

In order to identify a more helpful question for feminist moral theory to engage with, we have to return to the reasons why the question of feminist universalism was posed. At the beginning of this chapter, I suggested that at the heart of the debate over universalism for feminist ethics at the level of international politics is the problem of squaring a feminist commitment to judging and acting on behalf of all women with the fact that women's assessments of what is morally right to do do not coincide—taking into account a global context in which "difference" is not present horizontally as a diversity of equally weighted perspectives but is constructed by and mapped onto massive power differentials. I also suggested that this problem is acute for white western feminists, who are torn between commitment to certain moral values on the one hand and to the democracy implicit in feminist politics on the other. Feminist, universalist ethics appeared to allow for moral debate as such by providing cross-cultural reference points and, more important, for the possibility of moral intervention and critique without guilt. I have argued that feminist universalism not only does not but cannot live up to its promise but that still leaves unresolved the problems posed by difference and hierarchy to morality. So where do we go from here?

My suggestion for the way forward for a feminist international ethics is that a new version of the "how is moral debate possible" question should be asked. In this version, rather than asking the question of whether there are epistemologically valid grounds for moral judgment, feminist theory would focus on examining the actual conditions of moral judgments in different contexts and in the context of difference. This entails a turn from moral epistemology to moral phenomenology. What I am suggesting has been a feature of some recent moral theory of both a feminist and communitarian kind, but the preoccupation with the issue of universalism, plus a rather narrow focus on the meaning of context, has tended to distract attention from what phenomenology can offer moral theory. The strength of Ruddick's and Benhabib's work lies in the extent to which they enhance the understanding of what morality involves, even though neither of them by any means exhausts the issue. Ruddick's notion of maternal thinking as inseparable from maternal practice and Benhabib's notion of moral judgment as inseparable from certain psychological capacities and political conditions represent a small step toward the comprehension of the material, political, and affective conditions in which morality is always enmeshed. Different sorts of moral claims will be linked to different kinds of enmeshment, and the work of phenomenology explores how and why this is the case and draws attention to the moral possibilities in any given nexus of conditions. The international system and the global economy—the multiplicity of ways in which individual lives are internationally or globally mediated—constitute the actual conditions of international or global morality. Moral theorists need to focus on understanding what the implications of those conditions might be for moral debate and the prospects for moral agreement or disagreement. This phenomenological work does not pretend to definitively answer questions of right and wrong; it seeks instead to give participants in moral debates as deep an understanding as possible of what they share and what differentiates them from each other. By beginning to explore material, political, and affective conditions that underlie different moral orientations, both Ruddick and Benhabib draw attention to how moral debate may be extended and deepened within an international context.

A consequence of this phenomenological focus is that feminists in general, and white western feminists in particular, will be obliged to cease to see the fact that values clash in a highly unequal political context as being something that has to be or can be neutralized prior to moral debate. Seeking to establish guarantees for moral claims closes off debate because it suggests that there is a point at which accountability of moral actors, particularly more powerful actors, ends. By accountability I mean literally acknowledging all the implications involved in a moral stance without the shortcut of an appeal to a higher ground. If the justificatory conditions for a claim are seen to both necessitate the rightness of the claim and neutralize its negative implications for others, then this implies that there is a point at which moral judgment or intervention would not be risky and might not fail. But I would suggest that this is precisely what characterizes moral judgment and moral intervention, most especially in an international context. A phenomenology of moral judgment demonstrates that it is not the case that you need a ground of right from which to speak in order to speak in moral debate. There is, however, a very complex set of conditions that determines the extent to which moral voices may be heard. This is not to suggest that the actuality of difference and hierarchy does not pose problems for moral debate, critique, and intervention; but these problems do not make debate either impossible or useless, although they render it always difficult and sometimes ugly. Instead of relying on guaranteed authority, if feminists want to address the problem of cross-cultural moral dialogue, we need to self-consciously acknowledge and be open to the vulnerability of any moral claim in theory and in practice and recognize that there are costs that have to be counted in any kind of committed intervention in the world. The more powerful an individual feminist is as an actor, the more necessary it is to recognize and open to further challenge the effects of power entailed by particular moral judgments and their practical implications. To strive for epistemological security, as if that somehow takes priority over all the other kinds of securities that so many women in the world lack, is to misunderstand the nature of moral engagement in an imperfect world.

NOTES

1. There has been a great deal of feminist work on international ethical issues, particularly on the ethics of war and global environmental ethics. I use Ruddick's work partly because it is a particularly well known and influential example, partly because Ruddick draws on the ideas of a feminist "ethic of care" and the notion of a "feminist standpoint," both of which have been frequently used in the literature as a means of criticizing mainstream moral theory. I will be focusing on Ruddick, *Maternal Thinking*. For other examples of feminist international ethics, see Warren and Cady, *Hypatia Special Issue;* and Harris and King, *Rocking the Ship of State.*

2. Although Benhabib is not specifically concerned with international relations, her work does focus precisely on the question with which this paper opens and provides a possible way forward for feminist international ethics, which has tended to remain dominated by the "ethic of care," "feminist standpoint" approach, even when it recognizes its limitations. I will be focusing mainly on Benhabib's collection of essays *Situating the Self.*

3. For overviews of the Kantian and utilitarian traditions in international ethics, see chapters by Donaldson, "Kant's Global Rationalism," and Ellis, "Utilitarianism and International Ethics," in Nardin and Mapel, *Traditions of International Ethics;* and Brown's chapter on cosmopolitan normative theory, in Brown, *International Relations Theory.*

4. Walzer's *Just and Unjust Wars* has undoubtedly been the most influential text in relation to the ethics of war in recent times. Walzer draws on a mixture of sources, including Mill's classic defense of self-determination. Although Walzer does not outlaw international intervention in all cases, he does set up strong presumptions against it (see Walzer, *Just and Unjust Wars,* pp. 86–108).

5. Examples in relation to war might be Walzer, *Just and Unjust Wars,* versus Holmes, *On War and Morality;* on rights, see Renteln, *International Human Rights,* versus Howard, *Human Rights and the Search for Community;* on justice, see Singer, "Famine, Affluence, and Morality," versus O'Neill, "Transnational Justice," and so on.

6. Benhabib, *Situating the Self,* pp. 148–170.

7. Ibid., p. 170.

8. In Ruddick's *Maternal Thinking* she pays tribute to the notion of a femi-

nist "ethic of care" and links her argument to that of Gilligan (Ruddick, *Maternal Thinking*, pp. 94–95, 182–183). Gilligan, a social psychologist who had been working on the question of moral development, took issue with the measures for moral development constructed by Kohlberg. Essentially, Gilligan's argument in *In a Different Voice* is that women tend to display different patterns of moral reasoning from men, ones that derive from an orientation to the specific patterns of responsibility associated with particular relationships and contexts. Gilligan claims that this moral voice has been denigrated in traditional conceptions of what counts as moral reasoning, which, she argues, have been dominated by the more abstract, impartial, and universalistic "ethic of justice." In this early work, Gilligan did not claim any superiority for the care orientation, but she did argue that it should be given an equal place with the ethic of justice in accounts of moral maturity. A large literature on Gilligan's work and the ethic of care has since developed (e.g., Larrabee, *An Ethic of Care;* Tronto, *Moral Boundaries;* Bubeck, *Care, Gender, and Justice*).

9. I am thinking here of MacIntyre, *After Virtue;* and Walzer, *Spheres of Justice.* Okin provides one example of a feminist critique of Walzer (Okin, *Justice, Gender, and the Family*). Benhabib distinguishes between "integrationist" (MacIntyre) and "participationist" (Walzer) versions of communitarianism, and she associates the charge of conservatism and lack of attention to plurality with the former (see below).

10. Benhabib, *Situating the Self,* p. 74.

11. Ruddick, *Maternal Thinking,* p. 123.

12. Ibid., pp. 129–135.

13. Hartsock, "The Feminist Standpoint."

14. Ruddick, *Maternal Thinking,* p. 135.

15. Ibid., p. 148.

16. Ibid., p. 150.

17. Ibid., pp. 141–159.

18. Obviously, feminist involvement in the antinuclear movement in the 1980s is important here (see Cohn, "Sex and Death in the Rational World of Defense Intellectuals"; Harris and King, *Rocking the Ship of State;* Warren and Cady, *Hypatia Special Issue*).

19. There is a huge literature in and around all these issues. See Nicholson, *Feminism/Postmodernism;* Hirsch and Fox-Keller, *Conflicts in Feminism;* Gunew, *A Reader in Feminist Knowledge;* Marchand and Parpart, *Feminism/Postmodernism/Development;* Mohanty, Russo, and Torres, *Third World Women and the Politics of Feminism;* articles in Grant and Newland, *Gender and International Relations;* Newland, "The Sources of Gender Bias in International Relations Theory"; Moser, "Gender Planning in the Third World"; and Goetz, "Feminism and the Claim to Know."

20. Benhabib, *Situating the Self,* p. 187.

21. Ibid., pp. 152–153.

22. Ibid., p. 187.

23. Ibid., p. 77.

24. In her first book, *Critique, Norm, and Utopia,* Benhabib argued that Habermas's communicative or discourse ethics provided a way through for the critical theory tradition, which has its roots in the work of Kant, Hegel, and Marx. The essays in *Situating the Self* set Habermas's critical theory against various alternatives and argue, overall, for some modifications to Habermas's ideas, particularly in the light of Arendt's work (see below); but they nevertheless continue to see Habermas as the best hope for a contemporary critical ethical and political theory.

In the book on Arendt, Benhabib continues to utilize the perspective of Habermas's critical theory in her critique of what she terms Arendt's "phenomenological essentialism" and as a corrective to Arendt's monological view of ethics and overly agonistic model of politics.

25. For a thorough discussion of debates over communicative or discourse ethics, see Benhabib and Dallmyr, *The Communicative Ethics Controversy*.

26. Habermas, "Discourse Ethics," pp. 71–73.

27. Benhabib, *Situating the Self,* pp. 105–106.

28. Ibid., p. 185.

29. Ibid., pp. 182–185.

30. Ibid., p. 185.

31. Ibid., pp. 158–161.

32. Arendt, "Thinking and Moral Considerations," p. 8.

33. Benhabib, *Situating the Self,* p. 141.

34. Ibid., pp. 90–95; Benhabib, *Reluctant Modernism,* pp. 123–141.

35. Benhabib, *Situating the Self,* pp. 124–133.

36. Ibid., pp. 137–141, 187–190.

37. Ibid., p. 230.

38. Ibid., p. 45.

39. Ibid., p. 45.

40. Rorty, "Human Rights," p. 118.

41. Ibid., p. 124.

42. Ibid., pp. 116–117.

43. It should be noted that Ruddick is aware of these arguments and in general is much more tentative in her claims to a feminist standpoint than Hartsock. Nevertheless, in invoking the notion of standpoint, Ruddick is continuing to be caught up in the theoretical preoccupation with *justifying* the exclusions that are effected by her theory. Even as she accounts for ways in which mothers have colluded with militarism, she is also engaged in establishing her right to say that such mothers are wrong.

44. Rorty, "Human Rights," pp. 124–125.

45. Hutchings, *Kant, Critique, and Politics*.

3

Explorations of Difference in Normative International Relations

Vivienne Jabri

Late modern feminism faces a multitude of challenges as it confronts conditions within global political and economic structures that differentially impact upon women, enabling some—primarily those located in the West—while constraining the majority of all those deemed "other," that vast expanse of a space named "nonwestern." The inequalities of the global politico-economic arena, coupled with manifest diversities in the lived experience of women that transcend the signifying divides of state or region, highlight the dilemmas that confront feminist theory and praxis, which for so long has sought to establish shared experiences and commonalities as the foundation stone for the universal emancipation of women. Women, or even feminists, can no longer claim to "speak with one voice," or respond as a unity, to the clarion call of a sisterhood at large. Thus bereft of its universalist aspirations, the challenge to feminism is highlighted daily with images of violence perpetrated against individuals named women, with socioeconomic conditions that confine primarily women and children within the poverty trap and with continuing exploitative practices that deny equal access to the public sphere for women.

Such structural inequalities that continue to define the present order must be juxtaposed with the increasing globalization of all aspects of social relations, generating a changing, multilayered contextualization wherein the global comes into direct confrontation with the local. The global public space has come to constitute an arena of contestation, where the excluded and marginalized struggle to acquire voice against a context of increasing abstraction of systems of knowledge and power. This global public space is also the location of migration, exile, and individual movements traversing bounded territories and identities. The narratives of self that emerge from such complexity highlight the proximities of the local and global, past and present, so that fragmentation and the reordering of

39

time and space relations suggest a move away from a singular, unchallenged locatedness.[1]

This complex interplay of the local and the global has clear implications for the construction of subjectivity and for our conceptions of the public spaces within which enactments of judgment and responsibility, the constitutive elements of moral agency, take place. How then does feminist theory respond? More significantly for the context of this chapter and others in the collection, is there a form of ethicality that we might label feminist and that focuses upon difference as the formative moment of a late modern discourse that seeks to reimagine the political spaces available to us?

The aim of this chapter is to explore the notion of difference and to problematize subjectivity as the baseline from which we could rewrite an ethical position for feminist theory and praxis. Drawing from major voices in poststructuralist and postcolonial discourses, I aim to articulate a normative position that takes into account questions of self-constitution and self-transformation as the baseline from which we may begin to reimagine both the agency of women and the political spaces that surround the diversity of women's lived experience. Arguing against the care and justice dualism that so permeates feminist ethics, I suggest that style and self-understanding are the formative moments of a late-modern subjectivity that is responsive to its constitutive other. What is therefore articulated is a form of *aesthetic ethicality* that interprets the individual as a location of multiple "textual selves,"[2] and that suggests a form of feminist ethics that recognizes the plurality of the self and the plurality of cultured subjectivity. This would entail a move beyond a singular definition of woman, or of feminism, suggesting instead a discourse of dissent that has a multiplicity of locations and styles, each with its differential set of enablements and constraints.

The first section of the chapter provides a brief evaluation of how feminist discourses on ethics have dealt with the question of difference. I show that a formulaic addition of culture to gender fails to account for the complexities of subjectivity and the multiple narratives that constitute the self. In attempting to establish a theoretical discourse on the question of identity and the challenge of fragmentation, the second section of the chapter concentrates specifically on the complexities of culture and cultural agency. Here we see an argument against originary conceptions of subjectivity, suggesting in place of such certainties the view that identity refers to a complex interplay of articulations of self and the typifications that constitute the self within social continuities. The refigurations of self that emerge across time may come to have manifest implications for the redrawing of the political and ethical domains of social existence. Using this as a point of departure, the final section aims to restyle the ethical subject in feminist discourse through the use of Judith Butler's reading of sex and gender as "corporeal stylization." The point of connection between Butler's approach to gender and the view of identity in terms of strategies of selfhood is a Foucaultian conception of ethics as the cultivation and transfiguration of self. The form of aesthetic ethics that emerges is finally illustrated through the use of the installation, and particularly the work of a Palestinian exile, Mona Hatoum, as a form of artistic expression that incorporates the themes of fragmentation and restylization as modes of dissent and subversion.

THE DOMAIN OF FEMINIST
ETHICS AND THE UNIVERSALIZED SELF

Gayatry Chakravorty Spivak, in an early essay on French feminism, asks the question, "What is the constituency for an international feminism?" She moves on to state that however significant the difference between French and Anglo-American feminisms may be, these must remain superficial compared with the seeming chasm that separates our discourses in a late modern West from all locations named "nonwestern." In Spivak's terms, "I see no way to avoid insisting that there has to be a simultaneous other focus: not merely who am I? But who is the other woman? How am I naming her? How does she name me? Is this part of the problematic I discuss?"[3] These are questions central to the concerns of this chapter, which seeks, along with others within feminist discourse, a form of critical ethicality that focuses on self-understanding and self-construction at one and the same time as our constructions of the other. This constitutes a form of vision that from the outset recognizes the dual sense of the ontology of moral agency as located both within the self and the self's relationship with its constitutive other. The other form of "double vision" is one Spivak suggests is the defining character of French feminism, where feminism is seen as both against sexism and for feminism. But can we claim one form of feminism, or must we realize that our discourses are always situated within a wider societal realm constituted by local institutional, discursive, and normative continuities that defy any universal ethic, any singular construction of woman, and (ultimately) a singular conception of liberation or emancipation?

The domain of feminist ethics is framed by a dualism between what Gilligan refers to as an "ethic of justice," identified with a Kantian ontological project of autonomous personhood, as opposed to an "ethic of care," the ontological project of which is centered on the relational self. Those, like Carol Gilligan, who espouse the latter suggest that the justice perspective is inherently masculinist, whereas care is associated with the lived experience of women.[4] The justice-care dualism parallels in form the normative project in international relations, constructed as it is around a Kantian-Hegelian opposition that has come to identify the cosmopolitan-communitarian divide.[5] This latter debate is founded upon a contending ontology of moral agency, with a Kantian, predetermined self, largely male, rational, and autonomous, critiqued by Hegelian conceptions of the self as communally constituted, realizing individuality within the public realm of civil society and state, confined to a male citizenry and built upon the exclusion of women. This ontological dualism came into sharp focus with the publication of John Rawls's *Theory of Justice* and subsequent communitarian critiques of the deontological liberalism that formed the focus of Rawls's Kantian-inspired ideas on the construction of a just society.[6]

One of the most influential texts in feminist ethics is Gilligan's *In a Different Voice,* which forms the baseline from which other feminist conceptions of moral agency derive. The central premise of this text is that the moral agency of women is situated in a so-called ethic of care, which is defined in opposition to the abstractions of a Kantian-inspired ethic of justice based on autonomous, rational individuality. Gilligan, a developmental psychologist, seeks to challenge Lawrence Kohlberg's moral developmental theory, claiming for women a "relational self" whose moral judgments are framed by affectional ties rather than by conceptions of justice based on the impartiality of a Kantian categorical imperative. Where Kohlberg defines an ethic of care as expressing an inferior subjectivity that he associates predominantly with his female subjects, Gilligan's claim, while not challenging the Kantian conception of the self, is that the ethic of care must be defined as equal and complementary to an ethic of justice.

Gilligan's association of an ethic of care with the lived experience of women has been effectively challenged on epistemological and ontological grounds and does not merit further consideration in this chapter.[7] What is important to highlight, however, and as Kimberly Hutchings's chapter in this book illustrates, is that Gilligan's formulaic account of the relationship between gender and moral agency has, despite the controversies associated with the early work, opened a space for a feminist discourse within a traditionally male-centered domain.[8] A second element that is more relevant to this chapter is Gilligan's more recent texts on the constitution of women's moral agency. The central focus of this work is the concept of "narrative" and the constitutive impact of gender as well as other societal factors in the formation of "moral voices."[9] In seeking to move beyond an absolutist discourse, Susan Heckman, using Gilligan as baseline, suggests that we should be concerned with the plurality of moral voices rather than with the one voice that an ethic of care would advocate.[10]

Recent feminist reconstructions of moral theory seek to formulate a concept of moral agency that is both constituted by the discursive and institutional continuities of local situations and is capable of resistance.

Drawing upon what she labels as the "postmodern subject" and using Wittgenstein's notion of a language game, Heckman articulates a position that, in significant respects, moves us away from the uniformities and implicit essentialisms associated with the relational self as the subject of the care perspective. The "discursive subject" that emerges from Heckman's Foucaultian-inspired account is one that is "both resistant and discursively constituted,"[11] where each act of resistance is also an act of self-creation: "At any given time we find ourselves confronted with an array of discourses of subjectivity, scripts that we are expected to follow. We can accept the script that is written for us or, alternatively, piece together a different script from other discourses that are extant in our particular circumstances."[12] This capacity for a rescripting of our narratives is not expressive of the enlightenment premise of autonomous, rational individuality but is rather a mode of recreation emergent from a plethora of discursive practices that surround the individual. Using the Wittgensteinian notion of a language game, Heckman defines feminism itself as a language of resistance emanating from a set of localized subjectivities. She identifies Gilligan's "care voice" as a

> distinct moral language game rooted in the particular experiences of most women in our culture. The logic and justification of this language game are different from that of the justice voice, but, as with the justice voice, the criteria of rightness are internal to the language game. The difference between the two moral discourses can be attributed to the fact that the "form of life" experienced by most women in our culture is distinct from that of men.[13]

The significance of Heckman's reformulation of the ethic of care lies in its recognition that moral voices are constituted differently in accordance with the positionality of the subject. However, the central problem with Heckman's approach is its failure to problematize subjectivity and self-understanding, so that it retains the foundational position that there is an already-existing identity through the category of "woman"—or one based on race and another on culture. The implication is that there is already a defined (and therefore unproblematized) subject of feminism or of ethics, a subject of culture, and so on. Such a restatement of what is essentially a communitarian position, with an ontology based upon what MacIntyre labels the "situated self,"[14] fails to account for the complexities associated with the self's capacity to negotiate the borderlines of ascribed affinities or cultural and gendered significations.

The other problem with Heckman's valiant effort to rescue Gilligan is that it seems to reiterate the dichotomous representations that associate the public and rational with masculinity, whereas that deemed private and emotive continues to constitute femininity. Moreover, the subjects associated with these categories are, respectively, men and "most" women. The "game" of the public is seen to be distinct from that of the private; the rational/autonomous self excludes and is excluded from the private realm; the lives of most women are, almost by definition, distinct from those of men. The paradox of first claiming a Foucaultian, creative "discursive self" only for this self to be so easily categorized is all too apparent. To simply suggest "a multiplicity of moral voices constituted by race, class, culture, as well as gender"[15] is to recognize a constructed difference among these social categories but to fail the creative self engaged in a constantly shifting articulation of these differences. It is furthermore an unreflexive naming of individuals that denies them their space, their subjectivity, their creativity.

It is therefore not enough to simply suggest, in a gestural salute to multiculturalism, that gender oppression differs depending on cultural context or that norms are associated with the contextualities of the local. Feminists have come to recognize that gender intersects with race, class, sexual orientation, and other modalities of discursively constituted identities. To claim for women a distinct moral voice—the ethic of care—is to strive for epistemological and ontological certainties, a form of systematized morality that has its foundational moment in gender. There is a sense in which this form of feminist discourse has substituted one foundation (reason) with another (gender or community) in an attempt to impose ordered explanations of why it is that the individual has the capacity for judgment and responsibility—a capacity to extend care and offer assistance to those less advantaged, to the imprisoned, to the tortured, to the excluded and marginalized. The feminist ethicality this chapter formulates argues against any singular foundational purpose to moral action, suggesting instead an acknowledgment of the ambiguities, spontaneities, and complexities that surround political identities and moral actions.

CULTURAL SUBJECTIVITY

The form of feminist ethics articulated in this chapter seeks to move the terms of debate so that we are no longer encumbered by the transcendental category called woman. It seeks a problematization of subjectivity where dissent may have a multiplicity of locations, each recursively constituted by these locations, while asserting a transformative capacity that is situated in contingent daily encounters. This is a feminism with a borderline shifting identity, recognizing its diasporic existence, its exiled position within that space of negation. It seeks no singular definition—as woman, feminist, mother, lesbian, lover, intellectual, peasant, worker, artist. Rather, it shifts within the interstices between these signifying categories, being at one and the same time reconstituted by and transformative of boundaries it does not respect. This is a feminism of the dissident. It does not seek conversion to a realm of true believers, those group affiliates whose wont is to pounce on dissent and difference. This is finally a feminism that does not seek a sisterhood at large or a constituency for an international feminism. Rather than drawing up parallels of experienced oppression, it seeks to celebrate that location of creativity wherein resistance takes place, where the dissent of the singular voice is articulated.

Feminist theory and praxis has sought to incorporate difference—the multiplicity of locations that constitute women's lives—through an acknowledgment of its own particular location within a western spacio-temporal setting. There is, however, a sense in which these locations remain unproblematized through discursive renditions of gender and culture, as if these are singular conceptual categories that easily situate the individual with respect to the social continuities that surround her/him. A move away from such singularities would place the focus of attention on the multiple sites of political presence and to inquire into practices of exclusion. As pointed out by Homi Bhabha:

> What is theoretically innovative, and politically crucial, is the need to think beyond narratives of originary and initial subjectivities and to focus on those moments or processes that are produced in the articulation of cultural differences. These "in-between" spaces provide the terrain for elaborating strategies of selfhood—singular or communal—that initiate new signs of identity, and innovative sites of collaboration, and contestation, in the act of defining the idea of society itself.[16]

Bhabha asks, "How are subjects formed 'in-between,' or in excess of, the sum of the 'parts' of difference (usually intoned as race/class/gender, etc.)?"[17] To inquire into culture's "in-between" is to reject any notion of difference or of identity as pregiven categories into which individuals may be typecast, for such would be a negation of alterity and a denial of the different positionalities that may exist within culture, race, or gender. What captures interest here is not so much the idea that movement across time and space produces complex arrays of experience beyond the point of origin, as Bhabha would suggest. What is pointed to in this chapter is, rather, the call for a refocusing of attention upon the moment where articulations of difference emerge, for it is such moments that point to the complexity of the subject as being always what Julia Kristeva would refer to as the "subject in process/on trial."[18] To therefore simply add culture to gender in some formulaic gesture toward difference is to preclude any discussion of the processes through which the self is constructed or of the political consequences that emerge from one mode of representation as opposed to another.

A complex array of memory, myth, symbolic orders, and self-imagery come to constitute the lifeworld of the situated individual. These constitutive aspects of the self are not necessarily articulated within social interaction but form a backdrop that enables the individual to go on and provide meaning in the daily encounters of situated individuals. Any articulation of a sense of self provides a marker and a continual reaffirmation of the locations the individual occupies in relation to structures of "signification" and "domination." Any such articulation is also at one and the same time a moment of interpretation wherein the individual or subject elaborates a form of "positionality" within the complex matrices of signification and power that constitute society.[19] Whereas articulations of identity constitute strategies of selfhood, the typification of the individual points to particular specifications that define the self through dominant social norms and symbolic orders. The mutually constitutive relationship between self-expressions and representations of the self suggest processes through which constructions of self and other emerge.[20]

To focus on those moments of self-expression and articulations of identity is by no means a reiteration of the self-contained, autonomous entity of Cartesian thought but rather a recognition that such moments constitute a capacity to move beyond the limits and confines of a conforming social order and the discursive and institutional constraints that constitute society's preference for classificatory control. Related to this is the view that the self situated within the continuities of social life is also recursively implicated in the reproduction of its discursive and institutional norms. It is this duality between self and society—one constitutive of the other, each action and utterance within daily encounters being both situated within and reconstitutive of the wider realm of meaning—that poses a challenge to any discourse that seeks universal legitimacy.[21] What emerges is a form of self-understanding situated within societal formations that are constitutive of the self but at the same time are subject to individual reflexivity and interpretative capacity.

In arguing against discourses that assume a pre-given subject, Butler illustrates the relationship between politics and inquiry into subjectivity when she states: "To claim that politics requires a stable subject is to claim that there can be no *political* opposition to that claim. Indeed that claim implies that a critique of the subject cannot be a politically informed critique but, rather, an act which puts into jeopardy politics as such."[22] The move away from a unified, originary notion of subjectivity does not deny the presence of the subject or the processes through which the subject negotiates its presence within the complexities of social life. Nor is there a rejection of the place of identity in what constitutes agency and politics and the multiplicity of ways in which the space of the political is drawn and redrawn. In view of the continual processes through which we interpret and redesign our spacio-temporal locations, or the different ways in which we retrace our histories, identities come to form what Stuart Hall refers to as a "politics of location," incorporating both mobilization and contestation.[23]

A politics of location conventionally conceived in the discourses of international relations would situate the self within the boundaries of the sovereign state just as a discourse of origins would locate the self in relation to an ethnic or cultural community contained within the construct "nation." Practices deemed to belong to the terrain of the political would thus be so only if contained within the signifying boundaries of state and/or nation. If, however, we conceive of the state and nation as merely hegemonic discursive constructs, we come to recognize the multiple sites of political presence and the complex array of spheres within which contestation and transformation may take place. The discursive hegemony that locates self-identity in relation to the state or nation emerges from a point of intersection where the positionality of the individual is defined through structures of domination and is continually constituted in relation to networks of meaning and normative expectations.[24] This point of intersection that comes to constitute the positionality of the self is, however, also a site for contestation and selection, where nonconformity is at its most visible and self-creativity, or self-refiguration, the ultimate expression of agency.

Identity is therefore constructed through discourse from a fund of interpretative possibilities, some of which, like national identity, come to constitute a dominant, hegemonic mode of discourse; but others actively express nonconformity and dissent from any homogenizing influence. Identity is always manifest in a linguistic public space, where the routine of daily encounters must be juxtaposed with the transformative moment of selection and contestation. In place of the certainties expressive of modernity's hegemonic/disciplining discourses, where the self is categorized within a form of "cultural totalization,"[25] I am arguing for a recognition of identiational fragmentation and the reordering of time and space relations. As Hall points out, "Identities are never unified and, in late modern times, increasingly fragmented and fractured; never singular but multiply constructed across different, often intersecting and antagonistic, discourses, practices and positions. They are subject to radical historicisation, and are constantly in the process of change and transformation."[26] The "narrativization of the self" is constructed within discourse and is produced "in specific historical and institutional sites within specific discursive formations and practices, by specific enunciative strategies."[27] Such narratives of the self are therefore always set against and constituted through modes of representation drawn upon and recursively reconstituted in the utterances and expressions of selfhood.

If we are to make the move away from representations of the subject as singular and unified, we come to recognize the fragmentation of subjectivity and therefore a rejection of singular representations of locatedness. What emerges is a form of multiplicity where the narratives and memory traces of the past merely form part of a complex collage that constitutes the lived experience of the individual. The narratives of the self come to derive from a complex interplay of past and present, the local and the global, where no singular representation has authoritative standing. In a statement that has manifold resonances for any feminist discourse that seeks to simply add culture to gender, Bhabha suggests that the "representation of difference must not be hastily read as the reflection of *pre-given* ethnic or cultural traits set in the fixed tablet of tradition."[28] There is, within a globalized setting, a sense in which there is an "on-going negotiation" where narratives of self are very much located at the borderline of a retraced history and a resignified present. The cultural hybridity that emerges from such "interstitial agency" allows articulations of difference without "an assumed or imposed hierarchy."[29]

The predominant project that frames postcolonial discourses is the theme of "crossing over," where the defining moments of "interstitial agency" include hybrid subjectivity, reinscriptions of history, and the refigurations of narratives of self that may no longer be confined within singular representations.[30] For Bhabha, the postcolonial perspective as a mode of analysis "attempts to revise those nationalist or 'nativist' pedagogies that set up the relation of Third World and First World in a binary structure of opposition. . . . It forces a recognition of the more complex cultural and political boundaries that exist on the cusp of these often opposed spheres."[31] What Bhabha calls the "in-between" of culture is also reflected in Edward Said's concern with processes of displacement and migration, articulating the position of the exile as existing in a "median state, neither completely at one with the new setting nor fully disencumbered of the old, beset with half involvements and half detachments, nostalgic and sentimental on one level, an adept mimic or secret outcast on another."[32] In seeing a parallel in experience between the exile and the outcast, Said's project has been concerned with challenging exclusionary practices through highlighting the life of the exiled intellectual as standing outside of unifying representations and defying simple identiational categories, projecting a self that is multiply positioned and resistant to a unifying conformity. The in-between location of cultural hybridity comes to represent a "diasporic habitation,"[33] threatening monolithic representation of the past and, in so doing, interrupting the givens of the present.

Such a rewriting of identity has implications not only for how feminist theory deals with difference but also for how we may reconceptualize ethics. Taking the themes outlined above as a starting point, I outline in the next section a restylized ethics that takes as its point of departure the problematization of subjectivity and refiguration as its defining elements. What emerges is a form of ethicality that takes account of difference and that does so through an acknowledgment of what Foucault terms the "aesthetics of experience."

RESTYLING THE ETHICAL
SUBJECT IN FEMINIST DISCOURSE

In developing a conception of feminist ethics that takes account of difference, I am arguing for an ethical and praxiological discourse of dissent.[34] In so doing, I am arguing that the formative moment of any such discourse is the problematization of subjectivity and the construction of self. These are elements emerging from a recognition that the self is multiply located, capable of forms of reinscription and refiguration that defy easy categorization or any complicitous engagement with gestures of recognition or representation. While structures of domination may have differential impact on the lived experience of individuals—constraining some while enabling others, promoting the cause of some while ensuring the invisibility of others— there is a sense in which the self emerges in and through such structures, being constitutively implicated in the reproduction and transformation of such continuities. The self is continually signified through the regulatory practices in society—as citizen, as gendered, as sexual being, as deviant, or other form of signification. These become, as Butler points out, the "multiply contested sites of meaning" that hold a possibility for disruption and subversion.[35] In a statement that has resonances for the restylization of feminist ethics this chapter calls for, Butler states,

> The very complexity of the discursive map that constructs gender appears to hold out the promise of an inadvertent and generative convergence of these discursive and regulatory structures. If the regulatory fictions of sex and gender are themselves multiply contested sites of meaning, then the very multiplicity of their construction holds out the possibility of a disruption of their univocal posturing.[36]

Just as sex and gender are multiply contested sites of meaning that open out the possibility of dissent, so too any singular or originary constructions of cultural identity become the sites through which the self retraces her or his mode of being.

The form of self-understanding that emerges from and engages with the disruption of dominant sites of meaning encompasses as its constitutive elements both creativity and critique. A Foucaultian conception of self-understanding is one that recognizes the social constitution of the self as an entity located and defined within a complex array of discursive and normative structures, but one that is at the same time both malleable and creative.[37] Self-understanding implies a recognition of the social norms implicated in the constitution of the self and the capacity of the embodied self to move beyond the limits of social discourse and normative expectations. Foucault's turn to the subject in his later writings, and specifically in the second and third volumes of *The History of Sexuality*,[38] is an acknowledgment that although the subject may be a product of the disciplinary continuities that constitute society, there is here also a reflexive entity, somehow aware of the plural subjectivities instantiated in everyday interaction and in locales of self-expression that defy conformity.

Foucault's subject encompasses critique and creativity. Characterizing this "critical ontology" in language that has clear reflections in the postcolonial discourse already discussed, Foucault calls for a "limit attitude" that moves "beyond the outside-inside alternative" locating the self firmly "at the frontiers" where the pre-givens of whatever is deemed universal and necessitous are recognized as contingent and arbitrary. Such a "practical critique" becomes a basis for a "possible transgression," a transformative moment that defies limits and boundaries. The transgressive moment emerges in a certain cultivation and stylization of self wherein the self sees herself or himself as a "work of art."[39] What we see, therefore, is a trajectory in Foucault's corpus from the technologies of discipline to the technologies of self, and it is the latter that define Foucault's thought on ethics and that I argue are central to a reconception of feminist ethics in terms of the aesthetics of existence.

What primarily concerns Foucault in his conception of ethics in terms of the cultivation of self as a work of art; and central to the form of discourse I wish to develop in feminist ethics is the juxtaposition of what he calls the "moral code" and the "aesthetics of existence."[40] Where the former refers to the regulative rules of social life, the latter points to style as the expressive moment of transgression and transfiguration—the self-forming activity that not only subverts categorical notions of identity but also allows an expression of difference that is beyond systematization or even certainty. In summarizing Foucault's position on ethics, A. Davidson points to the centrality of style to the form of aesthetic ethics that is apparent in this discourse:

> Foucault thought of ethics proper, of the self's relationship to itself, as having four main aspects: the ethical substance, that part of oneself that is taken to be the relevant domain for ethical judgement; the mode of subjection, the way in which the individual establishes his or her relation to moral obligations and rules; the self-forming activity or ethical work that one performs on oneself in order to transform oneself into an ethical subject; and, finally, the telos, the mode of being at which one aims in behaving ethically.[41]

Difference emerges from the particular combinations of each of these elements, where such difference expresses a "style of life" that "gives expression to the self's relationship to itself. To indicate what part of oneself one judges, how one relates oneself to moral obligations, what one does to transform oneself into an ethical subject, and what mode of being one aims to realize is to indicate how one lives, is to characterize one's style of life."[42] Style comes to express that moment of creativity that takes the individual beyond the regulative rules of the moral code toward a transformation of her or his mode of being. Such individuality is not expressive of the Cartesian self of logocentric reason but, rather, one located around an aesthetic subjectivity having a capacity for a redescription and reinvention of the lifeworld—a capacity made possible through a form of poetic ingenuity that even defies the rules of language and comes to create a mode of being that proclaims difference in the face of a conforming social order. As C. Venn points out, the subject envisaged here is a "Dionysian being whose will to power seeks not dominion over others but a form of plenitude— epiphanic perhaps—through the ecstatic and sublime experience of the artistic, inventive transfiguration of oneself."[43]

How does this translate into a form of feminist ethics that takes account of difference without denying difference its moment of emergence? In seeking to move beyond any foundationalist principles, Butler's approach to feminism starts from a Foucaultian conception of the subject and moves to reinscribe a subversive form of politics centered on notions of articulation and performance. As I will indicate, Butler's work on identity, subjectivity, and the body comes to inform and complement the postcolonial discourse I outlined earlier.

The radical critique Butler provides starts with the view that feminism, rather than seeking an international constituency at large—one that would simply incorporate the "other" within its terms—should remain "self-critical with respect to . . . totalizing gestures."[44] Butler suggests a number of points of departure that enable this critical self-reflection. The first is the move away from identifying the enemy as singular, for this amounts to a "reverse-discourse that uncritically mimics the strategy of the oppressor instead of offering a different set of terms." She also argues against the requirement for "unity" or "solidarity" as precursors of radical political action or contestation. Efforts to build up coalitions aimed precisely to take account of difference through a set of dialogic encounters enable women to articulate different modes or forms of identity in order to shape some form of unity in the midst of diversity. However, "despite the clearly democratizing impulse that motivates coalition building, the coalitional theorist can inadvertently reinsert herself as sovereign of the process by trying to assert an ideal form for coalitional structures in advance, one that will effectively guarantee unity as the outcome."[45] Furthermore, "the very notion of 'dialogue' is culturally specific and historically bound." What is at the heart of this critique of coalitional politics is that the latter assumes "in advance that there is a category of 'women' that simply needs to be filled in with various components of race, class, age, ethnicity and sexuality in order to become complete." To assume the category "incompleteness," however, would render it a "permanently available site of contested meanings."[46] For Butler, the "coherence" and "continuity" of "the person" emerge from "socially instituted and maintained norms of intelligibility" that allow certain configurations of sex, gender, and sexual desire and prohibit those that do not easily ascribe to such regulatory boundaries. Just as the body, following this Foucaultian analysis, is not a "ready surface awaiting signification," so too "sex" becomes a "performatively enacted signification" that, "released from its naturalized interiority and surface, can occasion the parodic proliferation and subversive play of gendered meanings."[47] And in a statement that has profound resonances for the feminist ethics I am articulating here, Butler describes her project as

> effort to think through the possibility of subverting and displacing those naturalized and reified notions of gender that support masculine hegemony and heterosexist power, to make gender trouble, not through the strategies that figure a utopian beyond, but through the mobilization, subversive confusion, and proliferation of precisely those constitutive categories that seek to keep gender in its place by posturing as the foundational illusions of identity.[48]

The form of subversion Butler envisages is defined in terms of performance and parody. Borrowing from Foucault's ideas on the inscription of the body by regulatory structures, Butler argues for a redescription of gender as "the disciplinary production of the figures of fantasy through the play of presence and absence on the body's surface, the construction of the gendered body through a series of exclusions and denials, signifying absences."[49] The "stylization of gender" amounts to a "fantasied and fantastic figuration of the body" in the service of a "heterosexual construction and regulation of sexuality within the reproductive domain."[50] The exclusionary signification that emerges suggests a coherence of identity that "conceals the gender discontinuities that run rampant within heterosexual, bisexual, gay and lesbian contexts in which gender does not necessarily follow from sex, and desire, or sexuality generally, does not seem to follow from gender."[51] Given that the norm of gender so established is a mere fiction, or "fabrication," the refiguration of this fiction through performance and parody is a subversion of the givens of identity and more specifically gender identity. Pointing to the practice of drag and cross-dressing as revealing the "imitative structure of gender itself—as well as its contingency,"[52] Butler makes a powerful case for the subversive potential that emerges from restylization and the refiguration of gender through what is in effect a rewriting of the body.

Just as gender is a form of "corporeal stylization,"[53] so too modes of cultural expression are performative in the sense of being contingent constructions of meaning that go through perpetual displacement suggesting a "fluidity of identities" with an openness to resignification and recontextualization. The parodic performance that restyles identity disrupts notions of originality or a core of being, suggesting instead a form of "variable boundary," which is the "body." That identity is performative—that it is an enactment of style scripted on the body—points to the question of how certain and particular modes of self-figuration and stylization may come to disrupt hegemonic discourses that seek to domesticate or discipline the self into some form of coherent, original identity.

The self that emerges from this discourse is an expression of a Foucaultian "limit attitude," a self-understanding that is neither inside nor outside, that occupies a liminal state, and that is as troubling in its borderline location as it is in its capacity to redraw boundaries that seek exclusion. This is a diasporic habitation of the metaphorical exile, performing and articulating a fragmented identity, the (dis)locations of which find their expressive moment in the text.[54]

In an exhibition of late-twentieth-century art held in 1995 at the Tate Gallery in London and entitled "Rites of Passage," the themes of exile, fragmentation, and self-understanding are apparent in every installation, just as the embodied self is seen as having no particular, secure location or representation. As described by Arnold van Gennep in a book, *The Rites of Passage,* published in 1908, the rite of passage involves three phases: separation, transition, and incorporation. It is the transition stage that Gennep refers to as the "liminal" stage, which describes the individual as being neither inside nor outside of society. As Stewart Morgan, in an introduction to the exhibition, points out, it is this liminal, transition stage that locates the works of art exemplified by artists such as Mona Hatoum, Pepe Espaliu, and Louise Bourgeois. In commenting on the exhibition, Julia Kristeva states,

> My overriding impression is that we have never been in such a state of crisis and fragmentation, in terms of both the individual—the artist, and the aesthetic object. The crisis is such that not only do we have difficulty with the question of the work of art, but also the question of beauty itself seems unbearable, as does the spiritual destiny of these strange and shocking objects. . . . So the questions to be asked are "Why do they do this? Who is doing this? What are the experiences behind these objects, objects which work with the impossible, with the disgusting, the intolerable?"[55]

The primary element of the installations included in the exhibition was a questioning of subjectivity and the portrayal of the constantly shifting boundaries between inside and outside, presence and absence. Kristeva's concluding comment on the exhibition, "The frontiers between sign and body, inside and outside, self and other are threatened," is especially pertinent to the work of Hatoum, which exemplifies the interstitial agency located in the in-between of culture—on the borderline, disrupting boundary—and within the work of art, articulating a form of ethicality that problematizes subjectivity and the relations with the other.

Hatoum's installation, *Corps étranger* (foreign body), points to the liminality and marginality that defines that space of negation where the subject is neither present nor absent, where the "I" and "other" dissolve into a common space of vulnerability. Born in Beirut to Palestinian parents, resident in London since the outbreak of the Lebanese civil war in 1975, Hatoum seeks in her work to reinscribe the body, her own body, as work of art. The "foreign body" exhibited in *Corps étranger* is Hatoum's own, the inside of which is opened to the scrutiny of the public via a camera used in endoscopy and coloscopy. *Corps étranger* is a tubular room in which a video image is projected onto a circular screen on the floor. The images captured come into being as the camera enters each orifice of the artist in turn, moving into the complex landscapes of a breathing, living body. The viewer encounters the distorted imagery projected on the floor by standing inside the tubular installation. The viewer becomes part of the installation: a "pure white cylinder pierced by two slender vertical apertures through which the viewer enters" and is "embraced within a dark circular chamber and enveloped in the soft rhythms and noises that emanate from speakers enclosed in the perimeter walls."[56] Frances Morris describes this work, in terms of Kristeva'a notion of "abjection," as one that "disturbs identity, system, order. What does not respect borders, positions, rules. The in-between, the ambiguous, the composite."[57]

There is no unity or certainty in the form of self-recognition that Hatoum describes in *Corps étranger,* the text upon which the artist's body is opened out and becomes at one with a viewing public. Both are inside and outside, standing on the liminal threshold. The in-between location that Hatoum gives expression to through her art disrupts the binary oppositions of public/private, mind/body, inside/outside, presenting a parody of these constructs, shattering any semblance of boundary. In another work, a video installation named *Measures of Distance* (1988), the themes of exile, fragmentation, the body, subjectivity, and representations of the other are shown to be intimately related. The video shows images of Hatoum's mother in the shower, with letters written in Arabic from the mother in Beirut to her daughter in London superimposed on the images. The voices heard on the video are of the daughter reading the letters in English and of

Arabic conversations between mother and daughter. The following is Hatoum's own description of this work:

> One reason for doing this work was because whenever I watched news reports about Lebanon, I was struck by how the Arabs were always shown en masse with mostly hysterical women crying over dead bodies. We rarely heard about the personal feelings of those who lost their relatives. It is as if people from the Third World are seen as a mass or a herd and not as individuals. Of course I was also influenced by the feminist slogan "the personal is political." The work was constructed around letters from my mother in Beirut to myself in London and a dozen slides I took of my mother under the shower. Although the main thing that comes across is a very close and emotional relationship between mother and daughter, it also speaks of exile, displacement, disorientation and a tremendous sense of loss as a result of the separation caused by the war. In this work I was also trying to go against the fixed identity that is usually implied in the stereotype of Arab woman as passive, mother as a non-sexual being . . . the work is constructed visually in such a way that every frame speaks of literal closeness and implied distance. The close-up images of my mother under the shower, a closeness also echoed by the intimacy of the exchange between my mother and myself, she is speaking openly of her feelings and answering intimate questions about her sexuality. Her letters in Arabic appear over her images and look like barbed wire or a veil that prevents total access to the image yet they are the only means of communication. Letters also imply distance. The sound track on the video is of me reading her letters in English, in a sad and monotonous voice which is contrasted with laughter and animated Arabic conversation that took place between us. The Arabic conversation is given as much emphasis as the English text creating a difficult and alienating situation for a Western audience who have to strain to follow the narrative.[58]

There is here what Bhabha refers to as an "interstitial intimacy," where the separation of spheres of experience into the private and the public, the past and present is questioned through an "in-between temporality that takes the measure of dwelling at home, while producing an image of the world of history."[59] There is in Hatoum's work an inscription of a borderline habitation, between home and the world, art and representation, art and the disruption of exclusionist and marginalizing discourses and representation. The ethical moment that emerges from this subversive work encompasses both a questioning of originary identities and modes of signification of self and other; and at the same time, it articulates difference and resistance against structures of signification and domination. The body that emerges is not the docile body, signified, framed in passivity. Proximity and distance, and the artist's body located in a spacial and temporal in-between, are again powerfully represented in Hatoum's work *The Negotiating Table* (1983). In a description of this installation, Hatoum states:

My work often refers to hostile realities, war, destruction, but it is not localized. It refers to conflicts all over the world while hopefully pointing out the forces of oppression and resistance to these forces—cultural, historical, economic and social forces. In fact, I can think of only one piece which referred specifically to the invasion of Lebanon. It was entitled *The Negotiating Table,* and it was more like a "tableau vivant." I was lying on a table covered with entrails, bandages and blood and wrapped up in a body bag. There were chairs around the table and sound tapes of speeches of Western leaders talking about peace. It was basically a juxtaposition of two elements, one referring to the physical reality and brutality of the situation and the other to the way it is represented and dealt with in the West. This piece was the most direct reference I had ever made to the war in Lebanon. I made this work right after the Israeli invasion and the massacres in the camps, which for me was the most shattering experience of my life. But in general my work is about my experience of living in the West as a person from the Third World, about being an outsider, about occupying a marginal position, being excluded, being defined as "Other" or as one of "Them."[60]

What we see in Hatoum's work is an enactment of what Foucault terms a "style of being." The reinscription of self coupled with the critique of the present come to define a form of aesthetic ethics that places the self's relation to self as the expression of subjectivity. Although the artistic installation may be seen as a site of subversion, the discussion raises questions relating to the subject within society at large. In particular, it points to the multiple sites in which the political comes into being, in which the excluded and the mariginalized come to refigure themselves as political actors.

CONCLUSION

Feminist orthodoxies on ethics and cultural difference have all too often presented a formulaic discourse, taking gender and culture as unitary representations that are then interlinked in a gestural salute to cultural awareness and feminism's own historicity. A consequence of this is a wholesale negation of the complexities involved in the politics of location, in the constructions of self, and in self-other relations. There is, moreover, a tendency that stresses understanding the "other" as a critical moment that seeks to transcend cultural diversity. But to seek an understanding of the other, to incorporate the other within our conceptual schema, is precisely a negation of alterity and a denial of the multiform presences that define the political. Such an approach leaves the self wholly unproblematized and as such represented as sovereign, reasonable, and coherent. The western subject comes to be represented as the reference point, the standard against which all others are judged. The certainties that emerge from this mode of discourse become the basis of domination and exploitation, of violence perpetrated by the righteous against all who question. The certainties that emerge from such discourse have their baseline in a failure to problematize the self, and such unquestioning results in a singular narrative of history where the dominant subject of modernity, the western individual, remains unimplicated in the perpetuation of the domination, exclusion, and inequality now structurated in our globalized human condition.

In questioning gendered and cultural subjectivity, and in using insights drawn from Butler's Foucaultian analysis of gender and the politics of the body, I have sought to argue for a conception of identity as the inscription of style and the performative. The narratives of self that emerge come to encompass both critique and creativity where the self is no longer amenable to singular representation. The ethical moment defined, following Foucault, as the "critical ontology of ourselves," seeks a re-creation of ourselves, where the constraints and limits of our present boundaries, our present narratives, are always subject to disruption and subversion through restylization.

Subjectivity comes to be seen in terms of a politics of location encompassing not only the multiplicities of the self but also the multiple locations of culture and cross-cultural relations. The spacial and temporal "in-between" of culture is a form of rescripting of the present and a retracing of the past that defy easy categorization of past and present, inside and outside. Self and other come to occupy a positionality representing a reconstituted "we," where—as illustrated through Hatoum's work—the artist and viewer, self and other come to be aspects within the same artistic installation. This is a contained space of a reflexive self-understanding that allows the outer space within. This is also a text placed firmly within a public space, where the private space of the self is also a public space, open to the gaze of the stranger invited in to form an integral part of the text. Critique and creativity are both present here, replacing epistemological and ontological certainty with a form of critical ethicality that seeks neither dominion over others nor a systematization of its terms in a universal discourse aiming toward an international constituency.

NOTES

1. Giddens, *Modernity and Self-Identity.*
2. See Jabri, "Restyling the Subject of Responsibility in International Relations"; and Jabri, "Textualising the Self."
3. Spivak, *In Other Worlds,* p. 150.
4. See Gilligan, *In a Different Voice,* for the conceptual distinction between "justice" and "care" as perspectives on ethics.
5. See Brown, *International Relations Theory;* and Linklater, *Men and Citizens in the Theory of International Relations.*

6. Rawls, *A Theory of Justice*. Prominant communitarian critics of the Rawlsian position include MacIntyre, *After Virtue;* and Sandel, *Liberalism and the Limits of Justice.*

7. Tronto, "Women's Morality." For a critical application of the care perspective to international relations, see Robinson, "Globalizing Care."

8. See Jaggar, "Feminist Ethics."

9. Heckman, *Moral Voices*, p. 19.

10. Ibid., p. 67.

11. Ibid., p. 79.

12. Ibid., p. 82.

13. Ibid., p. 119.

14. MacIntyre, *After Virtue.*

15. Heckman, *Moral Voices*, p. 163.

16. Bhabha, *The Location of Culture*, p. 1.

17. Ibid., p. 2.

18. See "A Conversation with Julia Kristeva," interview conducted by Ina Lipkowitz and Andrea Loselle, in Ross M. Guberman (ed.), *Julia Kristeva Interviews.*

19. See Giddens, *The Constitution of Society,* for the concept of "positionality." Giddens refers to structures of signification as those that constitute the realms of meaning, whereas structures of domination point to the realm of power.

20. See Jabri, *Discourses on Violence,* for the conception of political identity articulated here.

21. Giddens articulates the notion of the duality of agency and structure in his theory of structuration. See his *Central Problems in Social Theory* and *The Constitution of Society.* For an application of structuration theory to the question of identity, see Jabri, *Discourses on Violence.*

22. Butler, "Contingent Foundations," p. 36.

23. Hall, "Introduction: Who Needs Identity?" p. 2.

24. The "point of intersection" among structures of domination, legitimation, and signification is precisely what defines the positionality of the self, according to Giddens. See his *The Constitution of Society.* See also Jabri's discussion of self-identity and the state in terms of positionality in *Discourses on Violence,* Chapter 5.

25. Bhabha, "Culture's In-Between," p. 58.

26. Hall, "Introduction: Who Needs Identity?" p. 4.

27. Ibid.

28. Bhabha, *The Location of Culture*, p. 2.

29. Ibid., p. 4.

30. For an elaboration of the theme of "crossing over," its implications for a reconceptualization of politics, and as applied to the Muslim political community, see Mandaville, "Reimagining the Umma."

31. Bhabha, *The Location of Culture*, p. 173.

32. Said, *Representations of the Intellectual,* p. 36. For the implications of Said's reflections on migration and exile in redefining moral agency, see Jabri, "Textualising the Self."

33. Parry, "Overlapping Territories and Intertwined Histories, p. 31.

34. See Jabri, "Restyling the Subject of Responsibility in International Relations," for the Foucaultian ethics expressed in this section.

35. Butler, *Gender Trouble,* p. 32.

36. Ibid.

37. Hoy, *Foucault: A Critical Reader*, p. 17.

38. Foucault, *The Use of Pleasure* and *The Care of the Self.* Focuault's turn to the subject is most strongly highlighted in Foucault, "What Is Enlightenment?"

39. See Foucault, "What Is Enlightenment?"

40. Rabinow, *The Foucault Reader,* p. 352.

41. Davidson, "Ethics as Ascetics," p. 118.

42. Ibid., pp. 124–125.

43. Venn, "Beyond Enlightenment?" p. 2.

44. Butler, *Gender Trouble,* p. 13.

45. Ibid., p. 14.

46. Ibid., p 15.

47. Ibid., p. 33.

48. Ibid., pp. 33–34.

49. Ibid., p. 135.

50. Ibid.

51. Ibid., pp. 135–136.

52. Ibid., p. 137.

53. Ibid., p. 139.

54. See Jabri, "Textualising the Self."

55. "Of Word and Flesh," an interview with Julia Kristeva by Charles Penwarden, reproduced in Morgan and Morris, *rites of passage,* p. 21.

56. Morgan and Morris, *rites of passage,* p. 103.

57. Kristeva, quoted in Morgan and Morris, *rites of passage*, p. 104.

58. Interview conducted by Claudia Spinelli in 1996 and reproduced in Michael Archer, Guy Brett, and Catherine de Zegher, *Mona Hatoum* (London: Phaidon Press, 1997), p. 140.

59. Bhabha, *The Location of Culture,* p. 13.

60. Interview conducted with Sara Diamond in 1987, reproduced in Archer, Brett, and de Zegher, *Mona Hatoum.*

4

Wartimeviolence: Pulping Fictions of the Subaltern

Nalini Persram

Violence—war. Violence—silence. Violence—time, space, subject.

Pulp Fiction.[1] The film's controversy arose, in large part, from its interpretation as a blatant advocation and glorification of violence. On initial impulse, heroin chic over racy music and the (not so) usual suspects produced judgments about the film's potential for the vicarious enjoyment of illicit and hedonistic wealth and of casual and violent death. Understandable if one takes the initial for the essential—that is, leaves without further thought, allowing sensations to dictate sensationalism, but still hasty. It turns what is a serious farce into a tasteless joke.[2]

To assume that the film merely reflects the recognition of gratuitous violence and escapism as features of contemporary life in late modernity and that it works with them to an aesthetic end is not so incomprehensible given the film's seductive stylism and fetishistic tendencies. Still, it ignores the grander discursive and ideological gesture the work makes. That gesture directs itself toward the idea of civil society as the battleground for war.

In the middle of the screenplay appears an account about a "gold watch."[3] Worn by several generations of soldiers in such conflicts as World War II and Vietnam and having traveled vast distances in space, time, and backsides to arrive in the hands of its new owner, it symbolizes the glory and heroism of men in military battle and the timelessness of war as the ultima ratio. Once distinguished from the generic notion of violence, the idea of war as a very specific political concept begins to codify itself more visibly. This, ironically, occurs by virtue of an absence of anything resembling either what is considered to be war in traditional international relations theory or what are held to be sociolegally sanctioned forms of violence.[4] In the two instances in the film where it would be possible, we are not taken into World War II or the Cold War with the watch bearers, nor do we attend the boxing match. What we do see are different portraits of violence—variously in the forms of substance abuse, beatings, sexual and mental torture, killings, and murders. But it is not, of course, just violence. It is not left as that demonized and individualized quirk in the machinery of the liberal democratic state, that occasionally justifiable but never legitimate action,[5] that imperfect but nevertheless necessary regulatory phenomenon that is fundamental to the power of the state but never so recognized.[6] For with a watch always ticking and the time constantly telling, what we witness, for all political purposes and intents, is *war.*

The politicization of violence lies in the way it is named as war. On this reading, one transports the film to the terrain of political theory. Here, the notion of violence takes on a very specific meaning in relation to the political subject of modernity, if said to be constituted by the violence of human essence.[7] Violence is conceivable at the fundamental level of human existence, according to Hannah Arendt, since it is "the basic social system, within which other secondary modes of social organization conflict or conspire."[8] Once within the social contract, however, once inside the city limits, violence is relegated to the realm of the antisocial, the nonmodern, and the dehumanist. It is removed, in other words, from the order of things.

In a scene that could have been lifted right out of *Pulp Fiction,* Governor Mario Cuomo on the day the bomb went off at the World Trade Center declared that "normalcy" could not return "to this safest and greatest city and state and nation in the world until the culprits" were caught. This statement came in the same week in which six residents of the Bronx were lined up and shot through the back of the head. In asking himself what could possibly constitute "normalcy" under these conditions, one international relations scholar has answered, "abnormalized events such as this one."[9] In a society that for many is nothing more than a field where life is nasty, brutish, and short, the abnormal is the norm.

Warfare, as Arendt noted, has lost much of its effectiveness and nearly all its glamour due to the technological developments of this century.[10] In Tarantino's film, it retrieves its former glory. And this is not just by virtue of cinematographic techniques or narrative. The often humorous though brutal depictions of systematic dehumanization—of killings, murders, tortures, and narrow escapes from hallucinogenic disaster on slick urbanscape—are disturbingly familiar. Indeed, they call to mind some of the daily satellite pictures of action footage taken in the cockpits during what was, according to official U.S. government statements, one of the most cleanly executed wars of this century, the Gulf War.[11] Stylistic liberty therefore actually speaks to a very tangible historical content, and the theme of war exceeding violence aligns the film more closely to the genre of

Hollywood war movies (particularly *Apocalypse Now*,[12] the cult status of which *Pulp Fiction* probably far surpasses) than to American crime films. In fact, one could say that it collapses this distinction, as war is seen to explode the boundaries of anarchy—its traditional bastion according to international relations theorists—and to expand its horizons to encompass the realm of the political. If there is an element of black humor in the film, it looms large behind this dynamic.

With the symbolic device of the watch being activated almost exactly midway through the film and the subsequent folding of the narrative back on itself, the gratuitousness of a clever filmmaker suddenly appears before us as the reality of a world driving itself into madness, with those who are able forcing themselves into oblivion at the expense of those who are unable.

The story ends in a way that is not at all foreign to American filmmaking traditions. Looping back to the opening scene of the film, a circular determinism is escaped through the narrative diversion depicting, in quietly spectacular fashion, the agency and power of the individual. The message is that all resides in the individual—for better or for worse. With it is thrown out the possibility that a "war of all against all" is intimately related to the idea that the sociopolitical ideal has been exceeded by its own technological rationalism and the logic of its individualist ontology. It is up to the morally responsible individual to rise above urban smog, blood, and ruin, to see through the ideological smoke screen of "in government we trust" and refuse complacency. It is the only way out. And it can be done. Pending, of course, a little divine—and for Tarantino, comedic—intervention, or a little pulp fiction.[13]

The violent reactions Tarantino's film has provoked are in many ways comparable to those prompted by an essay written by Gayatri Spivak a decade ago. Like the film's director, the essay's author turns to glitter and polemics as the means of establishing visibility for a very difficult issue. But the parallels do not stop there. If clockwork is what thematically transforms the mediocrity of violence into the profundity of war in a postmodern movie, Spivak demonstrates how it is the epistemic in social and political theorizing that commits the violence of rendering speech total silence. If Tarantino asks the difficult question of whether or not we can seriously deny the state of war that contemporary society is in, she asks a different and dangerously rhetorical question: Can the subaltern speak? For both, the answer is no. And for both, the answer is dependent upon time and social space.

What the rest of this essay engages in is an attempt to move beyond sensationalism to the issues at stake, to the matter of what it means to enter into query about whether or not the subaltern can speak.

APORIA AND APHONIA

In the work of Spivak, the intersection of feminism, difference, and the global figures prominently. The Marxist insistence on keeping the economic under erasure makes visible the global division of labor and maintains the concept of "Third World" as one that describes singularly an economic condition. Spivak's feminist position involves a radical break between the epistemological category of "woman" and the feminist agent of the ethical/political. It allows for the use of an essentialism that is always dangerous and constantly subject to critique. Difference lies in the way this configuration allows for, first, the investigation of women as very specific subjects under patriarchy—overdetermined by a reproductive economy—and, second, brings to crisis the reducibility of the metaphor/myth of "woman" with the subject of feminist politics. One of the places where all of these axes meet is in the figure of the subaltern woman. It is she who serves as the ground for identifying the occurrence of epistemic violence and the operation of strategic essentialism.

According to Spivak, the homogeneous construction of the Other by reference to our own site within the Self/Same[14] is a prevalent feature of European theorizing.[15] This process, claims to the contrary notwithstanding, inhibits any grasp of the heterogeneity of the Other.

> It is impossible for contemporary . . . intellectuals to imagine the kind of Power and Desire that would inhabit the unnamed subject of the Other of Europe. It is not only that everything they read, critical or uncritical, is caught within the debate of the production of that Other, supporting or critiquing the constitution of the Subject as Europe. It is also that, in the constitution of that Other of Europe, great care was taken to obliterate the textual ingredients with which such a subject could cathect, could occupy (invest?) its itinerary.[16]

For Spivak, the "remotely orchestrated, far-flung, and heterogeneous project to constitute the colonial subject as Other is one of the most highly revealing examples of "epistemic violence."[17] Again, there is a laugh; this time it assumes the nature of a deep scepticism. It is the desire to know intimately the subaltern without affecting a shift in the relations between the knower and his object—the "meaningless piety"[18] that accompanies uncritical and unsituated theories of subaltern agency—that is the joke. In describing the site of the subaltern as being "on the other side of the international division of labor from socialized capital, inside *and* outside the circuit of the epistemic violence of imperialist law and education supplementing an earlier economic text,"[19] the uncritical assertion of agency is untenable. It is something that creates the appearance of a certain kind of conscious political action and resistance on the part of the subaltern where there is none and thus does more political damage than good, despite its ethical intentions. Rather than advancing the project of "learning to think differently"[20] it is an endeavor that merely maps the Self onto the Other and posits a reassuring identity where there must not, for quite significant reasons, be any.

A loaded statement such as this one requires some initial qualification and contextualization about the subaltern and epistemic violence. The concept of subalternity is one that arises from Antonio Gramsci's work and refers to subordination in terms of class, gender, caste, race, language, and culture. It signified the fundamental place relationships of dominance occupy in history. The Subaltern Studies group was established with the intention to promote the study and discussion of subalternist issues in South Asian studies. It was inspired by Ranajit Guha, a distinguished Indian historian who edited the first six volumes of *Subaltern Studies* before a rotating editorial team drawn from the collective took over publication. Guha rejected elitist history in favor of a perspective that came from subaltern space. Elitist nationalist historiography had portrayed, for example, "the peasant rebel merely as an empirical person or member of a class, but not as an entity whose will and reason constituted the praxis called rebellion." Instead, peasant rebellions were considered to be spontaneous eruptions, or reflex actions to economic and political oppression. "Either way insurgency was regarded as *external* to the peasant's consciousness and Cause is made to stand in as a phantom surrogate for Reason, the logic of consciousness." Although the project of the group did resemble the work of "history from below," developed in the West by such historians as E. P. Thompson, subaltern history writing on the Indian peasantry ran into difficulties that stemmed from two differences marking them off from these other scholars. The use of poststructuralist analysis that explicitly rejected the unified subject as the agent of history—and the absence of workers' diaries and other recorded sources that were available to British historians—complicated the analysis of the operation of power relations in the domain of colonial South Asia. Hence the difference in approach that Subaltern Studies represents.[21]

The concept of epistemic violence is directly indebted to Michel Foucault's analysis of *epistemes* in *The Order of Things: An Archaeology of the Human Sciences*.[22] It draws directly upon Foucault and his work, but I would suggest that it also functions metonymically to refer to the influential body of European-derived literature dealing with forms knowledge as political practice as well as metaphorically in relation to Europe as the Subject of Knowledge.

Foucault begins with the idea that the human sciences make man the center of all things by defining him against other marginalized groups, such as women or the mad. This organization around the figure of man brought about a unity to History. For Foucault, Marx's totalistic notion of history was based on an anxiety about the dissolution of its unity, hence his attempt to maintain its unity by aligning it with the natural sciences. Foucault, however, points out the theoretical paradox involved: By emphasizing historicity as a mode of being, the human sciences made themselves subject to it as well, thereby destroying any possibility of formulating universal laws comparable to those of the natural sciences. Foucault's work demonstrated that history could not be the stable ground of knowledge, that it could not claim an a priori privilege as the fundamental mode of being either. As two "countersciences," ethnology and psychoanalysis, have shown, history is only one possibility for the discursive form of understanding. What the *episteme* refers to is a "cluster of transformations" that enable the substitution of "differentiated analyses for the themes of a totalising history." The *episteme* is the sum of the "deviation, distances, the oppositions, the differences, the relations of its multiple scientific discourses: it is not *a sort of grand underlying theory,* it is a space of *dispersion,* it is an *open field of relationships and no doubt indefinitely specifiable.*"[23]

Encoded within Spivak's question is a series of issues relating to what is known as colonial discourse analysis. These include the relations of power and knowledge between the colonized and the colonizers, the recovery of the lost subjectivity of the subaltern, and the location of agency where imperialist historiography has buried it. Characteristic of her mode of critique, Spivak informs these urgent problematics with the imperative of maintaining a reflexive stance in interpretations of and dialogues with the Other if the project of reviewing the regard for the Other is to avoid a retreat into the more insidious tactics of neoimperialism.

The problematic can be seen to coalesce around two dynamics: subject-constitution and object-formation. In the theories of several European intellectuals, the latter, as Spivak's article emphatically demonstrates, comes to the fore in the guise of the former; the self-evident, autonomously constituted subject is, she argues, a comforting myth, an object of desire.

Imperialism was marked by the endeavors of "carrying knowledge into the realms of ignorance—of substituting peace for war—freedom for bondage—religion for superstition—the hope of heaven for the fear of hell."[24] In the era of postimperialist social and political thought, desire is what drives the task of establishing the subjectivity of the Other. Critiques of imperialism—often driven by guilt, nativism, or reverse ethnocentrism—advocate the quest for the understanding, emancipation, and elevation of the Other through a reconstruction or recuperation of subjectivity. An effort is made to allow the conscious, individualized subaltern to speak, unfettered by the western Self's political shackles, which with the legacy of colonialism had dictated not just the means of speaking (with deference) but what was heard (selective exoticism). The paternalism that abounds in such endeavors, however, is evident in the absurdity of the First World intellectual who masquerades "as the absent nonrepresenter who lets the oppressed speak for themselves."[25] The problem is that since the project of imperialism has "always already historically refracted what might have been the absolute Other into a domesticated Other that consolidates the imperialist self,"[26] postcolonial attempts at retrieving the irretrievable involve the asymmetrical "obliteration of the trace of that Other in its precarious Subject-ivity."[27]

Spivak's study is in many ways a parallel to Lata Mani's study on the debate on sati in colonial India.[28] Where Spivak points out the violent implications of effectively neo- rather than anti-imperialist benevolent intentions, Mani does the same with colonial policies but also rejects the idea of benevolent intentions (it should, however, be noted that the two scholars treat subjectivity in different ways). Mani's main argument is that the discourse on sati seemed to be about women and humanitarian approaches to them, but it was not. Rather, it was a discourse that served as the vehicle by which the British could rescue Hindu civilization (conceived, moreover, as lying essentially in its Brahmin scriptures) from the Indian fall from a prior Golden Age and return to the natives the "truth" of their own traditions. It was more about the civilizing mission—the idea of the colonizer as the Subject of all knowledge—and what constituted authentic cultural tradition than about the fate of women.

The British did not outlaw certain forms of sati because of its horrors; "On the contrary, officials in favour of abolition were arguing that such action was in fact consistent with upholding religious tradition, even that a policy of religious tolerance necessitated intervention."[29] For Mani, women constituted not the object, not the subject of the discourse of sati, but the ground upon which the discourse could take place. The significance of this shift in the location of women is crucial to Mani's argument. The abolition of sati by the British in 1829 has become a "founding moment" in the history of Indian women. Initiated mostly by colonial officials, it is considered to be indicative of the concern the British had for the status of Indian women in the nineteenth century. The direction of Mani's argument is toward the situation where for too long and at "face value" the idea that colonization brings with it a more positive appraisal of the rights of women has been accepted.

It seems that one important question arises from Mani's analysis that surrounds the idea about British motivations regarding the outlawing of sati. Although Mani's account is convincing, it is nevertheless unclear whether the British were using the tradition-modernity discourse as a strategy to inhibit a practice that was morally reprehensible but politically volatile. By appearing to be concerned with authenticity, and by overriding custom with scripture (something Mani criticizes), it is possible that a legitimacy was being created for direct British intervention that masqueraded as the revival of Hindu tradition. That is, the most politically pragmatic way of reducing the practice of sati may not have been to outlaw it across the board without any apparent consideration of Hindu history. It may have been less practically and ideologically effective to impose a new Christian moral order, as Mani puts it, rather than be seen (ostensibly) to be recuperating and returning Hindu tradition to the people. This would have been consistent with the convenient perception of British colonialism as opposed to, say, French colonialism as having an interest in maintaining cultural diversity rather than in imposing universal values. None of this, moreover, precludes Mani's point that the British profited greatly, ideologically and historiographically, from such maneuvering. Although the danger of such a query is obvious, the scope of Mani's analysis does not allow for any investigation into the question of whether the tradition-modernity theme in the larger context of the issue surrounding widow immolation, like women in the discourse of sati, was the ground rather than subject or object of the debate—the red herring to the strategic attempt to abolish sati. Mani's reply might be that satis actually increased in number after the legal prohibition of it was put in place, but this does not necessarily diminish the issue raised here.

Neither does the problem I identify undermine—logically or intentionally—Mani's argument that the voices of satis went unheard. I think it is important—particularly when revealing the ways in which colonialism's legacy operates in the contemporary world is an objective—to recognize the complexity of colonial domination. Linear, binary, and singular ways of viewing colonial practices (perspectives that cannot be attributed, on the whole, to Mani's work, except perhaps by their extended implications) will never be able to separate intention from effect, or, more specifically, recognize that authoritarian benevolence can entail contradictory politics. Part of understanding the majesterial sweep of British colonialism involves addressing the way in which legitimacy was created for colonial domination along all levels of the power hierarchy. Examining that can reveal how the power and legitimacy of the colonizers has historically been generated and maintained by the ambiguity surrounding the intention and strategy of authorial benevolence; that is, how emancipated subjugation under colonial domination contains numerous meanings and effects, each of which has a distinct politics and temporal momentum. It is precisely the dynamic among these contingencies that produces the (other) contention to which Mani's analysis alludes, and the ambiguity and ambivalence about which Homi Bhabha[30] (more fashionably and, coincidentally, with more political slipperiness) has written.

This is where Spivak enters. Where Mani argues that benevolent desire was not only absent but totally neglected the subject-position of the subaltern sati, Spivak elaborates on the way that it enacts a form of violence in the postcolonial era and, moreover, in the name of a critique of empire.

What the nuance and sophistication of the work of both these scholars suggests (to varying degrees of overtness) is that these two conditions are not
mutually exclusive but often intermingle to produce an extremely complex
politics, one that is not easily countered with either the erasure of desire or
its polemicization.

To return to the question of the way in which the subaltern voice gets
lost, another instance is provided by Spivak, although I would suggest
that it is not as effective an illustration as Mani's. Despite the fact that
Bhuvaneswari Bhaduri was not a particularly subaltern figure, given her
middle-class standing and limited subject status, her life serves to illustrate
Spivak's argument. Bhuvaneswari was a young woman who hanged herself
in Calcutta in 1926. The suicide was difficult to explain, as she had been
menstruating at the time of her death and was thus not illicitly pregnant.
Bhuvaneswari may have rewritten "the social text of *sati*-suicide in an
interventionist way" by displacing and denying the "sanctioned motive for
female suicide." In generalizing this motive by waiting for the onset of
menstruation and excluding the possibility of extramarital pregnancy, illegitimate passion by a single male that traditionally imprisons this motive
was erased by the "physiological inscription of her body."[31]

Bhuvaneswari's act nevertheless was read as absurdity by delirium.
Upon much later discovery of her involvement in the armed struggle for
Indian independence, however, her sati-suicide was assimilated by the
hegemonic account of the "fighting mother" and preserved through the discourse of male leaders and participants in the independence movement.
Thus, the story of nonrational "femininity" gives way to an account surrounding a quite modernist rationality; delirium is elided by nationalism. A
generation later, Spivak's personal investigation revealed (by account of
Bhuvaneswari's nieces) a return to the original motive of her suicide: illicit
love. Political rationalism again becomes erstwhile traditional culture-
based rationalization, realigned with expectations surrounding gender roles,
rituals, and obligations.

The point that Spivak is at great pains to make in her circuitously written and sometimes convoluted essay is that in the figure of Bhuvaneswari,
"one diagnosis of female free will is substituted for another."[32] In her
analysis of the British rewriting of sati, Spivak notes the following:

> In the case of widow self-immolation, ritual is not being redefined as
> superstition but as *crime*. The gravity of *sati* was that it was ideologically
> cathected as "reward," just as the gravity of imperialism was that it was
> ideologically cathected as "social mission."[33]

Reading Bhuvaneswari's sati-suicide against this backdrop, Spivak concludes that "between patriarchy and imperialism, subject-constitution and
object-formation, the figure of the woman disappears, not into a pristine

nothingness, but into a violent shuttling which is the displaced figuration of the 'third-world woman' caught between tradition and modernization." Within the two conflicting versions of freedom, "the constitution of the female subject *in life* is the place of the *différend.*" No space exists from which the subaltern female subject can speak.[34]

Yet her muteness is "something other than silence and nonexistence,"[35] an important assertion given the kind of critiques Spivak's article has illicited. It is not that the subaltern cannot "talk"—that she has nothing to say, nor any desire to be able to speak (metaphorical aphonia); it is a much more complicated and at the same time simpler argument than that. It lies in the notion that it is speaking as well as hearing that complete the speech act;[36] thus, on its own, the gravity of life-and-death efforts to speak do not necessarily make the subaltern woman audible. To claim that the gendered subaltern cannot be heard or read, contrary to those who have heard Spivak silence the subaltern, is to make a highly provocative but also specific observation about the "violent aporia between subject and object status."

There have been outraged responses from those working in the area of postcolonial studies to Spivak's "complicated" piece—one that, she admits, was "uncontrolled" and bears the marks of "struggle," "crisis," and a lack of "the courage of [her own] convictions."[37] One, I would add, whose important argument is not assisted by its exhibitionist intellectual acrobatics. The implications of Spivak's well-known query have been deemed totalizing, antinativist, elitist, and essentialist. Benita Parry's reply has been exemplary. According to Parry, Spivak presents a disabling theoretical position, one that is, moreover, at variance with the "evidence":

> Where military conquest, institutional compulsion and ideological interpellation was, epistemic violence and devious discursive negotiations requiring of the native that he rewrite his position as object of imperialism, is; and in place of recalcitrance and refusal enacted in movements of resistance and articulated in oppositional discourses, a tale is told of the self-consolidating other and the disarticulated subaltern.[38]

For Parry, Spivak's illustration of the obliteration of the native's subject position within colonial discourse effectively dismisses the two-hundred-year history of resistance under British colonialism in India and "writes out the evidence of native agency."[39]

THE SUBJECT OF EUROPE

Parry's point is crucial in its persuasiveness. It suggests an elitism and conservatism generating from Spivak's account that reflects at least two things. At best, it reveals more of an interest in demonizing the West than in looking at how the colonized have managed to resist their dominators; at worst, it highlights a desire for theoretical integrity that leaves behind the commitment to social change. Second, the exposure of the delusory nature of the endeavor to recuperate subaltern subjectivity furthermore threatens a paralysis over how to proceed with regard to undoing some of the legacies of colonial oppression without repeating them in other forms. Third, and most ironically, the seemingly totalistic (non)expression of subaltern subjectivity—the notion of its elusiveness—produces implications that reverberate with the idealism inherent in quests for native authenticity at the same time as they reject any nativist position. On the one hand, the claim that the subaltern cannot speak is based on the notion that her authenticity is never retrievable and relies on a valorization of the idea of authenticity. On the other hand, authenticity itself is a ruse. One might conclude that what Spivak has produced is an argument that adheres to the primacy of the epistemic over the political and the techno-theoretical over the historico-material—a position whose strategy is to combat uncritical totalizations with reactionary ones.

To stop here and go no further would be to forestall the polemic rather than allow it to do its job—to provoke investigation. It would also ignore the politics of theory, which, as I will indicate later, are not confined to academe. To begin, therefore, the "first-world intellectuals" to whom Spivak initially directs her critique are Foucault, Deleuze, and Guattari. Making a subversive and uncompromising link between some of the "most radical" contemporary criticism originating from the West and the desire to maintain the subjectivity of the West, or "the West as Subject," she identifies the neglect of the international division of labor, the rendering of Asia and Africa "transparent," and the reinstatement of the "legal subject of socialized capital" as problems that mark both poststructuralist and structuralist theory.[40] With specific reference to Deleuze and Guattari, she notes that, failing to consider the relation between desire, power, and subjectivity, they are left incapable of developing a theory of interests. This arises out of their indifference to ideology.[41] In the conversation between Foucault and Deleuze, there is an unrecognized contradiction: The elevation of the "concrete experience" of the subjugated exists parallel to an uncritical view of the historical role of the intellectual. Neither is aware that "the intellectual within socialized capital, brandishing concrete experience, can help consolidate the international division of labor"; they seem oblivious to the way in which their position "helps only the intellectual anxious to prove that intellectual labor is just like manual labor."[42] Forcing Spivak to the point, these two thinkers believe that their theorizations can produce social changes that are comparable to those effected by laboring for and with the subaltern. It has to be said that in putting the economic under erasure—that is, in retaining its fundamental importance for social change regardless of the kind of critiques it is subjected to—and in aligning herself with the Subaltern Studies group, she avoids making herself the direct target of the same charge.

An expansion of this critique begins with the recognition of the way the critique of the sovereign subject has severely damaged the idea that the subject is the self-conscious author of its agency and that the Subject par excellence is the rational, white, male European. It has exposed the fiction that the agent of History—conceived as technologically rational progress— is Europe. To then turn around and say, as the intellectualizations of Foucault and Deleuze effectively do, that European theory can dictate how to conceptualize non-European agency is hypocritical. Furthermore, it reveals the desire to maintain the upper hand politically on the global scale (the assumptions being that any practice is always related to theory and that theory itself is always a practice) while simultaneously being critical of the epistemes that allowed the European belief in the right to world dominance. The obligation to internally deconstruct the foundations of legitimacy of the Subject sits alongside the desire to maintain those foundations in exter- nal relation to the rest of the world. As Deleuze and Foucault fail to see the neo-imperialist dangers such desires, combined with the economic and political power of Europe and the contradictory treatment of the Subject, produce, it prevents them from including in their hypotheses any account of the interest Europe has in advocating this combination of theoretical ele- ments. It inhibits any theory of ideology. This (presumably unrecognized) crisis of the "radical intellectual in the West" is thus the "deliberate choice of subalternity, granting to the oppressed either that very expressive subjec- tivity which s/he criticizes or, instead, a total unrepresentability."[43]

This is an interesting statement, given that Spivak's use of the term *silence* is suggestive of precisely the same unrepresentability. The contra- dictions and hypocrisies that lurk in the background of Spivak's essay dis- solve, to some degree, upon further examination of the argument. It is instructive, first of all, to note what exactly Spivak considers her own pro- ject to be. It is, she says, the attempt to identify the "positivist-idealist vari- ety" of the nostalgia for the Other.[44] It was her insistence on "imperialist subject-production," "the imperialist subject and the subject of imperial- ism," that occasioned her confrontation with subaltern speak; it was what disclosed her politics.[45] The political agenda is made even more specific when Spivak asserts that "the 'subject' has a history and that the task of the first-world subject of knowledge in our historical moment is to resist and critique 'recognition' of the Third World through 'assimilation,'" a process that is apparent in "the ferocious standardizing benevolence of most US and Western European human-scientific radicalism."[46] Locating the subal- tern was not as difficult as entering into a relationship of responsibility with responses flowing both ways: "Learning to learn without this quick-fix frenzy of doing good with an implicit assumption of cultural supremacy which is legitimized by unexamined romanticization, that's the hard part."[47]

It was imperialism's interest in economic exploitation that "interests, motives (desires), and power (of knowledge) be ruthlessly dislocated" within the subjectivity of the oppressed. Even though her entire article is devoted to elaborating the problems associated with this dislocation—the problematic of epistemic violence—Spivak nevertheless warns against prioritizing dislocation over the economic, because to do so may be to perpetuate that rupture and unknowingly create "a new balance of hegemonic relations."[48] (The epitome of such prioritization in my opinion is exemplified in Homi Bhabha's conceptualization of the unity of the colonial subject whereby both colonized and colonizer embody a similar quality of ambivalence and ambiguity, such that the issue of the economic is subsumed in the interests of weakening the coherence of imperialism's agents while strengthening the subversive potential of its subjugated. Here the dislocation of which Spivak speaks is prioritized over the problem of the economic dichotomy created by imperialism.[49]) In the face of the possibility that the intellectual is complicit in the persistent constitution of Other as the Self's shadow, a possibility of political practice for the intellectual would be to put the economic "under erasure," to see the economic factor as irreducible as it reinscribes the social text, even as it is erased—however imperfectly— when it claims to be the final determinant or the transcendental signified.[50] In other words, class must be critiqued when it claims to be the structural basis of social life, but it must be preserved at all costs as a fundamental category of analysis—that is, as something that cannot be subsumed by another, such as gender—when examining the processes and legacies of empire.

SUBALTERN HISTORIOGRAPHY

The project of retrieving the consciousness of those who reside in the space that is severed from the lines of mobility in a colonized country[51] is what marks an entry into the social, rather than the more idealized libidinal,[52] text of the subaltern. European intellectuals, says Spivak, may be attentive to the problems of neocolonialism in their own national domains, but they have little knowledge about the history of imperialism and its particular mode of epistemic violence.[53] Their "nostalgia for lost origins can be detrimental to the exploration of social realities within the critique of imperialism."[54] This in itself is indicative of the dire inconsistencies and contradictions that one may run into if one draws uncritically upon their work to theorize colonial subjectivity:

[To] buy a self-contained version of the West is symptomatically to ignore its production by the spacing-timing of the imperialist project. Sometimes it seems as if the very brilliance of Foucault's analysis of the centuries of European imperialism produces a miniature version of that heterogeneous phenomenon: management of space—but by doctors, development of administrations—but in asylums, considerations of the periphery—but in terms of the insane, prisoners, and children. The clinic, the asylum, the prison, the university, seem screen-allegories that foreclose a reading of the broader narratives of imperialism.[55]

The appropriation by "Third World" scholars, namely the Subaltern Studies group, of the work of "First World" intellectuals is of particular concern with regard to an uncritical use of theories of European origin and content. The element of complicity in the strong tendency by the Subaltern Studies group toward totalization is particularly difficult for Spivak.[56] The problems across the divide are not identical, however, as the Subaltern Studies group faces "a predicament rather different from the self-diagnosed transparency of the first-world radical intellectual." The assumption of subalternist work—contrary to that of Deleuze and Foucault, who maintain that "the oppressed . . . if given the chance . . . *can speak and know their conditions*"[57]—is that the mode of subalternity disallows such (western) self-knowledge and its corresponding articulation of subjectivity.[58]

The subaltern is important for the project of the Subaltern Studies group, which is attempting to rewrite the consciousness of the Indian nation. Writing subaltern history means, fundamentally, attributing to subaltern subjectivity a supplement—an agency—that in imperialist traditions of historiography is denied. The whole point of identifying something as "subaltern insurgency" is to recognize an attempt to engage in a kind of representation that does not function "according to the lines laid down by the official institutional structures of representation." Even as the subaltern attempts insurgency—something that would bring to crisis subalternity itself and make a possible shift toward a so-called political movement— "the Cambridge historian's argument" (following Hobsbawms's definition of what is political) is that it is not worthy of study because of the failure of the attempt.[59] The subaltern will therefore always "necessarily" be elusive to history since history narrates "success" not "failure."

This question of failure is precisely related to the genre of non-speakingness, hence the idea of a "not-speakingness in the very notion of subalternity."[60] The subaltern's (non)location within the trajectory of history in turn can prevent the subaltern from entering (written) history. Since the subaltern is viewed as having no agency because agency is defined in terms of historical forward movement—that is, successful struggle—the group's strategy is to shift the location of agency from the indigenous elite (bourgeois nationalist) to the insurgent or subaltern. Unlike the French theorists under scrutiny who claim to know the subaltern and engage themselves in its subject-constitution, the group is attempting the challenging task of rewriting the conditions of impossibility of their own text as the conditions of its possibility.[61] Where in European theorizing the subaltern was ultimately *unknowable*—because even when it has been given a space on the basis of the assumption and construction of a consciousness or a subjectivity through the idea of the sovereign subject it is "as mute as ever" because its agency is cast as failure and thus emptied—the Subaltern Studies group attempts to restructure what is considered to be failure.

Thus, where Foucault and Deleuze only manage to cohere with the imperialist counterproject, "mingling epistemic violence with the advancement of learning and civilization,"[62] the group, on the other hand, challenges imperialism's monopoly on knowledge—and therefore its conceptualizations of politics—to rewrite the subaltern as nonsubaltern. What has been considered by both colonialist and nationalist historiography as being failure or irrelevance (encoded as "the discontinuous chain of peasant insurgencies during the colonial occupation)—as having no "permission to narrate"—thus becomes the mark of success through a functional change in sign-systems.[63]

Nevertheless, and not surprisingly, it is usually not registered, which is why Spivak, among others, presumably has found it her task to draw attention to the potential of the work of the Subaltern Studies group for not only Indian historiography but social and political theory globally.

In identifying its attempt "to investigate, identify and measure" subaltern consciousness, Spivak names the essentialism of the endeavor. She also defends it on the basis that "the violence of imperialist epistemic, social, and disciplinary inscription" means that "a project understood in essentialist terms must traffic in a radical textual practice of difference."[64] For the subaltern scholars, the essentialist notion of a unified conscious subaltern must be part of their strategy, just as the concept of the nonmonolithic or situated subject must characterize the antihumanist critique "on the other side of the international division of labor."[65] Historiography is also a matter of timing; it is politically unproductive to adopt a deconstructive position toward a subject that has no history. Theory is historically situated as much as the subjects about which it theorizes. This point deserves further elaboration.

Spivak claims that her critique of the project by the subaltern scholars that seeks to (re)construct the consciousness or subject is not an appeal to an essentialist identity or to the privileging of experience.[66] The significance of the implications of this statement is that it undermines the notion that she is engaging in a totalizing enterprise that draws upon illegitimate forms of essentialism to render theoretical integrity dominant over social and political progress. Spivak attempts to explain.

The political necessity and pragmatism of adopting or identifying with a particular subject position is not mirrored by the process of knowledge production. Pure identity does not produce knowledge; difference does. Knowledge and its object are never each other's limits; the latter always exceeds the former.

> The theoretical model of the ideal knower in the embattled position we are discussing is that of the person identical with her predicament. This is actually the figure of the impossibility and non-necessity of knowledge. Here the relationship between the practical—need for claiming subaltern identity—and the theoretical—no program of knowledge production can presuppose identity as origin—is, once again, of an "interruption" that persistently brings each term to crisis.[67]

Spivak's "reinscription" of the project of the Subaltern Studies group is one that draws out this dynamic. It weakens the totalizing tendencies the work displays by the "lawful naming" of the subaltern as such through an appeal to the "critical force of anti-humanism." What is important to remember about the group's work is that the object of its examination is an "irreducible . . . essentializing moment";[68] its approach involves the "strategic use of positivist essentialism in a scrupulously visible political interest." It is "the usefulness of a dangerous thing."[69]

In this regard, Spivak refers analogously to a variety of "international-ist" Marxism that believes in a pure, retrievable form of consciousness only to dismiss it. This she identifies as the origin of the critical motivation of the Subaltern Studies scholars, something that is apparent in the constantly present suggestion in the group's work "that subaltern consciousness is subject to the cathexis of the élite, that it is never fully recoverable, that it is always askew from its received signifiers, indeed that it is effaced even as it is disclosed, that it is irreducibly discursive."[70]

Being a historian of the subaltern means that the attempt to articulate the subject-position of the subaltern involves the simultaneous dissolution of that position: "Working for the subaltern *means* the subaltern's insertion into citizenship."[71] Spivak speaks of the "interventionist value," the "translating back" that occurs with the alignment of the subaltern historian with the subaltern. Indeed, Spivak suggests that the subalternity of the Subaltern Studies group arising out of their claiming a "*positive* subject-position" for the subaltern might be "reinscribed as a strategy for our times":

> What good does such a re-inscription do? It acknowledges that the arena of the subaltern's persistent emergence into hegemony must always and by definition remain heterogeneous to the efforts of the disciplinary historian. The historian must persist in *his* efforts in this awareness, that the subaltern is necessarily the absolute limit of the place where history is narrativized into logic. It is a hard lesson to learn, but not to learn it is

merely to nominate elegant solutions to be correct theoretical practice. . . .
This is the always asymmetrical relationship between the interpretation
and transformation of the world which Marx marks in the eleventh thesis
on Feuerbach.[72]

What must be attempted is the systematic unlearning of privilege through
"seeking to learn to speak to (rather than listen to or speak for) the historically muted subject of the subaltern." This "systematic unlearning" means
acquiring the skill "to critique postcolonial discourse with the best tools it
can provide and not simply substituting the lost figure of the colonized."
Paradoxically, these are the conditions in which "the postcolonial intellectuals learn that their privilege is their loss" and by which "they are a paradigm of the intellectuals."[73]

Spivak as critic is included among those whom she critiques. This is
evident in her account of the importance of viewing the subaltern as being
"out of reach" and her assertion that this is "more than a strategic exclusion": she freely admits that this notion is something that would destroy her
generalizations.[74] One would even go so far as to say she encourages this
step. Thus, when Robert Young observes of Spivak's Marxism that it operates as an "overall syncretic frame" in her work as a whole, that it acts as a
"transcendentalizing gesture to produce closure," and that therefore
"Spivak's supplementary history must itself be supplemented,"[75] he is
right; but it is also the case that this process is already in motion in her
intellectual production. For already in "Can the Subaltern Speak?" there is
a plea to regard certain formulations—ones that could lead to the closure of
grand essentialisms and totalizations—as persistently critiqued while
nonetheless being found useful.

The assumption, prevalent in the United States, that there is a desire to
preserve subalternity on the part of the Subaltern Studies group is false.[76]
The group does not hold any romantic attachment to pure subalternity.
This, it would seem, is the result of the work of the group being read
through—not just being informed by—the liberal utopianism of thinkers
such as Foucault and Deleuze.[77] Although by Spivak's account Foucault
and Deleuze uncritically accept the negativity of the subject-position
known as subalternity yet insist on attributing the "positive" qualities of the
sovereign subject in all its rationality—consciousness and autonomy—the
Subaltern Studies group undertakes the more radical endeavor of allowing
positivity via a shift in the logic of historical agency. Foucault and Deleuze
posit social and political presence in the larger context of a History that
asserts its absence. On the other hand, in retheorizing what can be considered "success," and in actively retrieving a consciousness in the name of a
highly visible political interest, the Subaltern Studies group engages in the
more difficult and precarious, but at the same time less idealistic and illuso-
ry, task of tracking a subjectivity that, in its elusiveness, is a constant

reminder of its inherent unknowability and thus of the (necessarily) hear impossibility of the group's project. This is vastly different from the idea espoused by European thinkers Spivak focuses on, who ignore the difficulty encountered by the subaltern in entering into "organic intellectuality" in their overwhelming desire to have cake and eat it too: to remain the Subjects of Europe and at the same time be in touch with the speaking subaltern.[78]

BACK TO THE ESSENTIALS

If the task of the Subaltern Studies group is to engage in "measuring silences,"[79] it also does not escape the problems attending the use of essentialism without an "against the grain" reading. Understanding how essentialism can, indeed must, be used is something that has pervaded Spivak's work, particularly that concerning feminism and gender analyses as well as figures constructed by oppression.

Within the context of Spivak's methodological and theoretical techniques, essentialism has very little political use outside the insights of deconstruction. Deconstruction, however, has very little political value as an enterprise in and of itself. The greatest gift of deconstruction is to be critical of the interrogator without rendering him or her paralyzed.[80] Paralysis occurs only when the "enterprise of deconstruction" itself becomes the exclusive interest.[81] Quoting herself from *Of Grammatology,* Spivak illustrates how practitioners who become idolators of deconstruction specifically as a theory or blueprint for politics miss the point:

> Operating necessarily from the inside, borrowing all the strategic and economic resources of subversion from the old structure, borrowing them structurally, that is to say without being able to isolate their elements and atoms, the enterprise of deconstruction always in a certain way falls prey to its own work.[82]

If strategy works through a persistent (de)constructive critique of the theoretical, as Spivak maintains, it entails an impossible risk, for the idea of a lasting strategy is a contradiction.[83]

One instance of a formulaic treatment of politics involves Spivak's conception of the use of essentialism as it has been drawn upon to endorse academic posturing.[84] In retrospect, Spivak has recognized how the "artifice or trick designed to outwit or surprise the enemy," encoded in her own idea of "strategic essentialism," has alternately become "an alibi for proselytizing academic essentialisms" or a means of "self-differentiation from the poor essentialists." But it is precisely the "critique of the 'fetish-character'" that allows strategy to remain true to itself, that allows for the preemption of solidification into essentialism. At its most dangerous—as a *theoretical* design—it is reduced to a ploy that ultimately empties the generative productivity of the politics of subject-positions and their constitutive characteristics. What was a contingent approach to politics has become the mark of intellectual identity. As such, Spivak's cautionary pragmatics has contributed to the (de)moralization of the participants in the surrounding debate.[85] The notion of strategic essentialism has turned out to be complicitous in creating the foundations for a new rivalry, particularly within feminist theorizing.

It is a situation Spivak herself finds unhelpful to criticism. Hence the reconsideration of her previous call for what by now would not be too inaccurate conceived as an hygienic essentialism—one that names a "scrupulously visible" political interest at work—and the "concept-metaphor" *strategy* employed alongside it.

> I, myself, had thought I was saying that since it is not possible not to be an essentialist, one can self-consciously use this irreducible moment of essentialism as part of one's strategy. This can be used as part of a "good" strategy as well as a "bad" strategy and this can be used self-consciously as well as unself-consciously, and neither self-consciousness nor unself-consciousness can be valorized in my book.[86]

Politics, Spivak reminds her readers, is asymmetrical, "provisional," and one must face the burden of having "broken the theory" when one becomes political. There can be no escape from essentializing tactics ("if you escape in the end, you lose"); and the attempt to maintain theoretical—and, failing that, moral—purity amounts to political stagnation and polemics.[87]

Deconstruction presents final and total positions because this is unavoidable; "to make your arguments stick for the next half an hour" you must presuppose final and total positions. Speaking elsewhere of situational unity (which has affinities with the problems that may be generated by universalism and essentialism), Spivak speaks of the "travesty of philosophy, a turning of philosophy into a direct blueprint for policy making, to suggest that the search for a situational unity goes against the lesson of deconstruction." Treating as dictum Jacques Derrida's warning in "Force of Law: The 'Mystical Foundation of Authority,'" she insists that since "imperatives arise out of situations and, however unthinkingly, we act by imagining imperatives we must therefore scrupulously imagine a situation in order to act. Pure difference cannot appear. Difference cannot provide an adequate theory of practice."[88]

In an interview with Spivak, Ellen Rooney has pointed out that to be theoretically weary of the debate does not excuse being wary of it outside in the teaching machine. For her, essentialism is "a kind of initial question, politically and intellectually, when students discover the possibility of a feminist discourse." Spivak's response is that one can use the terms of the debate as part of a strategy to teach "rather than talk about it *ad infinitum.*"[89] The tedium and sterility of the debate over essentialism is understandable. Yet one cannot help thinking of Spivak's analogy about decolonization. Once it is won, she says, the people want to enter into "the haunted house inhabited by the colonizers, a house that 'the best people' think is not such a grand hotel."[90] What springs to mind within the context of the academic debate at hand is that the "best" were, more often than not, the very ones who created the myth of the "grand hotel." For Spivak, however, this is truly a fact of life; there is nothing outside the text (of complicity).

Related to this is the charge that Derridean deconstruction remains trapped in the metaphysics of western philosophy. If essentialisms are part of the production of practice, epistemology, and ontology, deconstruction gives no clue as to the real. "The real in deconstruction is neither essentialist nor antiessentialist."[91] Rather, this form of rereading encourages the investigation of the "counterintuitive position that there might be essences and there might not be essences." Hence the deconstructive lesson on the impossibility of antiessentialism.[92] In terms of feminist critique, since there is no "discursive continuity among women," the fundamental goal is "situational anti-sexism." Without denying the importance or excellence of some of the work being done with regard to tracing the figure of women geopolitically or otherwise, Spivak maintains that it is the recognition of heterogeneity, rather than "positing some kind of woman's subject, women's figure, that kind of stuff,"[93] that matters most.

Spivak's reassertion of the importance of the critique of essentialism is therefore one that is somewhat different from and much less theoretically rigid than a simple antiessentialist position. The point is not to engage in the exposure of error by way of the critique of essentialism. The critique of essentialism is not to be viewed in the negative "colloquial, Anglo-American sense of being adversely inclined," but productively, as critique "in the robust European philosophical sense."[94] It is a stance that Spivak would support "as one stand among many." Clarifying with an example, Spivak notes that within the context of mainstream U.S. feminism, the concept of the relationship between the personal and the political is quite often reduced to the notion that the personal *alone* is the political. From there the voice from one's own ground or standpoint is given emphasis over "matching the trick to the situation." Identitarianism, specifically as something drawing upon a theory subjectivity, solidifies into an approach that cannot escape the negative that inevitably accompanies the positive. Its commitment to itself disallows shifts to more politically advantageous positions that, although never completely nor even nearly uncomplicitous, engage with the historical shifts of value coding in progressive rather than regressive ways. "The most serious critique in deconstruction is the critique of things that are extremely useful, things without which we cannot live on, take chances; like our running self-identikit. That should be the approach to how we are essentialists."[95]

Spivak even goes so far as to advocate doing politics "according to the old rules" while remembering the dangers and recognizing the inevitable contingency of such an approach. "Since one cannot not be an essentialist, why not look at the ways in which one is essentialist, carve out a representative essentialist position," and then proceed?[96]

> Essences, it seems to me, are just a kind of content. All content is not essence. Why be so nervous about it? Why not demote the word "essence," because without a minimalizable essence, an essence as *ce qui reste*, an essence as what remains, there is no exchange. Difference articulates these negotiable essences. There is no time for essence/anti-essence. There is so much work to be done.[97]

If so in deeds, so also in theory. Just as agency is not always in the interest of "progressive" change (the move from "identity" to "agency," as Spivak notes, says nothing about whether that agency is good or bad), so the journeys into the impossibility of subaltern space do not produce useful formulas. "The possibility of subalternity for me," says Spivak, "acts as a reminder. If it is true that when you seem to have solved a problem, that victory, that solution, is a warning." As soon as the possibility of subalternity is apparent, it is time to look for things to "upset the apple cart."[98]

POSTCOLONIAL PARADOX

> What actually happens in a typical liberal multicultural classroom "at its best"? On a given day we are reading a text from one national origin. The group in the classroom from that particular national origin in the general polity can identify with the richness of the texture of the "culture" in question, often through a haze of nostalgia. . . . People from other national origins in the classroom (other, that is, than Anglo) relate sympathetically but superficially, in an aura of "same difference." The Anglo relates benevolently to everything, "knowing about other cultures" in a relativist glow.[99]

"Can the subaltern speak?" is about the warm glow that does harm even as it claims to do good. The response is never a resolute answer. It depends on who is listening and how they hear her.

The work of the Subaltern Studies group, which, says Spivak, is much more complicated than her own, cannot abdicate the responsibility of refusing to represent the oppressed.[100]

> Not only because of their devotion to semiotics, but also because they are trying to assemble a historical *bio*-graphy of those whose active lives are only disclosed by a deliberately fragmentary record produced elsewhere, the Subaltern Studies group . . . must remain committed to the subaltern as the subject of his history. As they choose this strategy, they reveal the limits of the critique of humanism as produced in the West.[101]

The responsibility that comes with such endeavors brings with it the inevitability of error. On the other hand, "the alternative of *not* attending to the subaltern past with all of its difficulties would be not to attend to it at all."

Three conclusions arise out of Spivak's work on subalternity that seem ironic in light of the insistence on historical knowledge and specificity, subject-positioning, and the politics of theory. There is the assertion that "the historical predicament of the colonial subaltern can be made to become the allegory of the predicament of *all* thought, *all* deliberative consciousness."[102] We are, in other words, all subaltern to some degree and in some capacity: We must all work to be heard accurately, whether it be in terms of experience (the gender and race issues figure prominently), politics (the representation of children is a highly relevant example), the psychoanalytical (do we even know ourselves who we are?), or whatever. What is surprising in this admission is that it seems to undermine the importance of the main argument in Spivak's dense essay, particularly given her decision to put the economic under erasure. In its radical antiessentialism, it threatens to undo all the emphatic arguments about the crucial significance of class and gender, location, and (privileged) place. On the other hand, it makes the work of the Subaltern Studies group extend in relevance to any field of thought concerned with social change. And it undoes the privilege of Europe as the all-knowing and primary signifier.

The second conclusive point Spivak makes is about how history is larger than personal goodwill:[103] "You are, to an extent, distanced from it with humility and respect when you 'build for difference,'"[104] since history and language do not offer many choices in the way of strategy. For all its poststructuralist rhetoric, the argument under scrutiny defers quite explicitly to the deeply entrenched structures history has produced; what is important is that it does so without being deterministic, fatalistic, or, ultimately, even totalistic. The totalizations with which Spivak engages are usually contingencies that achieve their power through situated universalisms, essentialisms, and irreducibility, although they are shrouded in jargon and hyperbole.

Finally, and most revealingly, Spivak acknowledges that to act with responsibility requires potentially the existence of intention, even the privilege of subjectivity in order to be responsible.[105] If "Can the Subaltern Speak?" could have been retitled "One or Two Things the European

Subject Cannot Know About the Other,"[106] with its themes of ethically motivated politics working with the heterogeneity of historical contexts and the homogeneousness of internationalism, it could, with the position outlined now, be formulated as "Space, Time, and the Posthumanist Political Subject." It engages with the idea that, to quote Bruce Robbins, "we can neither deny representation nor self-effacingly make ourselves transparent so that others can fully and immediately represent themselves. While working toward greater democracy of representation, we can only affirm the value of one mode of representation over another." It is to recognize, in the words of another critic, that "people do it all the time, and the crucial issue is by what means, to what purpose, to what effect."[107]

Over the years since the 1988 essay, there seems to be a pragmatism that characterizes Spivak's theorizing. It is something that cools the rhetoric and situates the argument in a way that makes it much more productive, if one is still willing to endure its intellectual contortions and exhibitionism. But rather than being simply a matter of pragmatism, to admit the sovereign subject back into her poststructuralist analyses is to reflect the concern to undermine the misguided authority of an extremely influential figure such as Foucault, rather than to adhere dogmatically to the notion of the eternally fragmented subject and to flow with the history of theory. (It also, incidentally, illustrates the way poststructuralist critique works most productively—when it acknowledges structures rather than ignores them.)[108]

Spivak now emphasizes the need to "learn how to attend." And what about mistakes? "Big deal. One is making mistakes all the time."[109] One of her more recent advocations has been to move beyond the task of grasping otherness to recognizing agency in the Other[110] in the "emerging dominant" and the idea of solutions in an impossible future. In an era where the ostensible "open-mindedness" of multiculturalism is producing policies in business where comprehending the Other—through, for example, language courses and briefings on cultural difference—is absolutely necessary for the seduction by capital to take place successfully, the radical intellectual has little choice but to accept that operative knowledge of the Other may not be expert knowledge, but it still allows one to register rejection.[111]

> If by teaching ourselves and our students to acknowledge our part and hope in capitalism we can bring that hope to a persistent and principled crisis, we can set ourselves on the way to intervening in an unfinished chapter of history that was mired in Eurocentric national disputes.[112]

If, despite and no doubt in spite of this long investigation, it was tempting to conclude that if we could only recognize the limits and location of theory, perhaps we would be able to mobilize its (contingent) truths in the interests of inhibiting violence in the sphere of the social rather than remaining pre-occupied with the way in which violence is committed through our epis-temes. I hope this essay shows that to query the notion of subaltern speak is to imply that the first task cannot be accomplished apart from the second. Representation, as Spivak observes, is not about representing "them" (*vertreten*) but about learning to represent (*darstellen*) ourselves.[113]

There are reasons for being transported through the corridors of *Pulp Fiction* to enter and exit Gayatri Spivak's study on the subaltern. The most significant one has to do with heuristic analogy. Important things are being said; some say them better than others. The vision of one writer can enable the screening of another's.

Once again, both the film and the essay harbor a fetishizing tendency that obscures the fundamental message: visual and thematic sensationalism on the one hand, and blinding intellectual and theoretical glare on the other.[114] The danger is that style may be mistaken for content—something that is not as much a problem for the film, given the implicit political possi-bilities of the link between real war and screen war, as it is for the essay. It is tempting to say, however feeble it may sound, that the complexities of theorizing about theories of the subaltern mirror the many difficulties in the endeavor to write the subaltern into history.

If both works suggest unacceptable ideas, different elements in each of them respectively undermine and exacerbate this condition. The message is that social and political change requires that we must always be aware of what (historical) time, (sociopolitical) space, and (libidinal) subject-position we occupy. The lack of glamorous and unexpected destinies of all the (male) (anti)heroes of the film subvert the theory of glorification on, at the very least, the subconscious level. Nothing is as it should be, according to the formulas of stereotype: The heroes do not live in palaces and the women are just promises. This is also the case in the essay; however, its lack of elegance, its convoluted and scattered nature, and its insistence on always plunging both reader and writer into the deep end threaten to con-vince some audience members to walk out before the final scene. In this context, the metaphorical nature of the argument is in danger of being taken literally, and the radical is at risk of sliding toward the reactionary.

The last and most relevant overlap between film and essay as it has been presented here has to do with wartimeviolence. In transporting generic violence to the level of war in the screenplay, urban conflict is transformed from being a pathology of individualist society to the status of origin and ontology of society itself. In so doing, what could be neglected before (the gold watch) cannot be ignored afterwards, because the gravity of war demands a response. Similarly, the aggressive and oppressive language of violence and silence in relation to the subaltern is virtually immune to indifference.

The politicization of "violence" lies in the way it is named as war/benevolence. What narrative symbolism does in a film, poetic polemic achieves in an essay. As a watch tells of times of war, "subaltern silence" narrates the blindness of postcolonial desire. And where a little divine intervention, a little pulp fiction, shows up in one arena of social and political critique, what occurs in another is the deconstruction of the machinations of sovereign subjectivity in the ghost that is the subaltern.

NOTES

1. Quentin Tarantino, director; Tarantino and Roger Avary, writers; Miramax Films, A Band Apart/Jersey Films, 1994.

2. Other examples include Hélène Cixous's "The Laugh of the Medusa," and *Trainspotting,* directed by Danny Boyle, screenplay by Hon Hodge, Polygram and Noel Gay Motion Picture Company, 1995, after a novel by Irvine Welsh.

3. I would like to thank Dominic Marner for his elaborations on the relationship between the gold watch and war in this film.

4. Examples of the latter would include corporal punishment, child abuse, legal executions.

5. Arendt, *On Violence,* pp. 6, 52.

6. Arendt said that violence may appear where power is in jeopardy (Arendt, *On Violence,* p. 56). Power, on the other hand, gains legitimacy and authority where violence needs to be controlled.

7. This is the political theory problematic of the collection edited by Campbell and Dillon, *The Political Subject of Violence.*

8. Cited in Arendt, *On Violence,* p. 9.

9. This example and its quotes were taken from Der Derian, "A Reinterpretation of Realism," p. 364.

10. Arendt, *On Violence,* p. 3.

11. See Virilio, *War and Cinema.*

12. Coppola, *Apocalypse Now.*

13. This is a reference to the return to the opening murder scene where a "miracle" has allowed bullets to pass through "our heroes."

14. Spivak, "Can the Subaltern Speak?" p. 288.

15. In Spivak's essay, this generalization generally refers to the work of Foucault and Deleuze and occasionally Guattari.

16. Spivak, "Can the Subaltern Speak?" p. 280. The intellectuals Spivak is referring to are Foucault, Deleuze, and Guattari, but her point has wider significance in the context of this analysis. The texts of interest in this regard are "Intellectuals and Power: A Conversation Between Michel Foucault and Gilles Deleuze," in Foucault, *Language, Counter-Memory, Practice;* and Deleuze and Guattari, *Anti-Oedipus.*

17. Spivak, "Can the Subaltern Speak?" p. 281.

18. Ibid., p. 271.

19. Ibid., p. 283.

20. Cited in the commentary by Jon Bird on the exhibition by Alfredo Jaar in which Spivak collaborated, "Two or Three Things I Imagine About Them," Lower, Upper and New Galleries, February 14–March 29, 1992, Whitechapel, London.

21. This account of the theoretical approach of the Subaltern Studies group, along with the citations from Guha, is taken from Prakash, "Subaltern Studies as Postcolonial Criticism" (pp. 1477–1478), an excellent articulation of the Subaltern Studies project.

22. Trans. anonymous (London: Tavistock Publications, 1970).

23. This brief introduction to Foucault's idea of *epistemes* is derived from Young, *White Mythologies,* pp. 74–76. All citations in this paragraph are from Foucault in Young.

24. Spivak, "Three Women's Texts and a Critique of Imperialism," p. 268. Spivak cites St. John Rivers in Charlotte Brontë's *Jane Eyre* (New York: 1960).

25. Spivak, "Can the Subaltern Speak?" pp. 288, 292.

26. Spivak, "Three Women's Texts and a Critique of Imperialism," p. 272.

27. Spivak, "Can the Subaltern Speak?" pp. 280–281.

28. Mani, "Contentious Traditions," pp. 90, 95, 111, 112, 115, 117, 119.

29. Ibid.

30. Bhabha, *The Location of Culture.*

31. Spivak, "Can the Subaltern Speak?" pp. 307, 308.

32. Ibid., pp. 300, 308.

33. Ibid., p. 301.

34. Ibid., pp. 301, 306, 307. Spivak notes that if a more privileged subaltern, such as the middle-class Bhuvaneswari, can still not be heard, then the most oppressed in subalternity are even further in the depths; the idea of the subaltern as woman, as one salient example, thus becomes contaminated. If the subaltern is too buried to be able to emerge with an audible voice, the gendered subaltern is a figure that is doubly displaced and "more deeply in shadow" (pp. 287, 295, 306, 307). The notion of irretrievability seems to have affinities with the idea of the indeterminacy of the "feminine" within deconstructive criticism and certain forms of feminist criticism. Nonetheless, the two concepts operate in vastly different ways within each respective intellectual domain. It is the subject-positioning that differentiates the dynamics; subaltern historiography as an approach that is specifically concerned with one particular kind of subjectivity raises methodological questions that disallow the move toward indeterminacy. "For the 'figure' of woman, the relationship between woman and silence can be plotted by women themselves; race and class differences are subsumed under that charge. Subaltern historiography must confront the impossibility of such gestures" (p. 287).

35. Ibid., pp. 286, 306, 308. Spivak draws upon Pierre Macherey's idea that what a work cannot say is important (p. 286).

36. Spivak, in Landry and Maclean, *The Spivak Reader,* p. 292.

37. Ibid., pp. 287–290.

38. Parry, "Problems in Current Theories of Colonial Discourse," p. 38; originally published in *The Oxford Literary Review* 9(1/2), 1987.

39. Ibid., p. 37.

40. Spivak, "Can the Subaltern Speak?" pp. 271, 272.

41. Ibid., p. 273.

42. Ibid., p. 275.

43. Spivak, *In Other Worlds,* p. 209. The negation of this position occurs with the discourse of postmodernism, which leads to an "emptying" of the subject-position. This phrase is rather complicated by Spivak's accidental (?) use of the term *either* twice, with the first being misplaced. The first part of the sentence reads: "The radical intellectual in the West is either caught in a deliberate choice of subalternity, granting to the oppressed either that very expressive subjectivity which s/he

criticizes or, instead, a total unrepresentability." This renders her statement about postmodernism ambiguous. Is the issue one of representation, where one seeks to arrive at the point where one can still say "I" and, in the crisis of the radical intellectual, oscillate from complete representability to none at all? If so, how does postmodernism inform the crisis of these intellectuals with specific regard to their ignorance of the history of imperialism? If the choice, on the other hand, is one between representation (regardless of its own conundrum)—where the "I" matters—and annihilation of the subject—where the "I" does not matter—this makes more sense but still leaves a lot to be untangled.

44. Spivak, "Can the Subaltern Speak?" p. 281.

45. Ibid., p. 300.

46. Ibid., pp. 292, 294.

47. Spivak, in Landry and Maclean, *The Spivak Reader,* p. 293.

48. Spivak, "Can the Subaltern Speak?" p. 280.

49. Bhabha, *The Location of Culture,* especially the essays "Of Mimicry and Man: The Ambivalence of Colonial Discourse," and "Signs Taken for Wonders: Questions of Ambivalence and Authority Under a Tree Outside Delhi, May 1817."

50. Spivak, "Can the Subaltern Speak?" p. 280.

51. Spivak, in Landry and Maclean, *The Spivak Reader,* p. 288.

52. The reference is to Deleuze. Spivak, "Can the Subaltern Speak?" p. 285.

53. Spivak, *In Other Worlds,* p. 209.

54. Spivak, "Can the Subaltern Speak?" pp. 290, 291.

55. Spivak, *In Other Worlds,* p. 210.

56. She refers to the "'law [that] assign[s] a[n] undifferentiated [proper] name' . . . 'to the subaltern as such'" that is drawn upon by the Subaltern Studies group. Ibid., p. 201.

57. Spivak, "Can the Subaltern Speak?" p. 283.

58. Spivak, *In Other Worlds,* p. 253.

59. Ibid., p. 207.

60. Spivak, in Landry and Maclean, *The Spivak Reader,* pp. 289, 290, 306. Spivak distinguishes this moment from what she calls the general condition of subalternity where speech acts are captured by oral history or a discursive formation that is different from investigation.

61. Spivak, "Can the Subaltern Speak?" p. 285.

62. Ibid., p. 295.

63. Ibid., pp. 283–286; Spivak, *In Other Worlds,* pp. 197–221. Spivak draws upon the work of Paul de Man to assert the Subaltern Studies group's scrupulous annotation of the double movement involved in the shift: "The movement of signification adds something . . . but this addition . . . comes to perform a vicarious function, to supplement a lack on the part of the signified." De Man cited by Spivak.

64. Spivak, "Can the Subaltern Speak?" p. 285.

65. Spivak, *In Other Worlds,* p. 210.

66. Spivak follows Jonathan Culler in this particular formulation.

67. Spivak, *In Other Worlds,* p. 254.

68. Ibid., p. 205.

69. Spivak, *Outside in the Teaching Machine,* pp. 5, 15.

70. Spivak, *In Other Worlds,* p. 203.

71. Spivak, in Landry and Maclean, *The Spivak Reader,* p. 307.

72. Spivak, *In Other Worlds,* pp. 207–208.

73. Spivak, "Can the Subaltern Speak?" pp. 287, 295.

74. Spivak, in Landry and Maclean, *The Spivak Reader,* p. 293.

75. Young, *White Mythologies: Writing History and the West*, p. 173.

76. Spivak implies by the use of the word *we* that it is to the group to which she herself belongs that she is referring.

77. This is Spivak's criticism of Deleuze and Foucault. She does, however, generalize it to include western intellectuals interested in tracking the subjectivity of the "Other."

78. Spivak, in Landry and Maclean, *The Spivak Reader*, p. 292.

79. Spivak, "Can the Subaltern Speak?" p. 286.

80. Spivak, *In Other Worlds*, p. 201.

81. This, according to Seung, *Structuralism and Hermeneutics,* is a common—and destructive—phenomenon.

> The eruption of post-structuralist irrationalism can be accepted as a necessary reaction and even be used as a healthy antidote to the naive scientific optimism and dogmatism that have nurtured the various structural programs. But to exalt this irrationalism as the guiding spirit of a new era is to invite and establish an intellectual anarchy.
>
> As long as this anarchy is confined within a few professional journals, it may not exact any tolls heavier than deranging a few feebleminded pedants. But when it invades classrooms and ravages the tender minds of young students, it can produce disastrous consequences. (p. xii)

82. Spivak, *In Other Worlds*, p. 201.

83. Spivak, *Outside in the Teaching Machine*, p. 3.

84. Spivak refers to the sloganizing of strategy. Spivak, *Outside in the Teaching Machine*, p. 9.

85. Citations from the following discussion are derived from Spivak, *Outside in the Teaching Machine,* pp. 3–7, except where otherwise indicated.

86. Spivak, in Harasym, *The Postcolonial Critic*, p. 109.

87. Spivak uses the terms *counterproductive, paralysis, negative metaphysics.* See ibid., pp. 11–13, 45, 47, 52, 122.

88. Spivak, "Teaching for the Times," p. 181. The essay by Derrida that she cites is from "Deconstruction and the Possibility of Justice," *Cordoza Law Review* 11 (July/August 1990).

89. Spivak adds that, in any case, students at this point are "not ready to take sides." See Spivak, *Outside in the Teaching Machine*, p. 18.

90. Spivak, in Landry and Maclean, *The Spivak Reader*, p. 27.

91. Spivak departs from Derrida where he distinguishes "woman," described genitally, from the figure and question of "woman," insisting on her antisexist stance "which is against a sort of purity of the deconstructive approach." See Spivak in Harasym, *The Postcolonial Critic*, p. 14.

92. Spivak, *Outside in the Teaching Machine*, p. 10.

93. Spivak, in Harasym, *The Postcolonial Critic*, p. 58.

94. Spivak, *Outside in the Teaching Machine*, p. 5.

95. Ibid., p. 4.

96. Spivak, in Harasym, *The Postcolonial Critic*, p. 45.

97. Spivak, *Outside in the Teaching Machine*, p. 18. Spivak also notes the tendency to conflate empiricism with essentialism. The careful construction of an object of investigation is not essentialism. The main concern is to be aware that there is, for example, no feminine essence, no essential class subjects, etc. (p. 16).

98. Spivak, in Landry and Maclean, *The Spivak Reader*, pp. 293, 294.

99. Spivak, "Teaching for the Times," p. 183.

100. This, according to Spivak, is what Foucault did during his influential last period. The term *influential* is crucial in this context to Spivak's argument.

101. Spivak, *In Other Worlds,* pp. 207–208.

102. Ibid., p. 204.

103. Spivak, in Landry and Maclean, *The Spivak Reader,* p. 296.

104. Spivak, *Outside in the Teaching Machine,* p. 7.

105. Spivak, in Landry and Maclean, *The Spivak Reader,* p. 294.

106. This is derived from the title of Jaar's exhibition, "Two or Three Things I Imagine About Them," commentary by Jon Bird. I found that the extremely diffi-cult-to-avoid problems of representing the Other nonhierarchically were apparent in some parts of the installation, as was the attempt to displace, or at least minimize, the visibility of authority (the prominence and size of Spivak's albeit inverted image on looped videotape being one such instance).

107. The first citation is from Bruce Robbins, the second from Jonathan Arac, both in Robbins, "The East Is a Career, p. 51.

108. Hence Spivak's supposedly antithetical position as a Marxist, feminist, deconstructivist, poststructuralist.

109. Spivak, in Landry and Maclean, *The Spivak Reader,* p. 307.

110. Spivak, "Teaching for the Times," p. 182. Rajeswari Sunder Rajan, *Real and Imagined Women* (pp. 15, 22–23, 31, 35), is a novel and radical attempt to for-mulate a theoretical way of seeing agency in, specifically, women who commit *sati* (suicide usually by burning or live burial alongside the male body in order to exon-erate the sins of the recently deceased husband and guarantee the entry of both into heaven). Although it only barely sketches out any such formulation, I find it a prob-lematical but intriguing idea. Consider the following thematic statements made by Rajan. The study "explores, tentatively, how a western meditation on the subject of the body in pain may be appropriated for and contested by a specific historical and feminist project in the interests of the female subject as agent."

"It is important . . . to recognize that an inherent resistance to pain is what impels the individual or collective suffering subject towards freedom. It is therefore as one who acts/reacts, rather than as one who invites assistance, that one must regard the subject in pain . . . the sati is understood not psychologically, in terms of a predisposition to or a disregard of pain, but as a contingent self."

"By abandoning the commitment to construct the subjectivity of the woman who performs sati in terms of her motivation we may be enabled to break out of a methodological impasse. Since those who claim that the sati embraces death do not also claim that she embraces pain, but instead argue that she knows no pain, it is necessary and possible to contest the latter argument." "The sati is not a dead woman, but a burning woman seeking to escape, not a spectacle but the subject of action and agency."

"To conclude, while I am sympathetic to a feminist politics that seeks to resist intervention [Rajan here refers to the work of Chandra Mohanty, Lata Mani, and Spivak] I am also anxious, like many feminists in this part of the globe, to discover what might make intervention possible. If 'victim' and 'agent' are adopted as exclu-sive and excluding labels for the female subject, and if, further, victimhood is equated with helplessness and agency with self-sufficiency, all feminist politics will be rendered either inauthentic or unnecessary. To view the 'victim' as subject in my argument about sati (to anchor the argument once again within its specific social and historical context) is to maintain that pain is the very condition of a move towards no-pain, without, at the same time, obviating the need for the operation of sympathy." This is obviously a complex argument that requires very methodical and unambiguous elaboration if it is to avoid being misapprehended.

111. Spivak uses the term *literacy* instead of *knowledge* and is speaking more specifically about education; but juxtaposing her two statements allows a useful point to be made. See Spivak, "Teaching for the Times," pp. 183, 193.

112. Ibid., p. 184. We can hopefully move beyond the question of ability to that of desire on the part of the marginalized of history rather than its center-stage participants. In a recent paper by Ann Stoler, the theme was "will the subaltern speak," one that is fraught with another set of complexities and frustrations but is as deeply significant as that discussed by Spivak. It must be said, as a reminder to those who would imagine that the issue investigated in this essay is now dead, that Stoler received criticism from a few of her colleagues for presuming to be able to step into a culture (albeit one that she has studied for decades and has lived in bi- and trilingually for several years) and retrieve its hidden histories. Stoler, "Memory Work and Postcolonial Studies," paper delivered to the joint literature and sociology seminar held in the Department of Sociology, University of Essex, Colchester, UK, February 5, 1998. This is the paralysis referred to earlier. And it is a problem whose accompanying pressures often reduce the issue of "what to do" to the choice of either continuing on in unreflexive and unreflective nineteenth-century-style "observation" and "interrogation," or critiquing oneself and one's work out of any productive potential at all. True, there is an increasing number of nuanced studies arising out of the study of colonialism, postcolonialism, and their overlapping discourses, but this is not indicative of the evaporation of the problem of how to proceed in the least damaging of ways. And, as the whole point of Spivak's essay illustrates, the instructiveness of nuance can hide narrow narcissism.

113. Spivak, "Can the Subaltern Speak?" pp. 288–289.

114. Here, as before, I am reducing Tarantino's film to one narrative for the purposes of argument.

5

Writing Women's Wars: Foucauldian Strategies of Engagement

Eleanor O'Gorman

This chapter adopts elements of Foucauldian analysis to dislodge ideas of power, subjectivity, and methodology in feminist international relations (IR), with particular reference to the experiences of women in revolutionary struggles.[1] The works of Michel Foucault have proved rich pickings for the critical/poststructuralist turn in international relations. In particular, the adoption of Foucauldian analyses to the service of critical feminist theory has involved redefining gendered subjectivity and power in the conduct of research and the building of theory.[2] The critical import of such redefinition is in rewriting the ontological and epistemological premises of the discipline of international relations. The appeal of Foucault to feminist theorists has been his challenge to enlightenment understandings of knowledge and the political promise of his genealogical method in excavating previously marginalized voices and forms of knowledge.

In adapting Foucault to the service of critical feminist theory, I take as my terrain the theorizing of women's participation in revolutionary wars. The discussion is developed in three parts. By way of context, the first part outlines representations of women's participation in revolutionary struggles. The second part assesses the theoretical implications of Foucauldian reworkings of power/resistance and subjectivity with respect to representations of women's experiences in such struggles. It is argued that a poststructuralist shift challenges the rigid categories of experience and expression found in representations of women's revolutionary participation that reinforce gendered stereotypes of roles and political space. The third part of the discussion explores some implications of this theoretical turn for feminist practice. There are two aspects to the idea of feminist practice as understood here. The first refers to practices of research methodology and the implications of interpreting and practicing Foucault's ideas of genealogy. The second aspect refers to the "experienced" world of international relations and the strategies of engagement that a poststructuralist feminist politics would involve at the level of action and policy. In outlining a distinction between feminist practice and theory, the intention is not to reinforce a sense of autonomy between feminist constructions of theory and feminist forms of political practice. On the contrary, strategies of engagement are identified here to highlight the imbrication of both these aspects of feminism as the sine qua non of feminist IR.[3]

WOMEN, SUBJECTIVITY, AND REVOLUTION

The liberatory promise of revolutionary movements has been one focus of action and research for feminist IR. Nicaragua, Palestine, South Africa, and Zimbabwe are examples of such struggles. Revolutionary struggle has provided a unity of purpose and site of resistance in the context of decolonization in the second half of the twentieth century. The romantic appeal of liberating women through liberating states finds currency and resonance in an iconography that offers particular roles for women in support of a wider struggle. Why do liberation movements invite this possibility of women's emancipation in the course of revolution?

Cynthia Enloe and Christine Sylvester both see possibilities in the distinctiveness of guerrilla warfare and the decentralized structure of guerrilla armies. The distinction between conventional and revolutionary warfare is seen to enable qualitatively different experiences of women's participation. In the former, the aim is "to mobilise human and material resources for the sake of optimising military effectiveness," whereas the latter is aimed "to bring about fundamental alterations in the socio-political order."[4] One possibility is that combat roles opened up for women by guerrilla armies "can be less other-conceptualized than the labour of combat under the flag of an established state, and the participation of women within it turns everyone's expectations on their heads."[5] Sylvester suggests the woman warrior identity can be mobilized to antipatriarchal ends by countering such expectations of the ruling elite, by challenging stereotypes of female labor, and by building the possibility of new understandings of power relations.[6] This is due to the antistate aims and the nonstate nature of a liberation army as a decentralized organization that relies on flexibility rather than weaponry for success.

There is also optimism about the liberatory promise of guerrilla armies as they collapse the boundaries of public/private by eschewing the "gendered distinction between 'front' and 'rear.'"[7] The battlefront and the homefront become the same terrain of struggle. However, Enloe also cautions against the romantic appeal of revolutionary armies as a panacea for the transformation of gender relations. Issues of masculinity, femininity, roles, and the sexual division of labor can be just as contentious here as in state armies.

In terms of revolutionary struggles, the allocation of women's roles has involved the politicization of women's "traditional" roles, such as mother, wife, and food producer. The motives for such a strategy include a commitment to agendas for social change as well as the requirements of military effectiveness. Thus, the concerns of revolutionary armies are not simply about transforming the political order but also, like state armies, the military effectiveness of operations. In the pursuit of such effectiveness, strategies of allocating roles according to generation and marital status can perpetuate a gendered and generational division of labor as roles and political space become coterminous when "homefront" support tasks are carried out by married women while unmarried women enter the more militarized spaces of the training camps. In the case of Zimbabwe, some young women assumed the ultimate male military task of combat, but for the most part unmarried women in the camps "performed militarised though still feminine tasks, serving as cooks, nurses, and laundresses for the guerrillas."[8] This reflects tensions concerning the degree to which such generational allocation of tasks for women actually operates within an unspoken gendered division of revolutionary labor.

Gendered discourses that shape the representation of women's experiences of war pose another cautionary note for optimism about women's liberation through revolution. These discourses are embedded in the histories of such revolutions. The currency of such gendered representations includes an exoticized and fetishized notion of women in powerful military positions juxtaposed with the portrayal of women as victims of violence and propaganda in the course and cause of war. The heroic image of women as guerrilla fighters is a familiar trope in revolutionary art and propaganda. Linked to this is an iconography that evokes the presence of women in war and the contradictory tension of expected roles—for example, women as mothers/women as warriors. A classic image is that of a woman holding a rifle and a baby. This image conveys many messages. It is a call to arms for women; it shames men into military action; it reassures society that women are still feminine though involved in masculine activities; it reassures society that women will return to traditional domestic roles following a temporary aberration of the natural order through war.

There is implicit in this image creation an ambivalence of women warriors as role models. Are such images and roles an aberration in gender terms (neither man nor woman) or a liberatory role model for women generally?[9] These contradictions reflect the difficulty of creating categorical identities for women in revolutions. The subjectivity of women in revolutions arises not only from the ideological influence of revolutionary social-ism but also from the reclamation work undertaken by feminist historians and social theorists to highlight the actions and roles of women in revolu-tion and war generally. Cutting across such representations is an under-standing in the first instance of the public and the private as two distinct spheres of gendered activity—the private being imbued with female values and involving particular roles for women in that sphere. The public sphere is conceptualized very much as a male sphere and war an activity of this sphere. Such partition of space leads to the categorization of women into particular roles with respect to the conduct and experience of war. Thus, the presence of women in war is explained and located in respect of spatial and categorical ontologies. Women are what women do in particular roles in particular spheres. Such a "presence/absence" dynamic assigns different values and visibility to male and female roles but nonetheless involves interdependence for the overall functioning of power.[10]

This positioning is partially reinforced by the radical feminist critique of militarism as a structural and institutional type of power that determines the positioning of men and women in relation to war.[11] In such a critique, militarism and patriarchy are seen to be acting in concert to subordinate women; women enter war on male terms, and the roles of women are very much circumscribed by the needs of militarism as a masculinist form of power—to service the primary male role of the soldier/warrior. Women (even in the archetypal male role of fighter) must be constructed in such a way as to perpetuate male power and female subordination in this gendered process of militarization. This defines a public and private space where society sets sanctions and rewards for women's aberrant actions during war. It also sees women more readily in noncombat, but key, supporting roles as wives, defense workers, nurses, drivers, administrators, and prostitutes.[12]

Implicit in the gendered process of militarization is the devaluation and invisibility of militarism's dependence on female labor. Such devaluation involves redefining women's roles and the space of noncombatant activity as the "homefront" to ensure the primacy of male, combat, frontline space. This artificiality of space becomes a paradox when women as nurses, sol-diers, intelligence workers, and prostitutes may be physically located close to the front line but still viewed as located at the homefront in terms of activities.[13] It is also paradoxical in war situations where military tactics involve increased civilian involvement. This is the case in guerrilla wars, where a daily war of attrition along with counterinsurgent responses involve the development of local supply and intelligence networks that implicate civilians and place them on the front line. In such gendered repre-sentations, roles in militarized spaces are constructed to perpetuate a gen-dered understanding of power where "men fight and women weep."[14] A feminist critique seeks to reveal such structural power and suggests subversion of these roles as a site of feminist struggle and change.

Jean Bethke Elshtain's treatise *Women and War* challenges the binary logic of such representations in the tradition of western modernity that has reinforced and perpetuated this essential dichotomy of women as life givers and men as life takers. The convenience of such typologies is double-edged, as they are deployed by feminists and antifeminists, militarists and pacifists to buttress their divergent positions concerning gender identities and the activities of war. Elshtain dislodges such tropes by asserting a complexity rather than duality of categories for women and men in war. The complexity that underlies the apparent rigidity of dichotomies—military/male/brave warrior versus peace/female/beautiful soul—is witnessed by women in the military and guerrilla armies and male soldiers objecting to technologies of war.

The prospects of women's emancipation through liberation struggles also come to be seen in a dimmer light when postindependence realities are investigated. There are two conflicting images of the postindependent situations for women. In the optimistic version, women's traditional roles are irreversibly politicized and gain an increased importance and recognition in the new state. The pessimistic scenario is one that sees the new government adopting the structures of the previous state and reinforcing the public/private split that invites the demobilization of women from their revolutionary roles. The optimism of politicizing women's work in the course of revolution is often lost, as such roles are most likely to be demobilized and depoliticized in the return to public/private understandings of space in the postindependence context.

The domestic/political strategy is therefore one that does not necessarily ensure advancement for women through revolution. The participation of women has to be seen less romantically in the context of continuity in the gendered division of labor that leaves the way open for the demobilization of women and integration into a new old order.[15] The preoccupation with a return to normality and the institution of public order influences the postliberation phase in the rebuilding of the state. The family is central to this and, as such, the demobilization of women becomes paramount as the political tenor of their actions is stripped away and they are once again consigned to the private realm in the service of the public, state, male realm. Enloe argues that holding on to the perceived empowerment of women in revolution calls for collective strategies that self-consciously promote women in this crucial postindependence period. This can prove particularly difficult for women who have crossed the gender divide and been fighters. One reported problem for such women in the postindependence Zimbabwe was reintegration into their communities because they were often treated with suspicion and fear. Despite the comradeship of combat with their male brethren, women faced difficulties in finding husbands![16] Such a pessimistic narrative begs the question of how we can assess women's experiences of empowerment and disempowerment through revolutionary struggles.

One approach is to challenge the motivation for explanation. The question of women's participation in revolutions has tended to focus on how and why women are mobilized for revolution by revolutionary movements. The "how" question centers on women's roles and the essential politicization of previously domestic tasks as well as the assumption by women of "male/public" roles as fighters and leaders. With regard to the "why" question, the tendency is to talk of the unifying appeal of anticolonial, nationalist, peasant, or class claims.[17] Within this, more revisionist works seek to disaggregate unified agendas and point to gender agendas or local interests as a key mobilizing factor.[18]

Maintaining a focus on mobilization tends to bias research toward the needs and motives of the revolutionary organizations, and local agency becomes important only to the extent that it fulfills or thwarts those efforts. When the why and how of revolutionary struggle for women remain centered on mobilization, the consciousness and actions of women's agency will remain secondary to institutional requirements. In mapping out a poststructuralist account of power, subjectivity, and research methodology, the intention here is to shift the focus to the daily experiences of women's participation in revolution through the practices of power and resistance they forge, proactively and reactively. Rethinking power/resistance and subjectivity in revolution allows us to explore and write about the lives of women beyond that of subjects awaiting mobilization and beyond that of roles read off from domestic space and political necessity.

STRATEGIES OF ENGAGEMENT 1:
THEORIES OF POWER/RESISTANCE AND SUBJECTIVITY

Using Foucault's understanding of power and resistance as a starting point, we can construct a poststructuralist approach to gender identities, resistance, and revolution that takes fuller account of women's differentiated experiences of guerrilla war. Foucault's conception of power holds the possibility of subjection and resistance simultaneously. He writes not only of disciplinary power but also of power/resistance, which extends through and is imbricated within our entire social fabric. Through power/resistance the practices of power and resistance are intimately inscribed in mutual tension as a dynamic struggle that is "agonistic" in expression. Resistance is inscribed in power. "It would not be possible for power relations to exist without points of insubordination which, by definition, are means of escape."[19] This suggests an exercise of power that circulates through social relations and is not fixed. Such an understanding of power eschews the notion of power as mere domination, challenges power as a possession, and imagines power as being everywhere.[20]

This reimagination of power sees it as circulating within relationships between subjects and originating from inside struggles, from below. It is a relational notion of power (that is, power bound up in social relations) where there is a constant struggle to act and reply to action. This "agonism" has been described as a type of combat "in which opponents develop a strategy of reaction and of mutual taunting." It constitutes a "relationship which is at the same time reciprocal incitation and struggle; less of a face-to-face confrontation which paralyzes both sides than a permanent provocation."[21] The possibilities and operations of power and resistance coexist in this permanent provocation. "There are no relations of power without resistances; the latter are all the more real and effective because they are formed right at the point where relations of power are exercised."[22] This understanding of power/resistance opens up discursive spaces where power and resistance are creating, defining, and defying each other in a tense dynamic of renegotiation. The simultaneity of resistance separates this from a more classical zero-sum conception of power, which lies at the heart of realist power relations between states and from the binary logic of an exogenous point of resistance as a unifying source of opposition. In such a fluid context of power/resistance relations, difference and differentiation become both conditions and effects of power. This can be said of gendered power that manifests itself in the categorization of women in particular spaces and roles and implicates ideas of femininity to limit behavior.

This shift in understanding power relations as relations of power/resistance has implications for understanding the modalities of power and gender identities in a setting of revolution. It triggers a movement away from fixed categories or roles toward a recognition of the many contradictory "roles" or "positions" that women are called upon to take up or resist within revolutionary struggles. For the "subject," this is a map of compliance and resistance, losses and gains, in the constant struggle that defines the field of possible actions. Through the circulation of power/resistance, the subject and subjectivity itself are in a state of renegotiation. This dynamic is described by Jana Sawicki as "resistant subjectivity."[23] It works through Foucauldian power/resistance as a struggle "against that which ties the individual to himself [sic] and submits him to others in this way," such that "maybe the target nowadays is not to discover what we are, but to refuse what we are."[24] We move toward a more discursive notion of power/resistance where the subject of power is both exercising power and creating resistance as well as being subject to power and resistance. Subjectivity becomes a shifting terrain of struggle such that modes of identity are claimed, reclaimed, and refused. Such continuous struggle is linked to the roles/identities we may be attempting to fulfill at any one time—for example, lecturer, daughter, student, Irishwoman, mother, friend. The strategies of power/resistance hinge upon the nature of a resisting subject producing a field of possible actions within the mobile field of social power relations. These practices of power/resistance find materiality in the practical engagement of experience that forges subjectivity. Such resistant subjectivity arises not simply in relation to other subjects and social representation but in the tense dynamic of self-representation implicit in the actions and consciousness of agents. With respect to the strategies involved in the perpetual struggle of power/resistance, Foucault suggests the following hypothesis:

> I would say it's all against all. There aren't immediately given subjects of a struggle, one the proletariat, the other the bourgeoisie. Who fights against whom? We all fight against each other. And there is always within each of us something that fights something else.[25]

The power/resistance dynamic functions not only as resistant subjectivity but also as "differentiated subjectivity" in relation to the self and others. In terms of gender power/resistance, resistant subjectivity invokes a recognition of difference among women and within "woman" as political agents. Sandra Harding reflects this in her assertion that "not only do our gender experiences vary across the cultural categories; they also are often in conflict in any one individual's experience."[26] The practices of power/resistance therefore reflect the possibility of multiple sites of resistance. This challenges the idea of a unitary site of resistance tied to a particular subject position (e.g., class, race, gender) that is at the heart of revolutionary resistance:

> The points of resistance are present everywhere in the power network. Hence there is no single locus of great Refusal, no soul of revolt, source of all rebellions, or pure law of the revolutionary. Instead there is a plurality of resistance's [sic], each of them a special case: resistances that are possible, necessary, improbable; others that are spontaneous, savage, solitary, concerted, rampant or violent; still others that are quick to compromise, interested, or sacrificial; by definition, they can only exist in the strategic field of power relations.[27]

Thus, in one fell swoop we lose the notion of the revolutionary subject so beloved of peasant revolutionary writers and also the possibility of a shared worldview. But we do gain the imagination of possibilities of multiple sites of resistance enacted through resistant and differentiated subjectivity. Resistance is grounded in particular histories and relations and expands the possibilities of politics: The personal, in its many forms and positionalities, becomes political. In the context of revolution, such a shift reveals the localized practices of resistance such that the possibilities for action do not have to involve a sense of false consciousness that robs women of their power to act.

To challenge any imperative to categorize gender identities in revolution, we need to explore this terrain of difference, resistance, and subjectivity in a context of relations of power and resistance. Our understanding of discursive practices of gender power/resistance is furthered by Henrietta Moore's discussion of "processes of identification and differentiation."[28] Rather than embodied and fixed identities of categories, roles, or spheres, it is these processes that inform the fluid interpretation and reinterpretation of gender identities through the experience of social power relations. Through these processes, differentiation is seen to mirror the complex interactions of multiple subjectivities that cut across race, class, sexuality, and age in inscribing gender identities. This leads to a highlighting of the "performative aspects of gender identity and the possibilities that exist for the subversion of categorical identities."[29] These processes mirror the idea of power/resistance *practices* outlined above. Through such practices, difference, social identities, and resistance are bound up in this contested terrain of gender subjectivities and are underpinned by a practical consciousness of gender identities "forged through practical engagement in lives lived."[30] The resistant and differentiated subjectivity of gender identities has therefore to be seen in the context of experienced difference.

This practical consciousness of identification and difference is informed by understandings of "intersubjectivity" and "subject positionality" that posit a constant renegotiation of identity "in relation" to others and the self. Intersubjectivity refers to the way in which our identities are constructed in relation to others around us and in relation to our own self-representations. In the process of identification, the agency of the individual is reclaimed through an intersubjectivity that is concerned with "desire and the projection and introjection of images of the self and others."[31] Positionality with respect to multiple subjectivities refers to the different "speaking positions" or "subject positions" taken up by an individual at any given time. It goes beyond gendered dichotomies in problematizing identities formed through social relations. In this way, the discursive practices of gendered power/resistance lead to women taking up different subject positions in the performance of multiple subjectivities—for example, mother, food provider, collaborator, good citizen, community worker, and so on. Such multiple positioning allied to intersubjectivity leads to gender identities that are discursive, that is, provisional and subject to reinforcement and/or resistance. Women in revolutions can be seen to take up a number of "speaking positions," which are established through relation with self and others.

The interplay of intersubjectivity and positionality suggests that gender identities can emerge to resist as well as subject—not in a universalist, detemporalized sense but in a located sense of experience and possibility in different situations—and still unmask the workings of power. Gender identities are therefore not simply the passive outcome of a determinist process of socialization but rather are constructed through processes of practical and discursive knowledge involving agency in the form of resistance and compliance that reproduce and/or resist dominant discourses and categories. The fluidity of such dynamics finds expression as "conflicting loyalties" and "incoherent identities," in the descriptions coined by Sawicki and Sylvester.[32] This reflects the many subject positions women may be enacting at any one time and the actions arising from different subject positions, be they ones of compliance (with the state, with the guerrillas, with neighbors) or of resistance (against the state, against the guerrillas, against each other). The positions are further differentiated in terms of location and experience.

Such identities are often in conflict through "investment" in particular subject positions and through the "thwarting" of such positions. The tension of taking up and maintaining multiple and contradictory subject positions results in thwarting that reflects the "inability to sustain or properly take up a gendered subject position, resulting in a crisis—real or imagined—of self-representation and/or social evaluation."[33] This can also arise from "others" failing to fulfill their subject positions in relation to one's own (e.g., husband/wife, government/good citizen, revolutionary organization/revolutionary cadre). Thwarting can also reflect the failure to accrue benefits from adopting or investing in a particular subject position—for example, compensation from the independent government for cattle seized and food given to the guerrillas during the war by local people. In an everyday context of living through and participating (or not) in revolution, such positionality is reflected in the following scenario:

> Competing demands can force women to make painful decisions: the family may need her support and attention, while she feels impelled by events to be active outside the home—demonstrating for peace, participating in the struggle, organising welfare services and so on. Many women find enormous reserves of emotional and physical energy to fulfil both roles; sometimes they have instead to sacrifice one or the other, and cope with some form of guilt.[34]

In building a poststructuralist perspective on revolution, we come to an understanding of social relations in war that challenges any attempt at metanarratives of power (patriarchal militarism) or categories of being (fighter, mother, prostitute). These multiple positionalities, along with a terrain of conflict marked by discursive practices of power/resistance (which do not demarcate political and nonpolitical spaces), allow us to map out the ways in which women, through resistant subjectivity (refusal to be categorized), negotiate and renegotiate their relationship to war at an everyday and local level. The practices of resistant and differentiated subjectivity in war are thus argued to be manifest in the struggle over gender identities that lies at the heart of the contradictory practice of power/resistance. Such a perspective allows us to understand the "field of possible actions" as viewed by women from their various subject positions in relation to war. These actions of power, resistance, and survival inform and are informed by a practical consciousness of everyday experience.

The forms of actions are similar to those unearthed by James Scott in his writings on everyday forms of peasant resistance, which he terms "weapons of the weak." Such actions include "foot dragging, dissimulation, false compliance, pilfering, feigned ignorance, slander, arson, sabotage, and so forth."[35] The stories of resistant and differentiated subjectivity yield a war by women fought on the level of the everyday, where risk and change are constantly being renegotiated. The outcome of such practical consciousness incorporates the contradictory practices of compliance and resistance in which women engage to present themselves to the world and to understand the war around them in relation to their daily lives. These practices and consciousness I have termed "Gendered Localized Resistance."[36] The practices of Gendered Localized Resistance reveal continuous gender struggles that take the form of everyday resistance. The fluid way in which this dynamic permeates the lives of women challenges a gender analysis of war conducted through women's roles or actions confined to private or public spheres. Through the various relationships in which women are involved throughout a war, there emerges a repertoire of contradictory views and practices that reflect elements of power, powerlessness, and resistance within the experiences of war.

The dynamics of resistant and differentiated subjectivity have implications for feminist research in that the focus of interest is shifted away from the revelation of oppression toward the anatomy of struggle, which reveals not only the intricacies of power as exercised but also the possibilities of resistance as bound up in power. Such a rendering of women's relationship to war has implications for a transformative agenda of gender relations. The first of these involves the opening up of roles and categories for women in war to give space and voice to the agency of women even in the most circumscribed of situations. It allows women to bear witness to their own experiences, which may otherwise be ignored, defined as nonpolitical, or individualized to an extent that the lack of a collective manifestation of agency is read as passivity. In a practical sense, what this reveals is that far from certain actions and identities in a context of war, we find a struggle of identities wrapped up in the experiences of war itself. This is first evident in the various subject positions adopted by women in war that refute any attempt to demarcate space as public/private or to term any experiences as purely embodied in one subject position—for example, woman as soldier, woman as mother, woman as food provider, woman as victim. The public and private must be disestablished, because the center of spatially configured political subjectivity cannot hold once power/resistance struggles are seen to embrace subjectivity in pervasive, noncategorical forms.

The transformative potential of gender power also lies in the analysis of difference between women's experiences of the same war through acts of compliance or resistance within relationships. Some women may be widowed, have a husband who works away from home, or leave home as a young adult to join a revolutionary movement. Their perspectives on war may be very different in reflecting how women relate to the community and the state and in how they perceive themselves and wish others to perceive them. A telling example is the ambivalence I found, in the course of my research on the Zimbabwe war, toward women who were in relationships with government soldiers. Such women were sometimes vilified by others in their communities and were targeted as sellouts and thus subject to punishment beatings or accusations of witchcraft. Yet other women claimed to understand that the motivation for women in such relationships was often economic in a context of chronic shortages of food, medicines, and cash. As such, some of the women interviewed were forgiving of behavior that in the main was socially unacceptable. Still other women saw sexual harassment by guards as bringing about such relations and saw the women involved as victims. In this scenario of private relations between women and the state military, we find a mix of social approbation, moral outrage, political treason, witchcraft, and economic rationalization. These are all explanations of one phenomenon that defy categorization as private/public or woman as prostitute/camp follower. In fact, such women may be at the same time a mother, a wife, a guerrilla supporter, a state collaborator, an economic agent, a victim, and a survivor.

Rethinking gender, power, and resistance as dynamic practices of positioning oneself in relation to war through the local conduct of everyday social relations has implications of not only moving beyond stereotypes of femininity and war but also reconfiguring stereotypes of masculinity and war. Differentiating the experiences of men and the constructions of masculine identities in war raises the question of the extent to which men embrace or resist categorical identities as women do. If women, in patriarchal accounts and feminist critiques, have been categorized or silenced, then men's identities also have been constructed from metanarratives of masculinity and power. If women are trapped by the subjectivities and roles of preexisting modes of explanation concerning war and revolution, then it follows that perhaps men too have been stereotyped, albeit in relatively more powerful subject positions. In taking women's and men's voices and actions at the local level as a starting point for analyzing war and gender relations, we can imagine more flexible ideas of gender identities and identify opportunities for transformation.

The promises of resistance and subversion come through "agonistic" understandings of power and subjectivity. This continual interplay of subjection and resistance is very different from the apocalyptic promise of open revolt inherent in revolutionary adaptations of Marxism. The latter, which involve dialectical schemes of liberation through the categorical inevitability of class conflict, influenced anticolonial liberation struggles in the second half of this century. The former, which allows no such clarity of struggle, invokes instead a complex interaction of the power, resistance, and subjectivity that require more historicized and located revelation of how people become subjects in revolution and how power is exercised through the creation of subjectivity (the oppressor and the oppressed). Such explorations involve an excavation and exhumation of revolutions that seek out the assumed and the unexplained and give voice to the simultaneous operations and possibilities of power and resistance within and without revolution.

STRATEGIES OF ENGAGEMENT 2: FEMINIST PRACTICES

Genealogy and Research Methodology

The reconceptualization of power, subjectivity, and resistance I have outlined requires appropriate methodologies and coalitions of practice on the ground if an agenda of transformation is to be effected. Practices of resistant and differentiated subjectivity challenge not only claims to knowledge but also how we establish such claims. A Foucauldian strategy in this regard is the development of critical knowledge and practice through genealogy. Genealogy recovers power/resistance through the particularization of located struggles, and it grounds any attempt at building theory and action. This requires the imbrication of theory and method to create critical knowledge. The argument here is that such a genealogical method underpins the work of the feminist as critic. The practice of criticism, according to Foucault, involves "pointing out on what kinds of assumptions, what kinds of familiar, unchallenged, unconsidered modes of thought the practices that we accept rest."[37] Implicit in his genealogical method is the practice of criticism that displays a "local character of criticism . . . whose validity is not dependent on the approval of the established regimes of thought." Such criticism is nothing less than the "insurrection of subjugated knowledges"[38] and is a self-conscious strategy whereby "knowledge is not made for understanding; it is made for cutting."[39] Genealogy as methodology is implicated in power/resistance because the recovery of "subjugated knowledges" is central to understanding the workings of power and subjectivity.

The excavation of subjugated knowledges and the anatomization of particular struggles mean we "lose" any sense of a transhistorical subject, man or woman. The genealogies of dissipated subjectivity challenge the idea of history as the march of God or man on earth. Rationality is that engine of history that seeks an authoritative account of historical events in order to render them fixed in terms of an unfolding story of inevitability in which characters enter the stage of history on cue with roles readily performed and interpreted in the playing out of these events. Genealogy recovers an alternative myriad of possibilities, the "numberless beginnings" of history that refuse a unified self. It is nothing less than a liberation of "lost events."[40] History is therefore seen to involve many interpretations and many points of emergence where we, the agents of history, are embroiled in the constant forging of meaning through the subversion, inversion, replacement, and creation of power relations. In the refusal of absolutes, genealogy

> corresponds to the acuity of a glance that distinguishes, separates, and disperses; that is capable of liberating divergence and marginal elements—the kind of dissociating view that is capable of decomposing itself, capable of shattering the unity of man's being through which it was thought he could extend his sovereignty to the events of his past.[41]

There is self-reflexivity involved in such an approach that calls for a consciousness of discontinuity. This consciousness is one that takes the present moment as the moment of question. Thus, in seeking to reevaluate past events, we, as researchers, are posing questions rooted in concerns arising from our present circumstances. The impetus for change and the search for new possibilities of ways of being as our "selves" drives the search into the past to deconstruct metanarratives and constitute alternative narratives. The impetus for such criticism is the expression of "a historical ontology of ourselves."[42] This ontology transforms the way we create and understand history and knowledge in relation to our present way of being. It refers to the creativity of criticism that, through a genealogical search, leads to an exploration of the past from the perspectives and problems of the present. Such a focus lends itself to a knowledge concerned with the limits of our existence so that we may transgress those limits, not that we may contain ourselves within them.

To seek out "subjugated knowledges," to pose a "critical ontology of ourselves" in the present as we look to the past, to deny a transcendental historical subject the comfort of a millennial solution—these are all the marks of a subversive methodology intricately bound up in that of which it speaks: power, resistance, and the possibilities of freedom.[43] It is this promise of resistance that remains both elusive and seductive in the work of Foucault and poses the challenge for feminist writers wishing to take up Foucault in challenging the limits of IR as an academic discipline and feminist IR as a critical discourse within that discipline.

The deployment of Foucault's genealogy to the purposes of writing about women's experiences of revolution involves close attention to issues of voice and difference in the representations of women's experiences. The tradition of western humanism is itself a partial knowledge constructed on particular positioning of women and ideas about women. It is based on a binary logic that frames the construction of "others." This, as we saw earlier, involves a gendered valuation of subjectivity and experience such that a norm of western male agency is juxtaposed with a devalued feminized "other." This is raised by Chandra Mohanty with respect to the representation of the experiences of women in the Third World. She raises the specter of "discursive colonialism" in the work of western feminists who forge a new orthodoxy of "otherness" by reductionist representations of women from the "Third World."[44] The critical ontology of feminist IR must be one that seeks to manifest the polyvocality of experience and so reflect differences of location, identity, constructions of past experience, and ongoing resistance that occur among "women" as a sexed and gendered group and within "woman" as a particular subject in relation to her "self" and "others."

One implication of genealogy as a critical methodology is the need to explore appropriate research methods that do not create a new orthodoxy but do embrace difference and seek out subjugated knowledges. The methods of such excavation may be archaeological and documentary but in the case of feminist research are reflected in the increased emphasis given to voice and oral testimony in writing about women and war. This raises issues concerning the nature of experience and the methods used to represent experience.[45] This reconceptualization opens up spaces and opportunities to explore the actions, responses, and understandings that women themselves bring to war through various research methods, including oral testimony, autobiographical and literary analysis, and revisions of documentary evidence used to "authenticate" events and actions. This allows us to envisage practices of gender power/resistance that are accompanied by an empowering methodology of recovering subjugated knowledges.

The practice of criticism by feminist scholars in international relations is not now about taking the canonical texts of man, the state, and war and seeking to insert a "womanly" presence; nor is it to covet and define "feminine" agendas of health, education, and the treatment of victims of war. Rather we must excavate the many practices of gender power relations within the academic discipline that construct the knowledge of political practice, and also reimagine that state of political practice in itself. In the case of war, the why and how of revolution for women becomes transplanted by the wider knowledge of lives lived, strategies developed, hopes, fears, and feelings through which the questions become: What do women want from revolution and what is their relationship to it? This is the why and how of revolution from the perspective of those subjects on whose behalf a revolution is claimed. In terms of research methodologies, rethinking the practice of gender power/resistance and gender identities in war situations opens the way for an array of cross-disciplinary research and insights in challenging the preconceptions of gender and conflict that have influenced thinking in politics and development. The significance of difference and representation of women's experiences are two themes requiring further research and debate in the wider field of feminist IR. Equally important may be the humility of a discipline coming to terms with, and listening to, the voices of the "subjects" it claims as constituents.

Politics of Engagement

Rethinking power and subjectivity allied to genealogical method poses subversive possibilities and fears for feminist theory. It generates much enlivening debate at a time when feminist theory and practice is infused with critical self-questioning concerning its political direction, its constituencies, and its foundations. Viewing gendered identities as tied to discursive power/resistance destabilizes the idea of a fixed standpoint position to inform political actions, which has long been a tenet of feminist research and politics. It has been asked if in dismantling categories we are heralding the end of feminist politics as a politics of resistance.[46] The answer here is no. In fact, the relinquishing of a privileged standpoint feminist epistemology has positive political implications for feminist practices in opening up the "field of possible actions."

Far from killing the subject, it can be argued that Foucault reinvigorates the dynamism of subjectivity by refusing the determinism of an Enlightenment humanism. The political act of social criticism creates this proliferation and explosion that defies the knowledge we claim to hold and blinds the Cartesian cyclops we call history. As subjects in constant struggle we do not necessarily face the inevitability of struggle but may also always face the prospect of resistance, reversal, and change. Feminist politics is urged beyond fixed subjectivities of victimhood or liberation. For feminist epistemology this means the letting go of a singular standpoint, a privileged perspective from which to locate the experiences of women. The claim to a female truth can be argued to have universalized "otherness," restricted strategies of resistance, and elided important differences that shape resistance. There is no authentic truth to counter another truth. Gendered positioning is much more mediated than that.

From a feminist standpoint position, Nancy Hartsock accuses the post-modernist turn of at best suspicious timing, at worst forging a conspiracy aimed at robbing feminism of its oppositional power in challenging unitary subjectivity at a time when critical social movements are gathering force. Foucault is thus condemned as a "colonizer who refuses," who exists in "painful ambiguity" with the Enlightenment tenets of his own subjectivity.[47] *Pace* Hartsock, it can be argued that Foucault's understanding of power does offer epistemological value to feminist reworkings of power. In particular, she laments the possible loss of a material analysis based on categories of the dominant and the dominated (the oppositional "other"). However, while materialism in the strict Marxist sense may be eschewed, a sense of poststructural materiality can be read from Foucault's rendering of power/resistance and his method of genealogy. It is not that in the mapping of power/resistance and resistant subjectivity we lose the importance of material contexts in the construction of identities and the practice of power and resistance. Rather, experiences of multiple subjectivity and intersubjectivity, through power/resistance, give a discursive rather than determining influence to that materialism in shaping power relations.

A strict standpoint position holds on to key modernist premises such as the binary opposition, the division of political space, and the need for a transcendental revolutionary subject. As long as those remain non-negotiable elements of a feminist politics of resistance, poststructuralist strategies of engagement and resistance cannot be heard or evaluated. These latter strategies of engagement are not explicit in the work of Foucault and certainly are not directed specifically to struggles of gender power/resistance. Foucault's evasive positions on the precise forms of resistance and political action are well established. However, feminist adoptions of Foucault should not shy away from highlighting the dynamics of resistance through genealogies of the diverse struggles that can readily be identified as concerns of feminist international relations.

The arguments of standpoint feminism have been well rehearsed in feminist theories of war and peace and hark back to the politics underlying the representations of women in war outlined earlier. Embracing the maternal/peaceful stereotype implies essentially shared values among women qua women and reinforces the beautiful-soul image that has inspired feminist action in the promotion of peace. To counter such standpoint claims of "feminine authenticity," Sylvester argues for the consideration of difference between women involved in different struggles. The efficacy of viewing the oppression of women in war as a collective standpoint is questionable in contexts where experiences among women and the subjectivities of women in war may differ greatly. There is not a linear progression of political consciousness for women and indeed not even one privileged type of consciousness. She argues that "for postmodernists . . . multiple standpoints which derive from ways of understanding developed collectively, through self-conscious political struggle, are harbingers of political victories."[48] (I would add "individually" to "collectively," as most struggles involve these two aspects.) This multiple and contested creation of subjectivities reflects the "crowded and fractured" nature of women's identities that defy simplistic categorizations of maternity and peace.[49]

In fact, such essentialism becomes a threat to any feminist project. The understanding of difference among women in interpreting experiences of war and consciousness of struggle thus becomes central to developing feminist analyses of war. Multiple subjectivities crossed by race, sex, class, and roles give rise to multiple standpoints of experience that must shape any feminist understanding of politics and change. Precisely because such difference rests on "a certain foundational incoherence," it is difficult to embrace, particularly in the attempts to forge political action and mobilize for change. However, such mobilization for change may be more effective precisely because there is a keener understanding of the practical engagement of women's struggles of power/resistance. Sylvester poses an "aware cacophony" where "dissonance and disagreement . . . shows that feminism as consciousness and movement, is subject to interpretation based on differences in lived realities of the interpreters."[50] Women therefore who do not "fit" categories of authenticity, because feminist change will not be consigned to the false consciousness of the victim who needs to be saved from herself.

There are positive elements of tension between Foucault and feminism in moving forward. One such link is the creativity of subjectivity, which leads to the emergence of subjects, illuminating the possibility for creative resistance. The fragmented nature of women's social identities is at the root of understanding the contradictory nature of the impact of revolution upon women and women's responses to revolution. What is envisioned therefore is not the abandonment of feminist politics but rather a feminist politics grounded in the struggles of resistance and identities by women. Such a feminist politics grows from a localized understanding of gendered resistance. It is the understanding of difference that gives voice to a more meaningful and empowered feminist politics in advocating and shaping agendas for change. One of the implications of this is that the strategies of struggle and resistance are predicated on difference and not on Enlightenment generalizations of unity tied to fixed subjectivity. This shift gives way to a feminist politics that does not destabilize or depoliticize action by women but, on the contrary, acknowledges the agency of women in very different contexts.

Sawicki's Foucauldian analysis suggests the possibility of feminist

action through such a "politics of difference." She advocates a radical pluralism that politicizes social and personal relationships and does not place
boundaries on what is the concern of the political. Resistant subjectivity is
a theory and a practice aimed at unveiling domination and also enacting
resistance.

> It is based on a form of incrementalism in which the distinction between
> reform and revolution is collapsed. . . . It is an incrementalism that recog-
> nizes domination, but also represents the social field as a dynamic, multi-
> dimensional set of relationships containing possibilities for liberation as
> well as domination.[51]

It allows us to evaluate the effectiveness or otherwise of particular
power/resistance practices in particular struggles. The political practice of
difference is effected through "coalition building." In such coalitions, "our
basis for common struggle is a democratic and provisional one, subject to
recreation and renegotiation."[52] This involves an acknowledgment of the
shifting identities we are and also of the many social and political coalitions arising from experiences of multiple identities. Coming to terms with
such differences may be the creative source of change. The fragmentation
of subjectivity also offers feminist politics an alternative model of consciousness-raising to that of the shared experience of patriarchal oppression. It acts instead to challenge who we are, in all our differences, and
opens up spaces for other imaginings of who we might want to be. In this
way, Sawicki argues, consciousness-raising "can be salvaged from the rem-
nants of humanist emancipatory politics."[53] The fragmentation of subjectivity through the microapplication of genealogy does not therefore mean the
fragmentation of politics. It simply means that shared experiences and simi-
larities will not be assumed, or taken for granted, and that understandings
of struggle and strategies of resistance can be developed with a more sensitive ear to different possibilities and necessities.

In the world of daily survival for many women around the globe, issues
of difference must respond to the impetus for action. This is an argument
made by Anne Marie Goetz when she criticizes claims to cultural relativity
and epistemological problems of subjectivity as "paralysing and inadequate
in the face of the imperative to act posed by the survival problems of
women in the third world."[54] Yet she carries forward the importance of difference and multiple sites of struggle in her proposition of coalition building as a feasible form of feminist politics. In this project there is no privileging of perspectives, and all claims to knowledge are accepted as partial.
Also implicit in this coalition strategy is the coexistence of competing
claims of class, race, and sexuality, as well as gender. Rather than an equa-
tion of oppressions, there is a shifting coalition of oppressions that will be
tied to context and provide provisional knowledge claims. She argues that

coalition politics of this sort struggles to eliminate the elements of centre, unity, and totality that organize structures into hierarchical oppositions. It also allows for the fact that women experience simultaneously many oppressions and must engage in a multitude of struggles that conflict and supplement each other.[55]

Mohanty's criticism of the homogenizing effects of discursive colonialism within western feminism draws attention to the limitations of sisterhood based on the "erasure of difference and inequality."[56] Her impetus for such criticism springs from "the urgent political necessity of forming strategic coalitions across race, class, and gender."[57] The self-conscious awareness of difference is thus a necessary strategy of engagement for feminist theorists who would be feminist activists. The activity of writing about women, gender, and change is a political act requiring writers to reflect on the effects of their representations of women.

In terms of political action, collectivity and the "fiction of unity" are still necessary to mobilize for change. Collective engagements can also provide vehicles for personal transformations that allow wider expression of the types of practices discussed here.[58] However, such political engagements are not separate from the academic work of theory. How we imagine the world and act to transform it reflects the imbricated politics of being. This will to know and will to act must continue to be a necessary tension for the development of feminist IR as theory and practice. There is therefore a need for dialogue across disciplines in forging international knowledge and practice. There is also a need to set in partnership the validity of field research and the abstractions of theory if the political impetus of international feminism tied to difference is to be supported and nurtured. The strategic challenge is to create and grasp opportunities of collective resistance in a context of difference as outlined by writers such as Bina Agarwal in the context of women's land rights in South Asia.[59]

There are other implications of a poststructuralist analysis for feminist politics and policies, not least of which is the design of more appropriate development interventions in war-torn societies struggling toward peace. The inability to understand the intricate dynamics of the societies on whose behalf "we" have so often presumed to act has marked many such interventions. The recognition of women's many identities and actions in war pushes policymakers to move beyond discourses of vulnerability and responsibility through to self-styled agendas where whole communities, rather than women as mothers/carers, take charge of survival and recovery. Political and development interventions need to acknowledge the lives and actions of women at a localized level in ways that do not reinforce and appropriate women's roles (as mothers, carers, community developers, etc.) in the form of low-cost invisible local resources. The current humanitarian concerns arising from the changing nature and conduct of war (in the shift to more internal and intimate conflicts implicating civilian populations to a pervasive extent) also demonstrate the need for local understandings of the dynamics of gender in conflict situations. This local focus is the bubbling source that distills international debates on gender, violence, the breakdown of community, and the constant struggle to secure human rights. The knowledge and understanding of local relational dynamics can inform the prospect of an end to war and the rebuilding of society in a context of ordinary lives being lived in extraordinary circumstances.

CONCLUSION

Gendered Localized Resistance is proposed as an emancipatory vehicle for dislodging a universalizing discourse on women and resistance in revolutionary wars. It challenges the conceptual and practical value of viewing women in war as victims colluding in their own oppression or as heroic role models of self-empowerment. In reality, wars have rarely been fought for the advancement of women. Gender analysis based on resistant and differentiated subjectivity moves beyond the reductionist conventions of women's roles (mother, fighter, camp follower) and spheres of activity (public, private, personal) in placing the dynamic of social relationships and identities at the center of analysis. In place of a standpoint position that views women as a group speaking from a shared position of oppression, the emphasis is to explore the multiple standpoints of experience and identity between and within individual women. In refusing who we are, we also redefine and renegotiate continually who we are in relation to others and ourselves. The forging of identities, self-understandings, and "other"-understandings thus takes place through the practices and accounts of power/resistance. The potential for transforming gender power relations lies in unmasking such relational practices. The reconceptualization of such relations as ones of power/resistance allied to a struggle of identities reveals a central role for difference and resistance as part of a silent, mundane revolution taking place from below in the constant negotiation of such gender power relations and identities. The strategies of engagement for women in revolutions arise from these everyday heroics that we blandly call survival. If liberation is about emancipation, it is not to be found in the metanarrative but in the everyday, localized narratives of women's locations, actions, and identities in a context of war.

In the adoption of Foucault, feminists have embraced the understandings of power and the efficacy of genealogical method. What could be more appealing to a liberatory and emancipatory project than the idea of recovering lost voices and excavating marginalized knowledge? However, the fractured subjectivity that lies at the heart of these alternative renderings of power and method has proved a source of unease to a project dedicated not only to the building of theory to understand subordination but also to a politics of opposition in overcoming such subordination. The inscriptions of difference and the dissipation of identity through a myriad of social practices that are power relations mark the dislodging of the central unitary subject of "woman" and "women." The implications of this shift are twofold. In simple terms, it is whether we view our glass as half full or half empty! In the latter scenario, the fragmentation of identity and the renouncing of universals may mean the end of the millennial liberatory project as we have known it in the West through the liberal and Marxist traditions. The coherent revolutionary subject bound together with others in an apocalyptic struggle of dialectical change is the narrative we have to sacrifice. The clarity and certainty of such a narrative has served as a potent appeal in the mobilization of various groups in many struggles—workers, peasants, women, colonized peoples. Some feminists predict that the emancipatory project of feminism will lose its teeth if we adopt a totally rejectionist position with respect to the Enlightenment tradition and to the notion of essential subjectivity.

However, in the scenario of the half-full glass we may, if we are brave enough to imagine, embrace an alternative vision of resistance and subjectivity that allows women the multiplicity of their experiences in different times and cultures as subjects of race, class, sexual orientation, nationality, and age. It is this politics of difference that forges practices of coalition that some feminist advocates of Foucauldian analysis see as the liberatory promise of our age. Instead of one voice, one politics, we reclaim the shifting contexts of the many power relations in which women are differentially implicated. In this way, we can imagine a more inclusive and more grounded form of social criticism and political action. The many coalitions formed by women across a range of issues—birth control, environmental degradation, education, emergency relief, peacebuilding—are testimony to practices that involve contradictory positions for "women" and defy any natural cohesive coalition for all women at all times. The challenge of resistance opened up by Foucault is to forge resistance at the limits, to constantly build and renegotiate interstitial resistance. This a resistance that creates crevices and fills them, forges power relations and reverses them. These strategies of resistance demand the commitment and vigilance of the long-distance hiker aware of vistas and falling rocks, dangers and opportunities.

The ego-myth of the intellectual enlightening the oppressed and leading them to revolution is thus unmasked. The challenge for feminist international relations is not to ape the revolutionary intellectual but to self-consciously explore the limits of the academic discipline and forge new narratives of understanding the workings of international relations. This is a work of partnership that reaches across disciplines and creates coalitions of knowledge and political action. In a world of diversity we can celebrate the many revolutions of daily emancipation and coping strategies and also decry the daily oppression and risks that make the rhetoric of revolutionary transformation less spontaneous or inevitable. Such strategies of academic engagement require a self-consciousness that questions the view we create of the world through the disciplinary lens of IR and the interventions we advance for genuine transformations and understandings of gender power relations. The challenge remains for us to push the boundaries of the discipline more creatively and to place our ears to the ground, for there are many untold stories and long silences erupting under our feet.

NOTES

1. An early version of this essay was presented to the International Studies Association Conference in San Diego, April 1996. I would like to thank the panel participants for their comments. I am also grateful to Sarah White, Liz Trinder, Deirdre Collings, Polly Mohs, Ann Cotton, and Vivienne Jabri for their helpful discussions on earlier drafts of this chapter.

2. The term *critical feminist theory* is used consciously and is not to be confused with feminist Critical Theory, which implies an association with the ideas and theories of the Frankfurt School.

3. I had considered using the term *feminist praxis* here, as that seemed to connote a sense of imbricated theory and practice. However, the word *praxis* seems loaded with other theoretical connotations based on derivations of Marxist theory, so I have opted to use the term *theory and practice*.

4. Enloe, *Does Khaki Become You?* pp. 161, 164.

5. Sylvester, "Some Dangers," p. 505.

6. Ibid., pp. 502, 505–506.

7. Enloe, *Does Khaki Become You?* p. 160.

8. Ibid., p. 164. Also see Scott, "Women and the Armed Struggle," for an analysis of roles taken up by women of different generations in the Zimbabwe liberation war.

9. For more on this point, see Stiehm "The Effect of Myths," and Macdonald, "Drawing the Lines."

10. Peterson and Runyan, *Global Gender Issues,* pp. 7–8. The presence/absence dynamic is described as a situation in which "the presence of men depends on the absence of women. Because of this interdependence, a gender analysis of women's lives and experiences does not simply 'add something' about women but *transforms* what we know about *men* and the activities they undertake" (emphasis in original).

11. This is far from being a consensus approach as Burguieres suggests in her analysis of three schools within the feminist peace/war approach. See Burguieres, "Feminist Approaches to Peace." The starting point for her analysis is the existence of stereotypes in relation to men and war and women and peace. The first school embraces the maternal female stereotype and valorizes it as a vision of peaceful society. The second school rejects the female stereotype and seeks instead to prove women to be as capable as men in the defense of the state. The equality of women

in the military would be a strategy supported within this view. The third school challenges both male and female stereotypes in seeking to address issues of structural power in the establishment of a feminist critique of militarism. Examples of the women and war literature include Brownmiller, *Against Our Will;* Elshtain, *Women and War;* Enloe, *Does Khaki Become You?;* Isaksson, *Women and the Military System;* Macdonald, Holden, and Ardener, *Images of Women in Peace and War;* Ridd and Callaway, *Caught Up in Conflict.*

12. Enloe, *Does Khaki Become You?* p. 212.

13. Ibid., p. 15.

14. Pierson, "Did Your Mother Wear Army Boots?" p. 214.

15. Enloe, *Does Khaki Become You?* pp. 161–169.

16. See Seidman, "Women in Zimbabwe," and Sylvester, *Zimbabwe,* on the mixed fortunes of women in postindependent Zimbabwe.

17. For examples of this in the case of the liberation war in Zimbabwe, see Ranger, *Peasant Consciousness;* and Lan, *Guns and Rain.*

18. In the case of Zimbabwe, see Kriger, *Zimbabwe's Liberation War.*

19. Foucault, "Afterword," p. 225. See also Foucault, *The History of Sexuality,* p. 95, where he says, "Where there is power, there is resistance, and yet, or rather consequently, this resistance is never in a position of exteriority in relation to power."

20. Foucault, *The History of Sexuality,* pp. 93–94.

21. Foucault, "Afterword," p. 222; footnote 3, p. 222. The "combat" description is suggested by the translator to clarify the meaning of the term.

22. Foucault, *Power/Knowledge,* p. 142.

23. Sawicki, *Disciplining Foucault,* p. 26.

24. Foucault, "Afterword," pp. 21, 212.

25. Foucault, "Introduction," p. 126 (quoted in Sawicki, *Disciplining Foucault,* pp. 25–26).

26. Harding, *Feminism and Methodology,* p. 7.

27. Foucault, *The History of Sexuality,* pp. 95–96.

28. Moore, *A Passion for Difference.*

29. Ibid., p. 24.

30. Ibid., pp. 53–54.

31. Ibid., pp. 3, 41.

32. Sawicki, *Disciplining Foucault,* p. 41; Sylvester, "Some Dangers," p. 507.

33. Moore, *A Passion for Difference,* p. 66.

34. Bennett, Bexley, and Warnock, *Arms to Fight, Arms to Protect,* p. 12.

35. Scott, *Weapons of the Weak,* p. 29. These actions are seen to reflect the "prosaic but constant struggle between the peasantry and those who seek to extract labour, food, taxes, rents, and interest from them." Scott has mapped out a terrain of resistance he sees as lying outside of the great struggles and movements and in a sense as being a precursor to them in the shape of everyday forms of peasant resistance. However, the consciousness for such actions is based on a neo-Marxist understanding of local class experiences. Scott's concerns with such resistance remain locked within a move toward the grand narrative of peasant resistance through open revolt of the agrarian classes against the rent-seeking landlords. However, what he does reveal is a cornucopia of strategies and actions that bubble beneath the surface of open revolt and in fact mark more widely the practice of resistance on a day-to-day level. The consciousness of resistance understood here borrows Scott's notion of practical engagement in the everyday as the impetus to intention and form of action but sees that context of action as informed by manipu-

lations of power/resistance played out through negotiating identities in the form of various subject positions. Such practical engagement corresponds to Moore's understanding of gender identifications outlined above.

36. Eleanor O'Gorman, "Chimurenga and Change: A Study of Women and War in Zimbabwe," Ph.D. thesis, University Of Cambridge (1999). The gendered dimension refers to gender power/resistance as practices of gender identities and relations. In this context, these relations and identities are drawn from understandings of women's identities and relations within revolutionary struggle. The focus is not simply one of women in relation to men but also of women in relation to other women and in relation to themselves. The "localized" focus refers in the first instance to geospecific localities where microstudies of conflict may be conducted in building an analysis of gender power/resistance from below. In the second instance, "localized" refers to a discursive space wherein the *agonistic* understanding of power/resistance allows us to break the dichotomy of public/private that lies at the heart of positioning women in war and peace. In a wider, more discursive sense, the "local" is infused with a Foucauldian understanding of the acting subject caught up in many power relationships. As such, actions within a locality feed into understandings and experiences beyond their physical boundaries and, in turn, power relations within the locality draw on ideas, subjectivities, and realities beyond those geographical limits. The linchpin of "Gendered Localized Resistance" is the notion of "resistant and differentiated subjectivity" that brings together these operations of gender and locality to map out the actions and consciousness of women's experiences of war.

37. Foucault, "Practicing Criticism," p. 154.

38. Foucault, *Power/Knowledge,* p. 81.

39. Ibid., p. 88.

40. Foucault, "Nietzsche, Genealogy, History," p. 81; for an interesting discussion on Foucault and history, see Thacker, "Foucault."

41. Foucault, "Nietzsche, Genealogy, History," p. 87.

42. Foucault, "What Is Enlightenment?"

43. Ibid., p. 46.

44. Mohanty, "Under Western Eyes," and "Feminist Encounters."

45. Joan Wallach Scott, "Evidence of Experience," takes up this theme of the foundational claims of experience. In a critical historical turn similar to Foucault's genealogy, she sees the task of the historian to be the investigation of constructions of experience rather than the mere acceptance of experience as explanation: "Experience is at once always already an interpretation *and* something that needs to be interpreted. . . . The study of experience . . . must call into question its originary status in historical explanation. This will happen when historians take as their project *not* the reproduction and transmission of knowledge said to be arrived at through experience but the analysis of the production of that knowledge" (pp. 400–401).

46. Martin, "Feminism, Criticism, and Foucault," p. 17.

47. Hartsock, "Foucault on Power," p. 164.

48. Sylvester, "Some Dangers," p. 501.

49. Ibid., p. 494.

50. Ibid., p. 501.

51. Sawicki, *Disciplining Foucault,* p. 9.

52. Ibid., p. 45.

53. Ibid., p. 307.

54. Goetz, "Feminism and the Claim to Know," p. 134.

55. Ibid., pp. 151–152.
56. Mohanty, "Feminist Encounters," p. 77.
57. Mohanty, "Under Western Eyes," p. 61.
58. Sawicki, *Disciplining Foucault,* pp. 307–308.
59. Agarwal, "Gender, Resistance, and Land."

6

Gender and Development: Working with Difference

Sarah C. White

It is a Friday in Ramadan, the Muslim holy month. The director of a Bangladeshi development agency is visiting one of the field offices. She arrived yesterday from her home, half a day's journey away in the capital city. As the jeep comes to a halt, a small crowd gathers. Mainly her own staff, the group is thickened by some local government officials and the inevitable gaggle of children and passers-by, who pause to see what is going on.

Somewhat stiffly, the director climbs down from the jeep. No longer a young woman, she is feeling her age. She greets the people and they smile and nod in response. She fumbles in her handbag and a gasp spreads through the crowd. In this Bangladesh, where cigarettes and the streets belong to men—on this most holy day, when fasting prohibits anything to pass the lips—this woman stands where everyone can see, meeting their eyes, daring a challenge—shamelessly, defiantly smoking.

In the heady early days of the Bretton Woods conventions, there was little doubt that the project of development was emancipatory. A brave new world was envisaged of progress and modernity—a world free from poverty, rich in human rights. In the 1990s, things look rather different. Environmental degradation and the persistence of violence, economic hardship, and political oppression have cast doubt on the dominant development models. In academic circles the grand theories have been displaced by a concern with particularity, flexibility, and difference. Emancipation is now to be sought not through a universalist project but through the recognition and celebration of diversity.

In this context, gender and development (GAD) occupies a site of critical contradiction. On the one hand, it represents a fundamental attack on the universalist claims of development discourse: what was said to hold for all was in fact scandalously particular, excluding the experience of one half of the human race! On the other hand, as it has become incorporated within policymaking, gender appears as a handmaiden to the "master discourse" of development, its political challenge domesticated into a technical concern. GAD advocates see their project as emancipatory, but paradoxically gender is the most common focus for resistance from the South, either through low-profile foot-dragging ("these outsiders don't understand our local women") or by more overt charges of cultural imperialism.

This contradictory context in turn produces contradictory outcomes. Women's desks and even women's ministries adorn the state apparatuses of many countries of the South but are generally starved of economic or political power.[1] A gender or "women in development" section has to be completed for all programs applying for North American or European funding, but privately many in these agencies believe "the gender business" is overdone. By the 1980s, a "women's program" had become the sine qua non of any self-respecting agency, resulting in a rash of such programs being instrumentally established. One outcome of such "special programs" is to keep women marginalized, aside from the mainstream. At the same time, this policy context has nonetheless expanded the space for women to be employed as staff members and for women as clients to gain some access to aid resources. Furthermore, local feminists who had found it difficult to get outside support have found that the new priority given to gender enables them to strengthen and expand their activities. Paradoxically, although this often means small-scale project work with women, it can also involve more overtly political lobbying, including against mainstream development itself.[2]

The history of gender and development reads like a switchback between domestication and emancipation—between the suppression and eruption of difference. This chapter aims to chart some of this story. It begins by setting out the dimensions of difference identified in feminist theory and showing how difference is construed in development planning. It then looks at the practical ways that notions of gender difference have been deployed in colonial and development contexts: to justify intervention, to resist intervention, and to modify intervention. Threading through the chapter is a concern with the relationship between issues of difference and emancipation—the points of tension as well as complementarity between them. Clearly there are dangers in universalism and the suppression of "other voices" that it entails. But there are dangers too in a stress on difference and the essentializing of "otherness" that this can involve. Neither "sameness" nor "difference" is set or self-explanatory. Both simplify a complex reality, suppressing some truths as they express others. They are symbolic, not simply descriptive, highly malleable, and politically indeterminate.

The opening story hints at some of this. If the director had been an expatriate, she would have confirmed herself an arrogant outsider. But in fact she was Bengali and, by birth at least, a Muslim. The self-assertion— or cultural offense—that her smoking involved was thus calculated and deliberate. Almost all who were there condemned it, but on very different grounds. For some it was evidence of apostasy, for others loose living, for yet others the pollution of western influence. For many of her staff it seemed simply ill-judged, likely to make their work harder when the dust had settled back into the tracks left by the jeep's tires. For the woman herself it was an assertion of difference, of her right to do as she liked, to live by her own, not others', values. She was not being "western"; she was simply being herself. Her personal defiance of local norms was to her consistent with the cultural challenge that her organization's radical stance on gender implied. That the culture is not monolithic is shown in the range of grounds on which she provoked censure: religious, sexual/moral, national/cultural, and practical/pragmatic. These reactions also ironically affirm her cultural identity as one who belongs; the same actions from a non-Bengali would have excited comparatively little comment.

DIMENSIONS OF DIFFERENCE

The notion of difference is a slippery one. Before proceeding, therefore, it is important to set down some parameters for its discussion. In feminist theory, difference is construed in three main ways. First, there is the question of women's difference from men. How this is tackled varies widely. Very crudely, liberal and socialist feminists seek to minimize this, holding that a categorical emphasis on women's "difference" has been fundamental to their subordination. Radical feminists, by contrast, assert women's difference and celebrate it as the grounds for an alternative and superior set of values. The second dimension of difference stresses contrasts in the constitution of gender relations across cultures. This may provide an invitation to a more nuanced, sensitive exploration of gender/power or alternatively present a wholesale rejection of feminism as irrelevant to women on a global scale. Finally, postmodernism has focused attention on differences between and within women, emphasizing the multiple dimensions of subjectivity and the importance of context in the constitution of identity.

These three dimensions of difference are all reflected in gender and development debates. But the particular form they take reflects the fact that gender and development is, above all, a policy discourse. This does not mean that it is concerned exclusively with aid-funded programs and projects but that its concern with social change is never politically innocent. It aims not just to describe the world but to change it. And the ways that this change is configured are not random but reflect the values and assumptions of the enterprise of development more broadly and the process of managing change to which it is committed. Therefore, before considering the gender debates specifically, it is important to review briefly how contradictions with respect to difference are inherent in the way development itself is understood.

Historically, there has been relatively little discussion of cultural difference in the development context. It appears mainly in the writings of modernization theorists of the 1960s and 1970s, who argued over the extent to which "traditional values" constituted "an obstacle to growth."[3] Although such phrasing is now politically unacceptable, these debates hint at the fact that notions of difference are fundamental to the whole way that development is understood and undertaken. The treatment of difference in development is radically contradictory. On the one hand, development both assumes and construes a categorical distinction between the "developed" and the "under"- or "less developed." The subject-object relations this establishes are played out in myriad pairings: between donor and recipient states, majority and minority communities, urban and rural areas, planners and their "target groups," those who know and those who are known. As Edward Said points out in *Orientalism,* such asymmetries serve to suppress the diversity within the subordinate group; whereas "we" have names and faces, one "native" stands for all.[4] This tendency becomes a formal requirement where planning is involved: Planning must of necessity simplify reality, divesting many of the particularities to formulate a portable "model." As Wood argues, the process of labeling that this involves is an important exercise of power.[5] People's humanity and diversity are denied as they are refigured as the targets of planning—cases detached from the stories of their own life-contexts.

On the other hand, the irony of this process is that it serves to collapse not only the differences among "the people," but also the distinctions between them and the planners. As people become "cases" they are not only disorganized from their own worlds but also reorganized into the life-worlds of the planners. Of course, this process is asymmetric: The people enter the planners' world, but not vice versa. But this submergence of difference is significant and as essential to the process of planning as the original assumption of it. On it depends the vital claim that planners can know the people's needs and so prescribe the action that serves their interests best.

The silencing of discussion of difference indicates most immediately its political sensitivity but perhaps also—ironically—its centrality. What is axiomatic and taken for granted does not need to be discussed, and perhaps cannot safely be, without the whole edifice crumbling down. This view is supported by evidence from the main locus for discussing difference in contemporary development discourse: the area of human rights. Since the 1960s there has been dispute about how inclusive human rights should be—whether only civil and political or broadened/replaced by economic and social. More recently, the universal character of human rights has been challenged as western and claims made for the space for different interpretations by culture. The details of these debates are not something I can discuss here. Rather, I am interested in where the protagonists are coming from: the Arab Islamic world and East Asia. These are, of course, precisely those parts of the world that fit least easily into the categories of North and South and most radically challenge the established oppositions of developed and developing.

GENDER AND THE CODIFICATION
OF DIFFERENCE IN COLONIALISM

Although women appear to be relative newcomers to the development agenda, the implication of gender in policy debates regarding (post)colonial societies is nothing new. As indicated below, an important part of the original assertion of "difference" in gender and development was the desire to attack the inappropriate imposition of western stereotypes that had characterized colonial and development policy. Colonialism was itself, of course, deeply inscribed with gender imagery, which was used to elaborate many varying lines of difference, some of which had nothing at all to do with differences between men and women. For British children, and to some extent the population "at home" more generally, the pioneer/explorer became the type of a certain kind of male hero. In India, the British Empire was symbolized by the (male) lion. Gender was also used within the divide-and-rule policy of assigning to the regions different "races" with different qualities: the tall, "martial" Punjabis were contrasted, for example, with the short, "feminine" Bengalis. Such imagery can, of course, be subverted from below. Thus, the Bengali nationalist movement of the nineteenth and early twentieth centuries embraced this feminized identity by asserting India as the "motherland." This at once rejected the legitimacy of the British lion and reasserted the long-established veneration of the goddess Kali in Bengal.[6]

Gender relations were also used as a way of marking the divide between "modern" and "traditional." In southern parts of Africa, for example, the "modern" urban/industrial sector was defined as male—to the extent that in some places women were actually debarred from entering it without special permission. The "backward" rural areas were by contrast construed as feminine—both in terms of the majority of their inhabitants and as inert, passive, and residual.[7] In South Asia, the precursor to gender and development was the "status of women debate," which arose in the context of British colonialism. I offer a very brief summary of this debate to highlight some of the continuities between it and contemporary GAD discourse.

The first and most obvious similarity is that the status of women arose as a policy issue. Its highest-profile expression was in discussion of "what is to be done" about, for example, the practice of widow immolation, sati. Second, the discourses of modernity within which it was inscribed were also heavily racialized. "Barbarous" traditional India was set against "civilized" modern Britain, and the contrast was used to justify colonial intervention. This was further reinforced by taking the problematic as "women's status," which constituted Indian women as passive, attributed status *by* society, requiring "liberation" by outside agents, and indeed objectified by the debates themselves.[8]

Implicit in this, of course, is that "women's status" is something negative to be escaped. It also establishes clearly the significant lines of difference: those between Indian women and men on the one hand, and between Indian and British women on the other. This both blocked analysis of gender relations among the British and, most important, obscured differences among Indian women.[9] Finally, framing gender in terms of women's status identified it as superstructural, effectively divorcing it from relationship with other forms of social inequality.[10]

GENDER AND DEVELOPMENT:
THE ASSERTION OF DIFFERENCE

Gender and development (or women in development, as it was first known) began in the 1970s with the assertion of difference. The major concern was to make the case for including women in development, to redesign development planning so that it took better account of women's responsibilities and interests. Development was seen predominantly as a good thing, from which women had been left out. The challenge, therefore, was to count women in. The overall motif for this project was the need to remedy the "invisibility" of women. This was particularly resonant in purdah societies, where a veil was seen literally to have been drawn over women's activities, but it was also applied very forcefully to the methods and approaches of development itself.

The case for taking women into account has primarily rested on the first two dimensions of difference identified earlier: the differences of women from men and cultural differences in gender relations. The first case was generally posed either on welfare grounds—that women constituted a vulnerable group in special need, or on grounds of efficiency—that including women would enable development to get its work done better. In the second case, the dominant model of development was attacked for carrying western assumptions about gender that were inappropriate to many of the societies in which programs took place. Attention focused particularly on two dimensions of this: the division of labor and divisions within the household. In both approaches, while the argument was made in the name of "Third World" women, the terms of engagement were set by factors quite external to them. This section describes this for each of the approaches in turn.

The overall framework within which the case for women's "difference" is advanced is the distinction drawn between the deserving and the undeserving. This dates back in social policy at least as far as the Elizabethan Poor Law in England. This line of difference is yet another highly malleable one: In the UK under the premierships of Margaret Thatcher and John Major, for example, the list of the undeserving was seen to expand exponentially until there is now an almost perfect fit between it and any who might wish to claim state benefit. To qualify as deserving, groups need to prove themselves as either especially needy or especially virtuous. A third, but much less sure, alternative also exists. This is the claim for justice, if a group can show itself to have been discriminated against.

The claim for women's "specific" interests to be taken into account in development planning has been made on all of these grounds, although the equity grounds have had by far the least prominence. Rather than arguing from first principles, the case made for women assumes a particular set of values or view of what development should be and then relies very heavily on the presentation of a particular set of images of women that establishes them as "deserving" according to that perspective. This re-presenting of women according to different development policy agendas is pointed out by Caroline Moser in her discussion of the way that styles of women's programs vary according to wider development fashions.[11] In addition to this, there is some variation within each approach, allowing women to be painted as more active or more passive. Table 6.1 adapts and extends the framework Moser presents to express some of these dimensions.

There are obvious limitations to the construction of any typology such as this. In practice, programs often have a range of objectives, and the different elements are frequently found mixed up together. Thus, programs to promote girls' education espousing the language of "equity" or "empowerment," for example, may derive from an underlying concern to limit population growth, since "empowered," and specifically educated, women are believed more likely to limit their family size. In addition, the outcomes of programs are not predictable simply from their character. A welfare program may promote more efficient use of resources, and an empowerment program could result primarily in enhanced welfare. Plans are modified by those who implement them, and people respond to programs in ways the

Table 6.1   Motives and Interests in Women's Programs

Program Approach	Women	Emphasis	Development Model	Methods
Population Control	dangerous breeders; no choice mothers	control population	global limits	top-down; women targeted
Welfare	vulnerable group; mothers	family welfare	relief	top-down; handout
Equity	backward class; disadvantaged by development	equality; human rights	modernization	top-down; legal/admin structural
Anti-Poverty	mothers; poorest of poor	fight poverty	basic needs	top-down; women targeted
Efficiency	under-utilized resources; resource managers	economic development via market	Structural Adjustment Program	top-down; business
Empowerment	women as powerless; need question gender relations	gender as power; relations	liberation	bottom-up; struggle

developers did not foresee.[12] In addition, programs are packaged differently for different markets, so that the practical content of a program cannot simply be read off from the way it is described. A nongovernmental organization (NGO) in the South, for example, might represent the same program as welfare to its national government, as efficiency to multilateral donors, and as empowerment to a more radical northern NGO. Furthermore, the issue of instrumentality may be read at least two ways. The tailoring of "women" to fit a particular agenda may indicate the instrumental incorporation of women to serve other objectives. Alternatively, it could reflect the political necessity to use the dominant ideology against itself, making the case for including women in terms the planners will recognize and accept.

Both of these dynamics certainly exist. There is, however, no doubt that an ambivalence runs throughout the area of gender and development with respect to its ultimate objective. Is the chief aim to improve the situation *for women,* or is it to promote the more effective *use of women* for other development goals? Slippage between these two is evident across the different program approaches and so cannot simply be mapped onto the typology above. As fashions in development have changed, there has been a clear shift from an early predominant stress on the needy/welfare/vulnerable set of images to the virtuous/efficiency/capable axis. It is important, however, not to assume too quickly that more "positive" images of women necessarily represent their interests better. The current stress on women as active, competent agents seems more progressive than that on women as a "vulnerable group." But the image of women as budding entrepreneurs, whose self-help initiatives simply need a little outside support in order to raise themselves out of poverty, also dovetails rather neatly with the global dominance of neoliberal politics and its interest in minimizing outlay on welfare or public services. The promotion of women in development undoubtedly does afford them new opportunities. There is, however, a distinct propensity for the advocacy of gender equity to metamorphose into an instrumental concern to use women as the means to achieve other ends. This shadows the tendency mentioned above—for the political challenge of a feminist perspective to be recast as a technical concern servicing the mainstream project of development.

Along with this emphasis on women's difference from men, women's inclusion in development has been argued on the grounds of cultural differences on gender. The first line of attack concerned the division of labor. In particular, the assumption that men were breadwinners and women housewives was claimed to have harmed the interests of women in the Third World and the interests of development itself. It was pointed out, for example, how all male cadres of agricultural extension workers had targeted male farmers for their advice and support, whereas in Africa, particularly, much of the farming is in fact done by women.[13] An allied, but somewhat more critical, account maintained that women had always been involved in development but only on male terms. Rather than being simply left out, this meant that they had actually been disadvantaged by development, either relatively by losing out in comparison with men or even suffering actual decline in absolute terms. Again in the case of agriculture, for example, it was argued that the assumption that farmers were men had resulted in a bias toward "men's crops"—predominantly those produced in whole or part for sale—in agricultural research stations and extension support. New opportunities for realizing cash incomes had encouraged men to concentrate on crops for sale, leaving less land on which women could grow food for subsistence. Divisions within the household meant that the cash men earned was construed as their personal income, leaving women to carry a heavier burden in sustaining the family's livelihood.[14]

Recognizing these intrahousehold conflicts over resources further challenged western models of the "family wage," the "common pot," or a division between outside "competition" and an inner domain ruled by "love not money." Admitting differences within the household also removed legitimacy from the formerly accepted practice of interviewing the male "head" as representative of the whole household. He might not *know* what other members of the household did or thought, and even if he did know he might misrepresent them where his interests were in conflict with theirs.

Similarly, the conventional view of a household as containing a husband, wife, and their children was overturned as culture-bound. Exposing this stereotype showed a high proportion of households without a male head, which had been previously overlooked. These were important in program terms not only because of their numbers (30 percent of households in much of Latin America and approaching 50 percent of households in some parts of the Caribbean, for example) but also because they are particularly common among the very poor.

Embodying these tensions, the inclusion of women was advocated both as an equity issue and as a means to increase the efficiency of the development enterprise. Targeting men only meant failing to access the points at which agricultural decisions were actually made, particularly with respect to crops grown purely for subsistence use, cultivation of which was overwhelmingly women's responsibility. Failing to engage with women could therefore restrict the expansion of "modern" farming techniques and have a negative impact on family welfare.

For some, recognition of male bias within the structures of development discourse and practice had indicated the need for a much more fundamental critique. National labor force statistics, for example, were shown to have been constructed according to a bias that privileged those parts of the economy in which men predominated and discounted those in which women figured more largely. Moving beyond issues of gender as such, this could be used to question the underlying values it betrayed: the priority given to cash crops over subsistence, or production for the market over family welfare. The gender critique of structural adjustment programs similarly moved on from seeing women as a vulnerable group that suffered disproportionately to questioning the gender bias implicit within macroeconomics itself.[15]

Still others have gone a step further and called for a rejection of development itself. McCarthy, for example, maintained that the agenda for "bringing women in" reflected a concern not for the interests of women but rather for capitalist expansion.[16] Women and the subsistence sector, she claimed, were now being targeted as new sources of capital formation, labor, and markets. Targeting women through gender-specific programs introduced false lines of differentiation within the working class and thus obscured their common interests and the real nature of their exploitation. An allied argument has been made from a radical feminist standpoint by the ecofeminists. They maintain that the entire project of development is inherently imperialist, founded on the exploitation of the Third World, women, and nature. Although open to criticism on diverse factual and theoretical grounds, taken as a poetic statement there is undoubted power in its critique of development as violence, dispossession, and desire.[17]

Such fundamental critiques of development are very much a minority

voice. By contrast, the dominant thrust of the assertion of cultural difference has been to demand an adjustment in the technical apparatus of development. Accepting the dominant values of "productive labor" and engagement in the market as read, the chief concern was to demonstrate how
women were in fact involved in the first and to promote their fuller
involvement in the second. Assertion of the importance of women to production was mounted on two lines. The first was to reevaluate the significance of women's domestic work, combating the "my wife doesn't work"
or "I'm only a housewife" syndrome. The *extent* of women's work was
stressed, resulting in a rash of time-use studies counting up hours and min-
utes that men and women spent working. These showed that women often
worked longer hours on a daily basis than men and more consistently
throughout the year, because demand for their labor was less subject to sea-
sonal fluctuations.

Second, the *significance* of domestic work was a topic of fierce debate.
Divisions between public and private spheres were challenged. The importance of domestic work to the reproduction of the labor force (servicing
children and employed family members) and to the overall system of production (e.g., by stretching household income and supplying necessary
labor without pay) were stressed. At the same time, a critique of the pro-
ductive/domestic division was launched on another tack: that it was an
invention of capitalism, and no such distinctions could be applied within
other kinds of societies (the term *family farm* expresses this neatly). For
development agencies, this led to suspicions of stereotyped women's
domestic projects, such as sewing and handicrafts, many of which had been
in existence since colonial times. How far did they reflect the existing division of labor between men and women, and how far were they the imposition of inappropriate stereotypes from outside?

The second line of attack was to stress that women were already
involved in productive labor—that which generated income. The notion
that men were the sole supporters of their families was shown up as a myth.
As already noted, in Africa particularly, men and women within the household might be allotted separate fields with differing responsibilities for providing for the family. In much of Asia, women worked in the family fields
alongside their male kin or were wage laborers, particularly among the
poor. Even those who did not work *outside* (a term whose definition varies
by context) were shown to do "production-related" work such as, in
Bangladesh, seed germination, crop processing, and storage. The boundaries between social and economic were seen to be much more permeable
than had been assumed. Picking up on anthropological perspectives, kinship, for example, construed in western society as a private matter, was
shown to have political and economic aspects vital to people's livelihood
options. In light of this, the women's work of family networking and gift

giving could be shown to be of much more than simply personal importance.[18]

A clear irony will be evident to anyone acquainted with western feminist debates. This is that the arguments for attending to cultural difference are in fact made on very similar terms to those advanced by feminists within the western context. The critique of productive and domestic spheres, the studies of household budgeting, and deconstruction of the myth of the sole male breadwinner are all very familiar. At one level this is not surprising, as the vast majority of these studies were made by western women; and even when they were made by women from the countries concerned, it is western analyses (and often western research funding) that have set the terms of the debate.

A further irony, which is common to much of at least the liberal and socialist schools in western feminism, is that the argument for women's "different" interests has been made largely on male terms. Women's work is important because it is *really* "productive" (like men's) even when it seems "just domestic" (like women's). The major way forward envisaged for women in poverty is through income generation—production for the market—seen hitherto as the male public sphere. Of course, it is a vast generalization to identify market participation as a male gendered activity. In West Africa, for example, women have long been established as highly adept market traders. Nevertheless, the economic model that dominates development analysis is not derived from West African livelihood systems. It is difficult to deny that in the dominant economic model such terms as *productive* and *domestic* do carry gendered associations.

In gender and development, notwithstanding its change of name from the earlier *women in development,* the onus for change has been squarely placed on women. The failure to problematize male gender identities, or (with a few honorable exceptions) the male bias in how economic value is assigned, has various contradictory outcomes. Women's difference from men becomes itself the problem, not something to be celebrated. Their development involves taking up more male activities, but without shedding any of their traditional responsibilities for reproductive labor. The typical women's program replicated repeatedly in countries all over the South thus sees women organized into groups to foster income generation, along with a cocktail of literacy training, contraceptive distribution, and health and welfare advice. The obvious result of this is the familiar problem of the double day for women. Lack of interest in domestic labor means that no effort is made to challenge men to compensate for women's expanded workload by taking on more of the responsibility for running the home. Development planners collude with the view that housework is not real work, that women's time and labor are largely without value and therefore endlessly elastic. As D. Elson has pointed out, this is of more than academic interest.[19] At the national level, it results in donor-imposed development policies, such as structural adjustment programs, systematically shifting costs from the public to the private sphere, from the state to the women.

The priority placed on productive labor is so taken for granted within western culture, and even within many feminist perspectives, that it can be difficult to see any other way of validating women's activities. The following example indicates that other alternatives exist:

In September 1988, Bangladesh suffered disastrous flooding, seriously affecting large areas of the country, including the capital, Dhaka. Food was an urgent necessity, as people's homes were flooded, with many living on the roofs of their houses and fuel and cooking areas waterlogged. Oxfam decided to set up a kitchen in the Dhaka office. The whole office area, inside and out, was given over to makeshift cooking facilities. At the peak of operations they produced more than 90,000 chapatis a day. It was run by volunteers, the wives of the office staff. They also employed 115 women from the relief camps on a daily wage basis. Male staff and volunteers then took the chapatis out in boats to distribute them to those marooned.

As one of the team evaluating this program, I was uncomfortable with the way that it so obviously reconfirmed the existing gender division of labor. The women were in the kitchen and the men were the heroes, doing the dangerous, high-profile work of distributing the food outside.[20] Worse even than this, the one female Bangladeshi staff member[21] was consigned to the kitchen, her gender overriding her professional status. On the other hand, this might have been simply the sensible deployment of comparative advantages: the women were better at making chapatis and the men at handling boats. A national emergency is not, perhaps, the time to launch a radical gender policy.

The local staff and their wives were angry with my interpretation. First, the women stressed how glad they were to be able to do something positive in the height of the crisis. Second, they pointed out the importance of giving wages to the women from the relief camps, who usually found it harder than their men to find casual paid work. Third, they were proud of having responded themselves, with something that they could do better than outsiders, rather than waiting on the foreigners to drop a relief program from the skies. But finally, and most important from the gender perspective, the "Oxfam kitchen" made absolutely clear just how essential and skilled women's domestic work is. This is something that is usually difficult to do, just because such work is so ordinary; but the spotlight of the crisis allowed it to be seen. While the program did not reverse gender roles, it certainly politicized them. My desire to see a challenge to the gender division of labor offended and frustrated the women volunteers. To them it was the denial of a legitimate source of their pride, both as Bangladeshis and as women.

DIFFERENCE BETWEEN WOMEN

Distinctions between women is the dimension of feminist concerns with difference that is by far the least explored in gender and development. In part, this is due to the general tendency of planning to telescope difference. The need for a tangible target makes an awareness of the multiple dimensions of subjectivity, for example, rather hard to take on. The use of women's groups as the medium of development intervention also tends to ascribe homogeneity, suppressing difference within the group as a unit as well as within the wider population of "women" at large.[22] Reflecting a common pattern, although men are also organized into groups by development agencies, these are typically characterized by occupational or landholding status (e.g., as fishermen or marginal farmers) rather than by gender.

On the other hand, recognizing the diversity of interests within households and the variety of household structures has opened up the possibility of exploring differences between women, as well as between women and men. Attention has tended to focus on conflicts within particular sets of relationships, such as those between co-wives or between mothers and daughters-in-law. D. Kandiyoti, for example, introduced the idea of the patriarchal bargain to explain why women collude in gender subordination: They know that even if they suffer while young, their conformity will be rewarded by their gaining some power in later life.[23] Predominantly, however, gender has been seen as a basis of solidarity and differences between women attributed to other factors, such as ethnicity or class. One of the most influential statements of this position was made by Maxine Molyneux in an article questioning how far women's involvement in the Nicaraguan liberation struggle had resulted in the recognition of "women's interests" in the postrevolutionary state.[24] The diversity of *women's interests* led her to jettison the term and suggest the notion of "gender interests," to characterize those that are derived specifically from structural inequality by gender. She further divided gender interests into practical and strategic. Practical interests lie in bettering one's situation within the overall system (such as women having access to cheap and affordable child care). Strategic interests relate to structural change of the system itself (for instance, challenging the assumption that domestic work is women's responsibility).

Molyneux makes three additional points in relation to gender interests. First, women may not recognize their strategic gender interests nor desire to achieve them. In part this may reflect "false consciousness," where women internalize the dominant culture. Another reason, however, is that strategic objectives may not serve, and may even threaten, women's immediate practical interests. Women's ownership of land, for example, would constitute a strategic gender interest in Bangladesh. But in most cases, even women who have formal rights of inheritance do not claim the land to which they are entitled. If they claim the land, they risk alienating their brothers, thereby jeopardizing their main form of "social security" if problems arise between them and their husbands. Their practical interest is in keeping relations sweet with their brothers in case they should need to turn to them in a crisis. This takes a higher priority than the strategic objective of owning land. Molyneux therefore argues that strategic objectives must recognize and politicize women's practical gender interests if they are to secure women's support.

Second, Molyneux points out that gender interests will be formulated in very different ways according to context. Solidarity must be forged rather than simply assumed; key issues in one situation may not translate to another. Third, women may not prioritize their gender interests over others that divide them. Even where women do mobilize around a particular issue, this unity is always conditional. In a situation of class, community, or national conflict, unity on gender lines tends to break down.

This framework furthers exploration of differences among women along two dimensions. Most obviously it brings out that women, like men, are divided among themselves by class, ethnicity, and so on. More innovatively, the division between practical and strategic gender interests carries the potential for seeing how gender itself may form the basis of contradictory interests among and within women. As in Kandiyoti's "'patriarchal bargain," it is the practical gender interests of older women that limit most strictly the gender interests of their younger kin, both practical and strategic. The practical and strategic dimensions of gender interests thus set up difference, and the potential for conflict, both *within* women and *among* them.

The dominant usage of this framework, however, has been as a tool for introducing gender into development planning. The more tangible needs are substituted for interests, and gender needs become a proxy for women's needs. The way this is done involves an interesting example of the concertinaing of notions of difference through planning. In a telling occlusion, Moser in the original article setting out this framework elides *the planners'* need to take women into account with *the women's* needs for certain types of action or resources. The main aim of Moser's "gender planning framework" is to distinguish women's needs from men's, thus ironically completing the circle to where Molyneux began it.[25]

The irony of this repeated emphasis on the difference of women to men is that it fails to problematize male gender identities and the way that these are written into the basic framework of analysis. Molyneux, for instance, though she mentions that men also may have gender interests, does not pursue this. The model seems to be essentially additive, that women have (specific) gender interests in addition to those of class or ethnicity that they share with men. This fails to question how ideas of the "general" interest by class or ethnicity may be implicitly male gendered or the dynamic way in which these interests are interrelated. Studies of liberation wars, for example, recognize that women do not lose their gender when they become involved in national struggles. Rather, patterns of how women are mobilized may be gender specific—such as South African mothers being politicized by their children's radicalism—and their modes of struggle embody, even if they redefine, their womanhood.[26]

The obvious corollary to this is to analyze the gender politics also implicit within male "nationalist" or "class" positions and so question the identification of men with the general/subject and women with the specific/other. The collapsing of differences between women is clearly consequent on their continued identification as the deviation from the male-defined norm. Again, this permits a relatively differentiated male subject with respect to "public" identities, but ironically it also involves the suppression of differences within and between men as these relate to gender. In the development context, the generally poor recognition of private and personal dimensions of human life becomes an almost total occlusion for men. This has three negative implications. First, it reinforces the opposition between men and women as constituting mutually exclusive categories, denying that what are considered masculine and feminine attributes (which clearly differs by social context) are found within both men and women. Second, it also deflects attention from the conflicts and contradictions within and between men and how these support or contradict public ideologies of masculinity.[27] Third, it sustains the tendency to abstract gender from other forms of social difference.

This last point is important not simply to the analysis of gender but to the wider political import of GAD. In drawing attention to the fallacy of development's pretensions to universality with respect to gender, the way was opened up to explore other biases, such as those by culture, class, or race. Instead of this, however, the focus on difference by gender has tended to block out other dimensions of difference and the power relations they sustain. Gender became *the* justice issue, women *the* "minority" whose interests should be considered; "social development" became, at least in some agencies, very largely commandeered by "gender specialists." Retraining the focus to explore how gender *for men and women* is articulated with other social relations should therefore sharpen awareness of other justice issues. Gender would become not the endpoint but the entry point for further questioning, which would broaden and deepen both the understanding of power and the vision of emancipation.

DIFFERENCE AND EMANCIPATION

I began his chapter by outlining some of the contradictions experienced in gender and development; I want to close by considering some of the contradictions the development context of external intervention raises for feminist concerns with difference, and for GAD in particular. There are, of course, many who would deny that GAD is in any way feminist. On the one hand, those hostile to feminism argue that gender differences are simply a reality that planning needs to take into account without any kind of emancipatory intent. On the other hand, feminist critiques of GAD point to its instrumental use of women and the prioritizing of efficiency over equity objectives. In this section, however, I wish to sidestep such objections and consider GAD at its best: as a feminist movement committed to fostering emancipation.

The major point on which the contradictions in GAD turn is the legitimacy of feminism as an intercultural initiative. The critical issue is this: that the feminist project is *both* countercultural *and* culturally embedded. The logical conclusion of this is that there must be different feminist projects in different cultural contexts. Stated in this way this seems relatively straightforward. In going on to explore what this means in practice, however, multiple difficulties arise.

The major difficulty concerns the understanding of culture. Colonialism, development, and globalization have resulted in highly permeable cultural boundaries. The implication of educational systems in all these three means that the continuities are particularly evident at the level of political theory and academic analysis. This means that there is at least a family resemblance between critical theorists working out of very different national contexts. The most radical rejections of western imperialism have frequently made reference to Karl Marx. It is very difficult to identify a voice that is wholly, and self-critically, other.

Alternatively, the frontiers of culture may be endlessly subdivided. The "same" society may be viewed as made up of multiple cultures—by class, age, place of residence, ethnicity, religion, politics, kinship, and so on. The logical extension of this to a culture of one is clearly absurd. And yet the assumptions on which it is based are common to much of the advocacy of difference: that culture can be described in primarily structural terms and that a common culture demands internal homogeneity. This highlights a key danger in the concern to avoid universalism: the risk of reifying cultures so that acceptance of difference between them closes the space for difference within.

It is ironic that a sometimes rather static conception of cultural difference has accompanied a sophisticated appreciation of the multiple dimensions of subjectivity at an individual level. An alternative approach is to view culture relationally and so accord it that same flexibility and indeterminacy, that same responsiveness to context. In this view, to share a culture would mean to recognize one another as belonging. This implies, as in the example with which the chapter began, that what characterizes shared culture is not the denial but the comprehension of difference.

The primary culture out of which GAD arises is development itself. Historically there is no doubt that this is a western-inspired project. GAD is countercultural in offering a critique of development; it is culturally embedded, as this review has shown, in the terms on which that critique is mounted.

The contradictions of GAD as an emancipatory project lie in the fact that development can itself be seen as countercultural within the societies that undergo intervention. The current emphasis on "good governance" explicitly advocates multiparty democracy against alternative political systems; economic prescriptions clearly privilege neoliberal values. What distinguishes this from a genuinely countercultural project is that these criticisms are offered from without, grounded in an assumption of categorical difference rather than affinity. In this context, a concern for transforming gender relations may be the vehicle of the most invasive form of intervention, the point at which the local culture is most openly denigrated. In such a case, a commitment to emancipation would seem to require siding with "local society" against the "developers"; but to do so would risk losing the critical edge of the feminist vision in failing to address patriarchal relations within the "local" culture.

Part of the way out of this conundrum is clearly for GAD advocates to support and form alliances with local feminist movements within the societies targeted for development. This means building toward an international feminist culture that can comprehend and celebrate difference. GAD's own implication in development hegemony, however, means that this process will not be without conflict. To some degree GAD will itself form the culture that feminists of the South are engaged in combating. For GAD to pull loose from its roots in the assumption of difference, and re-root in an embracing of affinity, will involve a painful dispossession. It means disavowing the priority of its own perspectives and becoming open to respond to the challenges of others.

This would mean opening to debate the whole question of how much difference can be accommodated within an approach that could still be labeled "feminist." The primary challenges to recognize difference have been made with respect to ethnicity and sexual orientation. What is not clear, however, is how far there is space within feminism to recognize and accord equal value to difference of perceptions with respect to gender itself. Even at-home, lay beliefs regarding the "natural" basis of gender difference or the "complementarity" of gender roles are regarded as "false consciousness" that needs to be liberated. In the development literature, perhaps the thorniest issue that repeatedly arises concerns the universality of individualism. Many Indian writers, for example, argue that women genuinely perceive their interests as intrinsically bound up with those of their families, particularly their children. To deny the validity of this and seek to distinguish the "real" (submerged/subordinated) individual interest is rejected as a form of cultural imperialism. This is very difficult for a feminism configured in the West to deal with. To embrace this on the basis of affinity means to move beyond the exoticism of reifying the "difference" of another culture and to bring the issue "back home." This opens up the question of whether even within the western context the presumption of the individual interest is wholly adequate or if for women in particular the boundaries between self and others are less clear-cut.

In closing this chapter, I present a final example from Bangladesh, which expresses both the permeability between cultures and the flexibility within them.

A nongovernmental organization (NGO) in Bangladesh wished to employ more women as field staff, but it faced a problem. The work involved traveling from village to village visiting development groups to offer training or practical support. Purdah norms meant that women were less mobile than men. They were unused to being out on their own, and it was considered unsafe for them to travel after dark when many meetings, especially for men, took place. Although more senior male staff had motorbikes, others traveled by bicycle; but the rough condition of most roads made this physically very demanding. In any case, both bicycles and motorbikes were very much a male preserve. As a result, female staff had tended to cover a far smaller area than men (walking or taking a bus where possible). This, combined with women's generally lower educational qualifications and apparent reluctance to take responsibility, had introduced inequities between male and female working conditions, which was causing considerable resentment.

The NGO management was split on how to tackle this. One group argued that they should formalize special arrangements for women staff: different norms for male/female responsibilities for area coverage or provision that women should be able to work in pairs. Gender sensitivity should mean that women should not be forced to compete on male terms and that it was legitimate to have criteria of achievement differentiated by gender. The other group fiercely disagreed. The NGO, they argued, should commit itself to providing motorcycles for female field staff and make learning to drive and using them in their work a condition of employment. They should show in their own actions that women could challenge local gender norms and still be "respectable."

This is what happened. The villagers were at first surprised and amused to see women on motorbikes but very soon accepted it. Rather than being stigmatized, the women saw their standing in the community enhanced by their having command of a motorbike, which was itself a status symbol. Within a short time it became a commonplace to see the women NGO workers riding about the countryside, a living symbol of the potential to transform apparently intractable obstacles into problems to be resolved.

NOTES

1. Goetz, "The Politics of Integrating Gender to State Development Processes."

2. Based in Bangladesh, for example, UBINIG lobbies forcefully at an international level against reproductive technologies, which represent a major part of many donors' women-focused interventions in Bangladesh.

3. See, for example, Morriss, "Values as an Obstacle to Economic Growth in South Asia."

4. Said, *Orientalism*.

5. Wood, *Labelling in Development Policy*.

6. Sarkar, "Nationalist Iconography."

7. See, for example, Parpart and Staudt, *Women and the State in Africa*.

8. One of the protagonists in this debate, a British woman married to an Indian, Frieda Hauswirth Das expresses this much more eloquently and forcefully than I can. See White, *Arguing with the Crocodile*, p. 2.

9. The "status of women debate"—as pursued by Indian modernizers as well as British colonials—in fact concentrated very largely on more elite women, who implicitly "stood for" the majority.

10. Links were made, of course, between caste differentiation and the status of women. It is, however, interesting how British government policy to promote "backward castes," etc., made no connection with gender debates, leaving the subjects of caste/tribe reservations explicitly neuter and implicitly male gendered.

11. Moser, "Gender Planning in the Third World."

12. Goetz, "The Politics of Integrating Gender to State Development Processes."

13. See, for example, Rogers, *The Domestication of Women*.

14. See Whitehead, "'I'm Hungry, Mum.'"

15. Elson, "Male Bias in Macroeconomics."

16. McCarthy, "The Target Group."

17. Mies and Shiva, *Ecofeminism*.

18. Sharma, *Women's Work, Class, and the Urban Household*.

19. Elson, "Male Bias in Macroeconomics."

20. The danger was very real. One volunteer was killed when his boat capsized.

21. The ratio of women to men in the Oxfam office has increased since that time.

22. See, for example, Araki, "Women's Clubs, Associations, and Other Relations in Southern Zambia."

23. Kandiyoti, "Bargaining with Patriarchy."

24. Molyneux, "Mobilization Without Emancipation."

25. Moser, "Gender Planning in the Third World."

26. See Beall, Hassim, and Todes, "'A Bit on the Side'?" Also see O'Gorman, "Writing Women's Wars," in this volume.

27. White, *Arguing with the Crocodile*.

7

"Supposing Truth to Be a Woman"? Pragmatism and the Feminist Problematique

Nicholas Higgins

Supposing truth to be a woman—what? is the suspicion not well founded that all philosophers, when they have been dogmatists, have had little understanding of woman? that the gruesome earnestness, the clumsy importunity with which they have hitherto been in the habit of approaching truth have been inept and improper means for winning a wench?
—Friedrich Nietzsche, *Beyond Good and Evil*[1]

If woman *is* truth, *she* at least knows that there is no truth, that truth has no place here and that no one has a place for truth. And she is a woman precisely because she herself does not believe in truth itself, because she does not believe in what she is, in what she is believed to be, in what she is thus not.
—Jacques Derrida, *Spurs*[2]

In contrast to the other contributions to this volume, and before making a step into the international, this chapter raises the central concern of all the contributors to the project but does so in an oft-overlooked location. Although it inquires as to the nature of difference, it does so within the context of what Richard Rorty has called the "North Atlantic liberal democracies." Not only has liberal democratic culture become the only dominant international political project considered suitable for all developed and developing nation-states, but these democracies are also home to the white male majority of educated and active practitioners and scholars of international relations, and it is thus to them that the invitation and challenge of supposing truth to be a woman is addressed.

In supposing truth to be a woman, however, it is not simply being suggested that the voice of women should be heard and believed, although this is still a necessary reminder in many an (inter)national locale; rather it asks that such scholars and practitioners take seriously the challenge of a feminist problematique. In searching for a truth in the subject of women, one is necessarily taking up a position of interrogation from where the claims of liberal democracies freedom must face the critical inquiry of their female citizens. But not only female citizens, for what is being proposed is that woman *not* be conceived as a single, all-encompassing, and solitary definitional category—on the contrary; and just as with truth, woman must admit to the multiplicity of meanings and inscriptions that she has come to host and might yet come to create. What this signifies is that difference itself must be recognized as that which is enfolded inside the very heart of feminist discourse.

Supposing truth to be a woman therefore becomes better understood as an epistemological stance, a stance that is exclusive to neither women nor men. Philosophical pragmatism as a school of thought that claims to hold just such an antiessentialist and antifoundationalist position thus provides this chapter with its theoretical orientation. By placing two of its foremost practitioners—one a man and one a woman—in a dialogical setting, I hope to explore the possibilities offered by pragmatist philosophy for feminist thought. I therefore proceed by allowing Rorty, as one of America's most seductive advocates of liberal democratic government, to explain how he interprets the challenge of feminism in today's advanced liberal societies. In response, Nancy Fraser, a veteran of the "woman's struggle," and also a self-professed democratic-pragmatist, proposes an alternative construal of our current democratic culture, one that remains very much at odds with that of Rorty.

In attempting to untangle the nature of the disagreement between the two theorists, I further hope to highlight the often uncontested experience in advanced liberal societies of the practices of freedom—and in particular to consider the role of women as they find themselves implicated within such practices. For Fraser it is through contestation of the classic liberal division between the public and the private domains that the character of her definition of a feminist politics takes shape. Unlike Rorty, who hopes to exploit the unsettled relation between the public/private, Fraser wishes to open such classifications to a greater degree of democratic scrutiny. The democratic method thus becomes integral to Fraser's conception of a feminist political movement, this being so because the adoption of such a process is seen as the best available means to justly and fairly mediate among the diverse and multiple positions inherent in a feminist politics. In contrast, rather than wishing to settle the inherent tension between plural feminist viewpoints, Rorty negates the salience of the liberal-democratic process and looks instead toward the cultural practice of linguistic self-description as the principal means to escape and reconfigure our present cultural understandings of woman. Rorty thus posits an understanding of self that has the capacity to resist the cultural dominance of existing descriptions of woman—descriptions that act to both limit the political and social possibilities available in our contemporary liberal culture.

Both political theorists might therefore be fairly described as concerned with unraveling the complex relationship between freedom and difference as now understood within advanced liberal societies. Nonetheless, it is through the course of their academic exchange that the costs and consequences of adopting a particular conceptual style begin to make themselves more clearly visible. The conclusion of this chapter therefore assesses such social and political costs and consequences and suggests how they might be both explained and best avoided. The very parameters of modern liberal freedom and practice thus come to be seen as both positive *and* negative, an insight that hopes to provoke a more sensitive appraisal of such liberal practices in place of an almost overwhelming, and uncritical, international assumption of their global applicability.

RORTY ON FEMINISM

Richard Rorty has elaborated on the cultural and political role a philosophical pragmatist can play in support of a contemporary social issue that calls for radical cultural transformation.[3] In focusing on the feminist problematique in his 1991 Tanner Lecture on Human Values, Rorty has clearly identified feminism as the contemporary social issue with the greatest revolutionary potential of resulting in positive moral and ethical change in the existing liberal communities of the North Atlantic democracies today. However, in keeping with his pragmatic historicist perspective, Rorty does not approach feminism in the manner of a free-floating sociopolitical project; on the contrary, feminism is firmly located as the latest in a long line of harbingers of intellectual and moral progress. And as such, Rorty comes to situate feminism within the broader historical parameters of a much larger, and continually evolving, political and ethical project—one that could ironically be called Rorty's postmodern liberal humanism.[4] Feminism viewed from this perspective thus avoids what Rorty believes would be the pitfalls of an essentialist movement, that is, a movement concerned solely with the emancipation of the female subject. This is because, from in the setting of a postmodern liberal humanism, feminism plays a much more inclusive sociocultural role—one that goes beyond gender distinctions and aims instead at "the production of a better set of social constructs than the ones presently available, and thus at the creation of a new and better sort of human being."[5]

In regarding feminism in such an evidently progressive light, Rorty clearly indicates that his postmodern liberal humanism bears very little relation to the classical universal liberal construct of the rational male individual, a construct that feminist theory, among others, has done so much to deconstruct. Rorty's humanism is metaphysically hollow; it does not claim to be universal in any useful sense. Rather, its content derives solely from the cultural and social context within which a human being might attempt to make the nature of her humanity intelligible. Such a stance therefore recalls the unavoidably ethnocentric nature of any human construction of identity; as a consequence, Rorty's postmodern humanism denies the validity of questions concerning the absolute ontological, or metaphysical, constitution of the human subject. In this respect, modernist ideologies, including liberal metanarratives, that base their political agenda on such metaphysical constructs are similarly dismissed.[6] Without an intrinsic nature, the question of human identity becomes a highly contested issue, yet such contestation shares a contingent reliance upon the cultural, social, and historical resources within which rival interpretations can only make themselves understood. Rorty's humanism is thus firmly situated within a pragmatic philosophical tradition that provides no extrasocial or extracultural perspective from where the nature of its humanity could be settled once and for all.

It is the very open-ended nature of Rorty's humanism that also informs the character of his liberalism. In much the same way that his humanism cannot be addressed without recourse to ethnocentrically situated historical and cultural resources, so too does liberalism come to function as the minimal sociological structure within which such resources might have the political space to coexist and blossom. Rorty's liberalism thus stands as a loose political framework within which various human natures might have the freedom to pursue their various self-interpretations, untrammelled by the imposition of one version of what humanity can be shown to be. Contrary to the liberalism of the Enlightenment, Rorty does not seek justification for democracy by an appeal to transcultural criteria of rationality. Rather, in the spirit of liberal philosophers such as John Stuart Mill, John Dewey, and Thomas Jefferson, Rorty gives priority to the pragmatic and procedural nature of democracy over and above any philosophical claims.[7] However, unlike the cold utilitarian rationale of Benthamite liberal democracy, Rorty's democratic impulse recalls the romantic and aesthetic aspect of Mill's more sensitive political liberalism.[8] Liberal democracy in this respect functions as a means of limiting the interference of the state in the personal life projects of the individual. The logic runs that if there is no one correct way of being, then individuals should be free, in a romantic manner, to "create themselves anew." The liberal structure does, of course, impose limits upon the influence such life projects can assume. These limits, considered as both community and individual safeguards, manifest themselves in the classic liberal construct of an institutional division between the realms of the public and the private. The private domain in this analysis provides the cultural space within which philosophers and poets can continue to work freely on the creation of novel self-descriptions of what it means to be a human being. The public domain in contrast demands that the role of creativity adopt a self-consciously pragmatic and communal nature. Public politics thus comes to adopt the reformist and practical character appropriate to a political ethos whose contemplation of social problems does not include the radical restructuring of the central mechanisms of governmental organization within which its diversity finds its protection.[9]

Rorty's liberalism and humanism are thus closely interlinked, making little attempt to describe life within a postmodern North Atlantic democracy bar endorsing the necessary double bind of the sociological distinction between the public and the private. Necessary because if there is no ahistorical human being whose potential could be fully realized if only we were to apply the correct plans and policies, government and politics must be limited to a self-consciously defined public space. A double bind because many of the life projects of individuals are concerned with creating stories about who we are, stories that because they cannot be considered true or valid in any strong metaphysical sense must have their cultural impact limited to the private domain of their creators. Pragmatic liberals thus hope to insulate the central political institutions of the state from the adoption of exclusionary political vocabularies that run the risk of subverting a liberal pluralism in the name of an extracultural or ahistorical truth. Nevertheless, although Rorty's postmodern conjuncture of a liberal humanism might provide a convincing antifoundationalist framework with which support for our existing liberal democracies might continue in lieu of a better alternative, it is still far from clear how this pragmatic perspective can explain the achievement of the moral and social progress implicit in his support for a feminist attempt to create "a new and better sort of human being."

At first glance it might appear that pragmatists, in forgoing the supposed ethical clarity of a moral realism, have also reduced the prospects of societal change, which could be considered progress, to an inherently chancy affair. However, in understanding the social world in a nonrepresentationalist manner, pragmatists have also come to question the supposed limits of our existing systems of representation. In ceasing to understand representation as objective or true in any nonculturally relative sense, pragmatists have come to regard the manner in which phenomena are named as holding far greater importance than whether such names can be considered accurate or not. Thus, from the pragmatic historicist's perspective, it is the fashioning of new names, and their subsequent effect on our existing linguistic practices, that comes to shape our relations within the social world. This is to say, along with Susan Hurley, that "the existence of certain shared practices, any of which might not have existed, is all that our having determinate reasons . . . to do anything rests on."[10] It is also to take seriously the idea, "made familiar by writers such as Charles Taylor, that interpretation goes all the way down: that what a human being is, for moral purposes, is largely a matter of how he or she describes him or herself."[11] As a result, linguistic practice and its possible alteration becomes the engine of social and moral progress. Novel linguistic practices, or new names, do not, however, come to be adopted in light of their intrinsic logic or rationale. Such an assumption would, for pragmatists such as Rorty, suggest the existence of a fictitious "rational" community upon whose consensus new descriptions or redescriptions would become widespread. Rather, and in contrast to a realist account, change comes about only because of the creation of a new vocabulary that, in its provision of a new description, renders a new self-understanding possible.

Thus, in recognition of the possibility of change implicit in the fashioning of new names, Rorty has come to consider feminism as functioning in a culturally poetic manner and in this respect possibly even in a socially prophetic mode. Feminists, in finding new descriptions for the people they believe themselves to be, make themselves anew. It is therefore in supporting Marilyn Frye, when she rallies her fellow feminists to "dare to rely on ourselves to make meaning and . . . to imagine ourselves capable of . . . weaving the web of meaning which will hold us in some kind of intelligibility," that Rorty can be seen to take seriously the role of psychological agency inherent in the practice of feminist redescription.[12] He therefore advocates a feminism that is creative, echoing Catherine MacKinnon when she describes feminism as "evoking for woman a role that we have yet to make, in the name of a voice that, unsilenced, might say something that has never been heard."[13] Admiring feminists not for their revelation of truth but for their creativity and imagination, Rorty interprets such feminist pronouncements as a means of saying that "women are only now beginning to put together a moral identity as women."[14]

Such a statement may strike some as peculiar, for surely women have always had a moral identity and it has been the role of feminism to struggle for the recognition and respect that such an identity *should* command. But for Rorty, this type of response is both a misconstrual of the nature of a moral identity and consequently a misunderstanding of the sociocultural role that feminism might fulfill. Furthermore, it is the very impulse that makes such sentences seem strange that serves to highlight the philosophical service that pragmatism might render on behalf of feminism. "For pragmatism redescribes both intellectual and moral progress by substituting metaphors of evolutionary progress for metaphors of progressively less distorted perception."[15] So rather than criticize past social practices for their failure to respect a preexisting and fully formed moral identity, pragmatists instead "identify most of the wrongness of past male oppression with its suppression of past potentiality, rather than in its injustice to past actuality."[16] Pragmatism thus functions as a philosophical road clearer for the far more heroic and ingenious task that contemporary feminist "poets and prophets" have undertaken. Regarded less as radicals and more as utopians, feminists come to be viewed as social and cultural visionaries. The inventive and courageous attempt to create a moral identity as woman is for Rorty "indistinguishable from the imagination it takes to hear oneself as the spokesperson of a merely possible community, rather than as a lonely, and perhaps crazed, outcast from an actual one."[17] It is therefore Rorty the philosophical pragmatist who volunteers himself as an academic Sancho Panza for the more daring cultural crusader of a feminist Don Quixote.

Like Don Quixote, feminists are encouraged to break away from the dominant linguistic practices that currently give womanhood its sociocultural content and to take it upon themselves to fashion the language of a "new being." This is because, after exhausting all the available political and moral space afforded by the existing linguistic practices, feminist separatism presents itself as a temporary strategy whereby women might escape the restrictive gaze of the "arrogant eye" of the moral realist and be free to engage in the linguistic experimentation necessary for the creation of new self-descriptions. The creation of a "new language," however, is not concerned solely with the invention of new words but also with the "creative misuses of language—familiar words used in ways which initially sound crazy."[18] Eventually, however, such words and descriptions will become assimilated into wider society whereby their popularity will serve to extend the previously available logical and psychological space "by making descriptions of situations which used to seem crazy seem sane."[19] Thus, feminist separatism, paraphrasing lesbian activists like Adrienne Rich, has little to do with sexual preference or civil rights and a lot to do with making things easier for the women of the future to define themselves in terms not now available.[20] Yet the prophetic nature of feminism cannot be solely about the role of women, "for roles require a community—a web of social expectations and habits which define the role in question."[21] Prophetic feminists like MacKinnon and Frye thus envision a totally "new being" not only for women but for society. And the society they foresee is one in which "the male-female distinction is no longer of much interest."[22] But whether their vision will be realized can only be determined by the fallibility of an as yet unknown future, a future that Rorty's postmodern liberal humanism hopes to engender but cannot guarantee.

FROM IRONY TO POLITICS?

Because Nancy Fraser regards her roles as both feminist and academic as not only compatible but politically interdependent, it comes as no surprise to find that she remains fundamentally dissatisfied with Rorty's characterization of feminism in a prophetic light. More unexpected, however, are the grounds upon which Fraser has chosen to contest Rorty's division of philosophical and cultural labor. It is Fraser's contention that her disagreement with Rorty is a disagreement within pragmatism. Fraser thus argues for a more "politically engaged" conception of the feminist movement—one that not only stems from a "zero degree" pragmatist stance but in doing so also offers a greater prospect of social change than that of Rorty's poetic separatism. But before we turn our attention to Fraser's self-proclaimed, pragmatic socialist-feminism, we must first ask *if* this is the result of a pragmatic stance—a stance Rorty takes to result in a politics conceptualized in a fragmented, localized, and issue-specific manner—and what Fraser might mean when she claims to take Rorty's analysis a step further from "prophecy to politics."

Fraser's conception of politics is most clearly articulated when she introduces the reader to her book of collected essays, *Unruly Practices*. It is in outlining the ground upon which her own essays might be considered as examples of intellectual political engagement that Fraser comes to defend a broad conception of politics—a conception based *not* on pragmatist philosophy but on a "quasi-Gramscian view, in which struggles over cultural meanings and social identities are struggles for cultural hegemony, that is, for the power to construct *authoritative* definitions of social situations and *legitimate* interpretations of social needs."[23] Although Fraser cites Antonio Gramsci as the principal inspiration for her construal of political activity, her characterization of politics as an activity concerned with struggles over cultural meanings and identities might possibly also describe Rorty's feminist attempt to alter the effects of dominant linguistic practices. However, it is the very question of the priority of pragmatist philosophy to politics that comes to divide Fraser and Rorty.

Whereas Rorty's feminist politics is constrained by the logic of his pragmatist antifoundations, Fraser's feminist politics is empowered through the adoption of what I shall call a "politically pragmatic" approach. In this way, Fraser takes "political issues—as opposed to metatheoretical issues about, say, 'totality' or 'foundationalism'—as [her] point of departure."[24] She thus claims "not to affect a stance of supposed archimedian neutrality but rather to speak out of a sociologically specific, explicitly gendered, and practically engaged situation."[25] In this respect, she considers her academic endeavors to be "exercises in situated theorizing."[26] In other words, that in comparison to her male colleagues, she, being both a woman and a feminist academic, is placed in a different position with respect to the levers of social power and consequently to the movements that oppose them.[27] Fraser's approach is therefore pragmatic in the sense that her engagement with both theory and society starts from a perspective that places her "involvement as a feminist at the centre"; thus her assessment of different philosophical positions is based upon their ability to bring about the kind of social changes that she, as first and foremost a woman and a feminist, feels are necessary.[28] It is this politically pragmatic stance that makes it possible to accuse Michel Foucault of being both "normatively confused" and subsequently "conservative" in his own intellectual endeavors.[29] Furthermore, it is only this self-avowed political perspective that allows Fraser to question both the political utility of the French Derrideans and the critical bite of Habermasian critical theory.[30] It should therefore come as no surprise that when Fraser turns her attention to Rortian pragmatism, she does so in a manner that treats it "pragmatically," judging it on its ability to induce the type of political change that she believes feminism requires.[31]

In an essay written before Rorty made his stance toward feminism explicit, Fraser took issue with what she called the "partition position" of what I have referred to as Rorty's postmodern liberal humanism. The partition position relates to Rorty's classically liberal separation of society into the public and the private domain. Fraser's concern in this instance is that Rorty's sociological division leads to a narrow conception of politics as that which is conducted only within the domain of the public. This is because Fraser believes that the partition position does not function as a politically liberal insulation against the life projects of particular individuals from the state and vice versa, as Rorty initially intended, but rather that the public/private distinction has come to enforce a gender subtext within the contemporary U.S. social structure. The private sphere for Fraser has come to delimit the family-related domain, resulting in its implicit codification as feminine, whereas the public sphere has come to be associated with labor-oriented issues and as such becomes implicitly masculine in its social codification.[32] As such, Fraser argues, both domestic and personal issues come to be deemed inappropriate for discussion in the officially designated political arena, with the unpalatable consequence that many of the central claims of the feminist movement would also be deemed private and apolitical. It is Fraser's characterization of feminism as a social movement that is important here, because in addition to feminism, "a whole range of New Left social movements, as illuminated by Gramscian, Foucauldian, and . . . Althusserian theory, have taught us that the cultural, the medical, the educational—everything that Hannah Arendt called 'the social,' as distinct from the private and the public—that all this, too, is political."[33] For Fraser then, it has been the "social movements of the last hundred or so years [that] have taught us to see the power-laden, and therefore political, character of interactions that classical liberalism considered private."[34] From this broad sociohistorical perspective, the very act of classifying an issue as private is a "political" act, an insight that Fraser feels Rorty's partition position ignores, leading us instead to "turn our backs on the last hundred years of social history."[35]

Fraser would certainly have a strong case if Rorty had actually been in the business of classifying issues as either public or private. Furthermore, in suggesting that such domains are essentially contested domains, she might even find evidence in Rorty's own work that supports such a position.[36] However, what she will not find is a strict elaboration of the formal relationship between the private and the public. This is because Rorty's partition position is a loose and ill-defined framework that derives its content from the historical and cultural contestation of various social issues as they have come to be articulated at different times in the past. Thus, although Fraser's charge that all manner of diverse social institutions are political may well be true; for Rorty such a broad-ranging conception of politics is at best banal and at worst of little use in answering questions concerning just how the contemporary educational system is to be improved or how current medical treatment might be made better. It is probably best in this instance to recall Rorty's endorsement of John Rawls's method of reflective equilibrium, for his use of the public/private distinction is more akin to an essentially ambiguous relationship—that is, a relationship involving the "give-and-take between intuitions about the desirability of particular consequences of particular actions and intuitions about general principles, with neither having the determining voice."[37] It is Rorty's pragmatic historicism that refuses the temptation to dictate in any final or ahistorical manner what issues are to be considered either public or private. And as if to illustrate this very point, we may well regard Rorty's contemplation of the feminist problematique as a contemporary example of an issue that refuses the straightforward classification of an issue to be addressed in either the private or the public domain. In fact, it is Rorty's call for a feminist separatism that underlines his belief in the transitory nature of what a society might consider an appropriate political classification for both women and men. Although Fraser clearly recognizes the implications of Rorty's characterization of feminism for her strict interpretation of a public/private partition, she nevertheless regards such implications as a radical departure from, rather than a further elaboration of, Rorty's postmodern liberal humanism. She thus views his Tanner lecture as "an instance of the sort of paradigm-breaking transformation that feminists have long said must occur whenever androcentric modes of understanding are forced to confront the problematic of gender."[38] Furthermore, and in recognition of the "new" social space in which Rorty has situated feminism, Fraser feels that the structure of his thought has come so close to a profound transformation as to nearly warrant the shift being acknowledged as the long-awaited transition from "Irony to Politics," but not quite.[39]

THE NEEDS OF A FEMINIST POLITICS

Having already defined the political as that which is coeval with what Arendt called the social, Fraser's wish to create a feminist politics with "a more sociological, institutional and collective spin" is at least consistent with her own definition of how political change has come to manifest itself throughout history.[40] Unlike Rorty, Fraser considers "the agents of historical change to be social movements rather than extraordinary individuals," and as such she takes issue with the individualizing aspect of Rorty's characterization of the feminist project as poetic and possibly even prophetic.[41] With this in mind, it is entirely in keeping with Fraser's approach that she should choose to "advance" Rorty's interpretation with the help of both a historical and an empirical correction. However, it is Fraser's further claim—to provide a more consistently pragmatic approach than Rorty's— that appears incompatible with her socialist-feminist theory of political engagement. Although Fraser claims to hold "the historicist view that feminists are engaged in creating new moral identities and sensibilities rather than in realising or discovering latent or pre-existing ones," her very first correction of Rorty's existing approach clearly suggests the contrary.[42]

Correcting Rorty on his "empirically false" statement—that a positive moral identity was unavailable to woman prior to the advent of feminism— Fraser lays claim to "discoveries" in feminist scholarship that have proved that positive identities for woman have indeed existed in the past. This discovery is of no small consequence, for "if it turns out that there are usable traditions in which the term *woman* has figured as a positive moral identity, then we will need another way of characterizing the innovation of feminist movements."[43] On the basis of this unreferenced historical evidence, Fraser dismisses Rorty's characterization of the feminist movement as concerned with the creation of a positive moral identity. Instead, she suggests that a more historically appropriate characterization for the innovation of the contemporary feminist movement would be to view them as involved in creating a "collective political identity."[44] However, Rorty's ignorance of feminist history does not end here, for Fraser continues to advance her own politically pragmatic (as opposed to philosophically pragmatic) project by showing how Rorty's ideas have already proved obsolete for the existing feminist movement. In this respect, Rorty's second mistake is in fact linked to his first, leading his pragmatism to lose its political bite. This is because, although Rorty's characterization of feminism as engaged with the creation of new descriptions of woman as woman "was a plausible initial response to the discovery that the supposedly human identities constructed by men were actually androcentric, it has not proved a workable political tool."[45] The reason for this, Fraser flatly asserts, is that "feminism is at base not an exclusive club of prophets, but a mass democratic social movement."[46] In light of these empirical corrections, feminism for Fraser can be viewed politically, as continuing a pragmatic democratic tradition concerned with the creation of a "discursive space where 'semantic authority' is constructed collectively, critically, and democratically, rather than imposed via prophetic pronouncements from mountaintops."[47] But before we congratulate Fraser on her move from prophecy to politics, we may wish to ask on what grounds she makes her claims to empirical knowledge. And can such grounds be considered, as she claims, to be both coherent to a zero-degree pragmatism—that is, an "antiessentialism with respect to traditional philosophical concepts like truth and reason, human nature and morality" and, at the same time, constitutive of a feminist politics?[48]

Let us consider Fraser's first criticism of Rorty's claim that a positive moral identity was unavailable to women prior to the advent of feminism. We might ask whether, in this instance, Fraser has reified the role of empirical historical evidence over and above the language and methodological conventions that give such "evidence" meaning. In accusing Rorty of being "empirically false," Fraser bases her correction on recent feminist scholarship, which she writes "involves retrieving and revaluing marginalized traditions of women's power and agency that androcentric scholars have neglected and denigrated."[49] However, if Rorty's claim is "empirically false," then it necessarily follows that evidence, provided by feminist scholarship, is "empirically true." But surely such a claim serves to highlight Fraser's failure to account for the very historicity of feminist scholarship's claims to truth and falsehood. If we invoke Ian Hacking, we can, in a classic positivist manner, claim that a sentence or a statement is neither true nor false except insofar as such a statement is a "candidate for truth or falsehood."[50] The very laudable fact that there now exists a community of feminist scholars concerned with the description of women's history says much about the advance of "woman" as an academically legitimate category for historical inquiry without laying claim to an advance in any nonacademically relative domain of truth.[51] Such an admission merely admits that the institutional success of feminist scholarship is relative to the concerns and preoccupations of a particular group, in a particular place, during a particular period of time. In claiming that "we now know quite a lot about the cultural construction of womanhood in various periods as a moral identity," Fraser appears to privilege this latest form of historical knowledge in a manner that fails to reflect on the very contemporary cultural constructions that make such claims to knowledge possible.[52]

By accusing Fraser of failing to historicize her own claims to knowledge, we strike right at the core of her feminist project, and as such we are drawn back toward some of her earlier claims for a situated theory. This is because, although Fraser claims to agree with Rorty that social criticism does not require philosophical foundations, she nonetheless does not base her social criticism on empiricism alone; rather, she hopes to underpin social criticism with her own version of a critical social theory.[53] This necessity for a theory is in itself due to Fraser's self-confessed nonpragmatic conception of politics as that concerned with "struggles for cultural hegemony—that is, for the power to construct authoritative definitions of social situations and legitimate interpretations of social needs."[54] In accordance with this conception, if Fraser wishes to empower feminists, she must first identify an existing cultural hegemony and then define the grounds upon which her own definitions can be considered authoritative or legitimate, in contrast to those that already exist. Although her corrections of Rorty's work give some clue as to how this might be attempted, it is in Fraser's outline of a socialist-feminist theory of late capitalist political culture that we find a more explicit account of her feminist politics.[55]

After identifying the manner in which social needs have come to be interpreted in North American capitalist society as an existing cultural hegemony, Fraser sets about defining the terms of the political contestation of those needs. Because Fraser's definition of "situated" appears to suggest situated with regard to an existing cultural hegemony, her recognition that "needs are culturally constructed and discursively interpreted" nonetheless does not mean that "any need interpretation is as good as any other."[56] This should come as no surprise, for it is once again Fraser's conception of politics that requires her counterhegemonic need interpretation to be both authoritative and legitimate; she thus needs to "underline the importance of an account of interpretative justification."[57] Fraser, in moving away from an account that concentrates on social needs in themselves, turns her attention to providing an explanation of the considerations any justification of a need interpretation should take into account. First, an interpretation of social needs should consider the consequences of holding such an interpretation. Fraser explains that "this means comparing alternative distributive outcomes of rival interpretations." She continues, "For example, would widespread acceptance of some given interpretation of a social need disadvantage some groups of people vis-à-vis others?"[58] But is it really possible to have needs that do not disadvantage anyone? And if so, from what theoretical perspective could such an assessment be made? However, if such a question suggests the specter of a socialist realism lurking behind Fraser's theoretical stance, then the uncontested sociological position from where Fraser situates her next questions can only compound the suspicion. In asking "does the interpretation conform to, rather than challenge, societal patterns of dominance and subordination," Fraser appears to already know what it is that counts as either dominance or subordination in capitalist North American culture. This is also true when she asks if "need interpretations . . . [are] more or less respectful, as opposed to transgressive, of ideological boundaries that delimit 'separate spheres' and thereby rationalize inequality."[59] Fraser's position cannot help but look increasingly circular in light of the unreflective manner in which political assumptions function within her rhetorical stance.

However, it is when we consider Fraser's second stipulation for a justified need interpretation that her earlier claim *not* to adopt a position of archimedian neutrality appears most in jeopardy. Fraser writes, "All other things being equal" (a situation that previously Fraser argued just being a woman made impossible), "the best need interpretations are those reached by means of communicative processes that most closely approximate the ideals of democracy, equality and fairness."[60] Admittedly Fraser is aware of the transcendentalist implications of such an "interpretative justification." Nonetheless, although she acknowledges the Habermasian inspiration of her account, she nevertheless maintains that her pragmatism does not involve the transcendental or quasi-transcendental metainterpretation of which Habermas has fallen foul. She claims instead that, "whereas Habermas purports to ground 'communicative ethics' in the conditions of possibility of speech understood universalistically and ahistorically, I consider it a contingently evolved, historically specific possibility."[61] But surely Fraser is both ambivalent and mistaken in making such a claim. She is ambivalent about whether the United States has either "evolved" a communicative ethics or whether it is just a "possibility"; and she is mistaken in thinking that even if the concept of "communicative ethics" is made culturally and historically specific, it no longer carries any transcendental connotations. Is it not a metaphysical deceit to believe that democracy might attain, rather than bravely strive after, a linguistic exchange that is free from the influence of power, or any other divisive cultural influences, and as such could provide the grounds upon which "equality and fairness" might be decided—in a language that could communicate everything that might want to be said?

If we are to take Rorty's pragmatism seriously, in the manner that he takes MacKinnon's feminism seriously, we will need to recognize "that unless women fit into the logical space prepared for them by current linguistic and other practices, the law"—or in this instance communicative ethics—"does not know how to deal with them."[62] The very idea that we might reach a situation whereby we have achieved linguistic totalism and thus hold all the possible descriptions of woman within our grasp is once again to believe that we will finally hold a satisfactory description of what a woman is. Although Fraser has encouraged the pluralism implicit in the practice of "feminisms" in the past,[63] it is due to her own theoretical construction of politics as hegemony that when confronted with Rorty's poetic characterization of feminism she nonetheless cannot free herself of the essentialist impulse to ask, "Which new descriptions will count as 'taking the view point of woman as woman'?" and, "Which women will be empowered to impose their semantic authority on the rest of us?"[64] And it is in her refusal to accept Rorty's chancy and falibilistic account of how new descriptions for woman might come about that Fraser reveals a transcendentalist "need" to find a means of settling the issue once and for all. It is therefore in her own characterization of feminism as "a mass democratic movement" that Fraser provides an answer to a question that Rorty feels there is no need to ask.

Although Fraser may hope for the creation of an "institutional framework of a classless, multicultural society without racism, sexism or hetrosexism—an international society of decentralised, democratic, self-managing collectivities,"[65] it is far from clear that her own critical social theory does, as she hopes, "help to clarify the prospects for democratic and egalitarian social change by sorting out the emancipatory from the repressive possibilities of needs talk."[66] In fact, there is a sneaking totalism present in Fraser's attempt to cook up a sociological stirfry—evident in her ever lengthening self-descriptions (e.g., democratic-socialist-feminist-pragmatist)—that informs her desire to hold society and culture in all its "multivalent diversity" within the grasp of one large "politically useful" critical social theory.[67] And even if you share the utopia that serves to animate Fraser's hopes, it in no way follows that a critical social theory is required to engender its realization. Furthermore, what seems most apparent is that Fraser's claim to adopt a pragmatic approach in her social criticism has little to do with the pragmatic philosophical tradition and a lot to do with a utilitarian approach to theory construction, a construction founded upon an uncontested and self-fulfilling Marxist-inspired conception of what politics is.[68] We can thus argue that it has been Fraser's consistent endorsement of an unswerving identification of the political with struggles over cultural hegemony that has forced her to adapt and alter all manner of divergent theoretical and philosophical insights, sewing them into a unified body that might serve as a replacement for the Marxist working-class struggle in which she was once an active participant. Her hopes thus appear directed at the provision of a theoretical basis upon which to raise a feminist consciousness, a consciousness that might then join with others in a united social movement—one that finds solidarity under the one all-encompassing banner of a Feminist Politics.[69] All this I fear betrays Fraser's project as one more attempt to reclothe an old Marxist dummy in the latest feminist garb; such clothes, however, no longer fit comfortably with the diversity and pluralism of contemporary sites of cultural contestation. Surely Rorty is at least right in thinking that theory should no longer feel obligated to tailor its requirements to the now outmoded political template of sociologically clumsy structures, such as the apparatus of the ideological state.[70]

Nonetheless, before concluding that Rorty alone can lay claim to the insights of a pragmatist-feminist conjuncture, we would do well to recall that it is Fraser who has the greater personal experience of feminism, and this should not be quickly dismissed. Throughout Fraser's work we find examples of the type of change a feminist sensibility has already brought about—change that has occurred in a local and noncoordinated manner, like the creation of battered women's shelters, the provision of women's support groups, and the refusal to accept the sexual exclusion of various workplace practices and hierarchies. Feminists can also be seen to take on issues raised by the new reproductive technology, the right to life, sexual abuse, and sexual harassment—which in a politically oblique manner leads to an engagement with the more conventionally understood political issues, such as the organization of work and child care. Such feminist activities call for action from official political authorities and, more subtly and yet more important, for transformations in the ethical sensibilities of society in general. It is only Fraser's theoretical conception of the political that forces her to combine all these diverse activities into one social movement, leading her to identify transformations in power and morality with large institutional changes instead of considering the revolutionary impact of the small, personal, and incremental effects of existing feminist causes on a more loosely yet historically specific understanding of the relationships of freedom and practice as currently experienced in liberal democratic culture.

THE FANTASY OF FEMINIST FREEDOM

However, in refuting Fraser's "politically" pragmatic attack on Rorty's thought, are we forced to conclude that Rorty's feminist analysis stands uncontested as the sole inheritor of a pragmatist perspective? Possibly not, and on what better grounds to reconsider Rorty's position than his own? Although he encourages his fellow academics to read the historical record in the manner of Burke's comic frame to free them from "the idea that a materialism and a sense of historicity more radical than Marx's will somehow provide a brand-new, still bigger (albeit still blurrier) object—an object perhaps called Language or Discourse—around which to weave our fantasies," has not Rorty himself failed to heed what he has advocated for others?[71] And even though his intention may well have been to continue a process of cultural disenchantment, might not his own feminist poetics reveal the weaving of a Rortian linguistic fantasy?

Although Rorty agrees with Chris Weedon that "one should not view language as a transparent tool for expressing facts but as the material in which particular often conflicting views of facts are constructed," Rorty nevertheless wishes to claim that such conflicts occur in a positive dialectical manner.[72] This is because it has been Rorty's contention that moral and intellectual progress will be achieved only if "the linguistic and other practices of the common culture . . . come to incorporate some of the practices characteristic of imaginative and courageous [feminist] outcasts."[73] In light of this belief, feminists have to break away from mainstream linguistic practices because, as with other progressive movements of the past, "had there been no stage of separation there would have been no subsequent stage of assimilation."[74] Rorty cannot, however, provide reasons why a new feminist language might come to be assimilated into wider U.S. culture, and this is because he has forgone the once "comforting belief that competing groups will always be able to reason together on the basis of plausible and neutral premises."[75] As such, "prophecy . . . is all that non-violent movements can fall back on when argument fails."[76] Yet for feminist prophecy to be confirmed, our approach to the history of the future must also conform to Rorty's whiggishly dialectical account of how historical change, via the role of language, has come to take place. As a consequence, Rorty cannot provide any analysis of how "the new language spoken by the separatist group may gradually get woven into the language taught in the schools," at least not one that does not start to look increasingly circular. In fact, all he can offer on the back of his antifoundationalist pragmatism is hope.

Is it possible that Rorty has overplayed the extent of cultural agency available within the "fashioning of new names"? In holding that "all awareness is a linguistic affair," does not Rorty suggest the presence of a cultural and linguistic idealism at work within his analysis—that is, an individualist idealism that exaggerates the moral and social possibilities of freedom within his project of redescription? Even without adopting Fraser's Gramscian analysis of the political, we might nonetheless have more than a little sympathy with her attempt to engage with some of the institutional structures that influence the realm of possible redescriptions for contemporary woman. Might not woman be especially subject to the limitations of identifications determined by the U.S. welfare state? And even if we refuse to make an invidious distinction between appearance and reality "in favour of a distinction between beliefs which serve some purposes and beliefs which serve other purposes—for example, the purposes of one group and those of another," might we still not wish to contest that the playing field upon which such groups confront each other is not one of equality but one permeated with the differential effects of power?[77] After all, is Fraser not correct in thinking that some of our cultural institutions and social practices do have more power in the fashioning of names than others? And although Rorty might provide a convincing explanation of how language comes to shape our thoughts about ourselves (a position, borrowed from Wilfred

Sellars, that he calls psychological nominalism), he fails to provide any account of how such social practices and personal thoughts have come to interact.

Interestingly, it is also Sellars who appears to recognize the sociological failings present in Rorty's, and possibly even Fraser's, oscillating philosophical stance when he writes, "One seems forced to choose between the picture of an elephant which rests on a tortoise (what supports the tortoise?) and the picture of a great Hegelian serpent of knowledge with its tail in its mouth (where does it begin?)." Dissatisfied with either of the options available, Sellars concludes that "neither will do."[78] So, might there be another route through the philosophical minefield of history and metaphysics? Hacking believes there is. Calling attention to Rorty's own reliance on the historical influence of Descartes for his subsequent explanation of the dominance of a particular style of philosophical reasoning—that is, one preoccupied with the search for foundations—Hacking wonders whether "perhaps Richard Rorty's Philosophy and the Mirror of Nature, with its central doctrine of 'conversation,' will some day seem as linguistic a philosophy as the analysis emanating from Oxford a generation or two ago."[79] Although Rorty's linguistic stance is the result of a historicist approach to the practice of philosophy, Rorty has failed to recognize that a historicist approach to other cultural and social practices may yet reveal the durability of other historically specific styles of reasoning. Although not claiming to reveal any ahistorical truths, such historicist accounts may nonetheless provide novel descriptions of how it is that certain social practices have come to dictate what might count as the institutional parameters for the possibility of redescription in the present.[80] One such example that Hacking has provided is the history of statistics.[81]

REDESCRIBING FREEDOM

Hacking writes, "The bureaucracy of statistics imposes not just by creating administrative rulings but by determining classifications within which people must think of themselves and of the actions that are open to them."[82] Hacking's disagreement with Rorty is therefore not with his claim that a new type of being can be created through a project of redescription (the very project with which Rorty has come to characterize feminism), for Hacking too believes that "categories of people come into existence at the same time as kinds of people come into being to fit those categories, and there is a two-way interaction between these processes."[83] However, Hacking would have to contest Rorty's extension of the new philosophical freedom created by the acceptance of the pragmatist tradition within the discipline of philosophy to the whole of society. Although it would be difficult to identify limits in the creative and imaginative attempt to redescribe woman in the uninhibited realm of language, Fraser may well have a strong case for arguing that all the self-redescription in the world will not transform the governmentally mediated relationships of power within which many women find themselves subject.

I suspect that the answer lies in the tension between Rorty's picture of *the self* as a centerless and contingent web of beliefs and desires and his separate endorsement of the overriding desire of women to unite such contingencies into a unifying story about *oneself*.[84] In this respect it seems appropriate to think of the writing of Marie Cardinal, whose international best-seller, *The Words to Say It,* describes her personal experience of seven years of psychoanalysis.[85] It is Cardinal, in a similar way to Rorty, who writes of the personal freedom she has come to value through creating a personal vocabulary from within that she has been able to articulate what it means to be a woman. Like Rorty, however, Cardinal then goes on to extend this very personal experience of the liberating effects of language, as discovered through countless hours of therapy, to the more collective enterprise of a feminist politics. She writes, "Speech is an act. Words are objects. Invisible, palpable, revealing. . . . Men hermetically sealed these words, imprisoned women within them. Women must open them if they want to survive. It is an enormous, dangerous and revolutionary task that we undertake."[86]

Cardinal's writing thus makes explicit what Rorty assumes. It is clear that Cardinal's very conception of freedom derives directly from the comparatively recent "discoveries" of psychology and psychoanalysis. That the sense of self understood by such "psy sciences" (as Nikolas Rose refers to them) is taken for granted by Rorty says much for the cultural prevalence of the psy effect and little for Rorty's narrowly focused philosophical historicism. In much the same way that Hacking has come to approach the history of statistics and probability, Rose has provided a cultural history of the sciences of psy.[87] Like Hacking, Rose has attempted to redescribe the history of psychiatry, psychology, and psychoanalysis in order to understand how such linguistic innovation has enabled us to think and act in new ways, to fashion a new human existence, and as such to treat ourselves and others in new and historically particular ways. In this respect, Rose does not deny the freedom of which Cardinal writes and that Rorty takes for granted; rather he hopes to increase the prospects of freedom not by endorsing the practices of psy but by attempting to describe the manner in which such practices have become central to the government of human conduct in advanced liberal democracies.[88]

> The subjectifying effects of psy are not simply a matter of the symbolic violence of a particular meaning system: language is structured into varie-

gated relations which grant powers to some and delimit the powers of others, which enable some to judge and some to be judged, some to cure and some to be cured, some to speak truth and others to acknowledge its authority and embrace it, aspire to it or submit to it. And if, in our vernacular speech, we think of ourselves in psy terms, we do so only through the relations we have established with this truth regime: for we each play our own part, as parents, teachers, partners, lovers, consumers and sufferers, in these contemporary psychological machinations of the self.[89]

From this historicist perspective we might profitably view both Rorty and Cardinal as principally concerned with the creative freedom and individual agency possible within a psychologically and thus self-contained conception of the self at the expense of the very "public" languages, practices, and techniques that have come to constitute such a psychological understanding of personal agency in the first place. Freedom might therefore be redescribed in terms that neither privilege the psychological agency of the modern self nor underestimate the political relationships of power within which such selves are inextricably woven. International relations could therefore benefit from a distinction already proposed in sociology—that is, a distinction between "freedom as a formula of resistance and freedom as a formula of power."[90] Thus, the ubiquity of freedom as presented in both the expansion of the "free market" and the "free world," of liberal economies and liberal democracies, may come to be better understood as containing certain ethical and political costs, costs that might be better approached from an internal and "untimely meditation" upon our contemporary practices of freedom—freedom understood as constituted both economically, psychologically, and as such inextricably socially.

For international relations, such a distinction offers the possibility of separating "our" internal liberal political inquiries from the many international struggles whose participants may never have been subject to our particular historically specific brand of liberal freedom. This is important, because through invoking such a distinction we might remain at conceptual liberty to investigate the diverse international political and ethical issues presented by such struggles, without obscuring the "different" cultural and historical traditions within which such "foreign" struggles find their distinctive character. Far from discouraging empathy for the plight of fellow humans, such a distinction encourages us to contemplate the long-term and political effects of our actions without obscuring such inquiries under the knee-jerk responses of a normative liberal sentiment. We might then stop to ask questions concerning the cultural constitution of freedom before suggesting such freedom as the obvious solution to conflicts we may not yet fully understand. Moreover, such a perspective would not breed paralysis as some have argued, and although not immediately attributable to any one political persuasion, it may yet encourage the intellectual oxygen within

which novel redescriptions of our contemporary international transformations may avoid making overeager normative judgments as to the rightness
or wrongness of political change. Alternatively, academics may well come
to expel greater energy on questions concerning how such foreign struggles
for freedom might also be struggles of resistance from the increasingly
dominant power of liberal (or, more appropriately, neoliberal) freedom as it
is currently being promoted by our international liberal institutions.[91]
Greater attention might also be paid to considering relationships of obligation and commitment rather than encouraging the often emotional, sentimental, and short-lived political and ethical interventions that currently
masquerade under the normative neutrality of "humanitarian assistance."[92]
In this respect too, feminists might also benefit from such a distinction,
allowing questions of women's empowerment to take on a more culturally
sensitive international perspective, without denying the existence of what
Christine Sylvester has called "empathetic co-operation," in the face of
deep-seated, and possibly little understood, cultural differences.[93]

Proscribing such an "untimely meditation" within the practices of liberal democracy thus recalls the philosopher upon whose supposition this
chapter takes its title, for it was Friedrich Nietzsche who first suggested
that history might fulfill such a "political" task.[94] Such histories, in their
attempt to redescribe our contemporary practices of freedom, hope to create
new opportunities for future understandings—understandings that might
herald a time in which women and men may have greater freedom from the
current truths within which they often unhappily find themselves subject.
Rorty, in supposing women to be the creators of their own truth, can be
charged with overlooking the historical manner in which our contemporary
linguistic practices have enmeshed themselves with our contemporary practices of power. Fraser, although not guilty of Rorty's linguistic idealism,
and although keen to engage with a more detailed analysis of liberal political culture than that presented by Rorty's postmodern liberal humanism,
nevertheless fails to account for the "positivity" within many contemporary
governmental practices and subsequently falls into a metaphysical trap of
believing that we will one day not merely make things better but get them
right. Fraser, in trying to be all things to all women, thus comes to posit a
sociological truth—one that results in a totalizing feminist politics, which,
despite all her claims to do the contrary, fails to assist feminists in their
exploration of the often sociologically discrete links between the very personal experience of women in liberal culture and the larger political history
of how our current neoliberal governmentality attempts to give such experiences sociological and political authority.

In conclusion, I would like to draw attention back to the quotes with
which I prefaced this essay, for I hope to have demonstrated—although not
in sufficient detail—that Rorty's characterization of the conjuncture

between pragmatism and feminism is not the only possible means by which an interpretation of philosophical pragmatism can be of use to feminism. Although I consider Fraser's "politically pragmatic" approach to be philosophically self-destructive, I would nevertheless hope to have made some preliminary suggestions that will go some way to contesting Rorty's claim that "Deweyan pragmatism when linguistified . . . gives you all that is politically useful in the Nietzche-Heideggar-Derrida-Foucault tradition."[95] There is still plenty of work for politically inspired academics to pursue, and although our conception of politics may have radically altered from the Marxist-Leninism of old, it is in continuing to suppose truth to be a woman that we develop an ethos that both inspires intellectuals to create new possibilities for the future and guards against the dogmatism that both litters the past and requires our continued contestation in the present.

NOTES

1. Nietzsche, *Beyond Good and Evil,* p. 31.
2. Derrida, *Spurs,* p. 53.
3. Another good example of Rorty's reply to the charge of social conservatism raised by Hilary Putman can be found in his "Does Academic Freedom Have Philosophical Presuppositions?"
4. Feminism thus comes to be placed alongside such esteemed company as, "for example, Plato's Academy, the early Christians meeting in the catacombs, the invisible Copernican colleges of the Seventeenth century, groups of working men gathering to discuss Thomas Paine's pamphlets"; see Rorty, "Feminism and Pragmatism," p. 138.
5. Rorty, "Feminism and Pragmatism," p. 140.
6. As an example of his evenhanded antifoundationalist approach, consider Rorty's "Human Rights, Rationality, and Sentimentality." Also see "Priority of Democracy to Philosophy" and "Postmodern Bourgeois Liberalism" in Rorty, *Objectivity, Relativism, and Truth.*
7. See Rorty's essay "Priority of Democracy," in his *Objectivity, Relativism, and Truth,* for a full account of the ongoing "experiment" that liberal democracy comes to represent once foundationalist philosophical liberalism has been abandoned. In particular, see pp. 192–193 for the resigned admission that such a stance might entail an unavoidable condition of paradox and self-referentiality.
8. See Rorty's essay "Method, Social Science, Social Hope," in Rorty, *Consequences of Pragmatism,* pp. 203–208 (especially footnote 16), for an explicit account of his endorsement of the liberalism of Mill and Dewey. See also Rorty's "Moral Identity and Private Autonomy: The Case of Foucault," in Rorty, *Essays on Heidegger and Others,* for a further elaboration of the procedural role of the public/private distinction. In this instance there might also be good reason to assume that Rorty's conception of freedom remains particularly enamored of Mill's project of self-realization as expressed in *On Liberty.* In this respect, see Morris, *Versions of the Self: Studies in English Autobiography from John Bunyan to Stuart Mill.* Clearly Mill's early feminist thoughts are also of relevance here; see J. S. Mill, "The Subjection of Woman" (1861).

9. See Rorty, "Private Irony and Liberal Hope," in Rorty, *Contingency, Irony, and Solidarity,* pp. 73–95.

10. Rorty, in his "Feminism and Pragmatism" (p. 127), quotes from a review of Susan Hurley's *Natural Resources* by Samuel Scheffler in the *London Review of Books.*

11. Rorty, "Feminism and Pragmatism," p. 135.

12. Frye, *The Politics of Reality,* p. 80 (quoted in Rorty, "Feminism and Pragmatism," p. 132).

13. MacKinnon, "On Exceptionality," in her *Feminism Unmodified: Discourses on Life and Law,* p. 77 (quoted in Rorty, "Feminism and Pragmatism," p. 125).

14. Rorty, "Feminism and Pragmatism," p. 134.

15. Ibid., p. 128.

16. Ibid., p. 135.

17. Ibid., p. 132.

18. Ibid., p. 127. We might also consider Nancy Fraser's examples of *date rape, sexual harrassment,* etc., as examples of just such words; see Fraser, "From Irony to Prophecy to Politics," p. 158.

19. Rorty, "Feminism and Pragmatism," p. 127.

20. Ibid., p. 137. See Rich, *On Lies, Secrets, and Silence,* p. 17.

21. Rorty, "Feminism and Pragmatism," p. 140.

22. Ibid., p. 140.

23. Fraser, "An Apologia for Academic Radicals," in her *Unruly Practices,* p. 6 (italics added).

24. Fraser, *Unruly Practices,* p. 7 (italics in original).

25. Ibid.

26. Ibid.

27. Ibid.

28. Ibid.

29. Ibid., chapters 1, 2.

30. Ibid., chapters 4, 6.

31. Ibid., chapter 5.

32. Ibid., p. 149.

33. Ibid., p. 102, in particular, footnote 24.

34. Ibid., p. 102.

35. Ibid.

36. See Higgins, "A Question of Style," pp. 32–34. Furthermore, and in direct relation to the objective of this article, although I would still argue that identity remains an "essentially contested" human condition, I would also hope to emphasize that after coming to such a philosophical conclusion, the next step is to try and elaborate just how such contestations currently take place. See the section "Redescribing Freedom" in this article for some suggestions as to how this might be done with regard to feminism.

37. See Rorty, *Objectivity, Relativism, and Truth,* p. 183, especially footnotes 20 and 21.

38. Fraser, "From Irony to Prophecy to Politics," p. 156.

39. Ibid.

40. It is important to realize that Fraser's use of the term *social* differs significantly from Arendt's own use of the term in *The Human Condition.* Fraser writes, "Arendt and I both understand the social as a historically emergent societal space specific to modernity. And we both understand the emergence of the social as tend-

ing to undercut or blur an earlier, more distinct separation of public and private spheres." Revealingly, Fraser does not choose to criticize Rorty's use of the public/private distinction in such a straightforwardly historical and empirical manner when she deals with the matter in her "Singularity or Solidarity" (Fraser, *Unruly Practices*); this I believe is because Fraser wishes to judge and co-opt the idea of the "social" rather than merely assert its empirical existence as a specific historical event. Thus, although agreeing with Arendt that "one salient defining feature of the social is the emergence of heretofore 'private' needs into public view," Fraser goes on to explain that Arendt's own negative interpretation of this occurrence was simply a consequence of her assumption that "needs are wholly natural." In contrast, Fraser's own assumption (informed by her own reading of Foucault) "that needs are irreducibly interpretative and that need interpretations are in principle contestable" makes her consider the event as "a generally positive development." Fraser thus considers the emergence of the social as heralding the "(possible) flourishing of politics," unlike Arendt who views the events as leading to "death of politics." However, whereas Arendt's interpretation is also based upon a more empirical claim—that the social has led to "the triumph of administration and instrumental reason"—Fraser's optimism is premised upon the belief that there is another possible outcome from such events, namely: "an alternative socialist-feminist, dialogical mode of need interpretation and a participatory-democratic institutionalization of the social." See Fraser, *Unruly Practices,* p. 160, footnote 32. I make this point simply to illustrate the manner in which Fraser approaches both historical and empirical information. This is because I believe she conflates two approaches that do not sit easily together. For although Fraser has argued that feminists can still embrace both "large historical narratives" and what she calls "analyses of societal macrostructures" because of the need for "large theoretical tools . . . to address large theoretical problems," Fraser's own interpretation of the historical event of the emergence of the "social" merely illustrates the imposition of a theoretically prescriptive analysis onto a decontextualized empirical historical "fact." I suspect that in Fraser's haste to build a large theoretical feminist edifice, she has only increased the locations in which problems can occur. For treating the "social" as an idea without due care to historical context, see Skinner, "Meaning and Understanding in the History of Ideas." Also, for a more recent and broad-ranging defense of the uses and abuses of history, see Skinner, "Reply to My Critics." Also for an alternative, and in my view more historically sensitive, account of the social, see Donzelot, *The Policing of Families.* Also see Riley, who concentrates explicity on the relationship of women to the social, in her *Am I That Name?* (chapter 3). In relation to the last two references, it is not that Fraser is unaware of the scholarship surrounding the social, but it is her claim that such work can be made consistent with her own critical social theory that is being questioned.

41. Fraser, *Unruly Practices,* p. 107.
42. Fraser, "From Irony to Prophecy to Politics," p. 156.
43. Ibid.
44. Ibid., p. 157 (italics in original).
45. Ibid., p. 158 (italics added).
46. Ibid., p. 158.
47. Ibid., p. 159.
48. Fraser, *Unruly Practices,* p. 106.
49. Fraser, "From Irony to Prophecy to Politics," p. 157. Fraser does not provide references for such scholarship, but this may be because the article is a pub-

lished version of a conference lecture. Nonetheless, the use of history and empirical "evidence" within her other publications remains questionable: see note 48.

50. See Hacking, "Language, Truth, and Reason."

51. This community of inquirers is by no means a homogenous group, and the very plausibility of a research methodology based on the category of woman is in itself contested; see Riley, *Am I That Name?* Also see the impressive series, edited by Duby and Perot, *A History of Women.* Fraser's more recent attempts with Linda Gordon to co-opt historical research for the feminist cause do not escape the criticisms raised here. See Fraser and Gordon, "A Genealogy of Dependency." Also see Fraser and Gordon, "Reclaiming Social Citizenship: Beyond the Ideology of Contract Versus Charity," in the same volume, for an example of how the same old metanarrative of capitalism and ideology come to undermine any claims to a Foucauldian genealogical method.

52. Such possibilities are what Rorty views as one of the advantages of liberal democratic culture, for Rorty claims his ethnocentric stance is still one that offers "a lot of opportunities for self-criticism and reform." See Rorty's introduction to *Objectivity, Relativism, and Truth,* p. 15, especially footnotes 28 and 29, for direct mention of Fraser.

53. See Fraser and Nicholson, "Social Criticism Without Philosophy." Also see note 47 with regard to the following criticisms of Fraser's approach.

54. Fraser, *Unruly Practices,* p. 6 (italics added).

55. See Fraser, *Unruly Practices,* pp. 161–187.

56. Ibid., p. 181.

57. Ibid. For how such a final account stands in direct contradiction of a pragmatist philosophy, see Fish, "What Makes an Interpretation Acceptable?" pp. 253–266. Such interpretive criteria also recall the methodological criteria of Karl Popper; for why such criteria only inhibit experimentation and progress rather than guarantee it, see Hacking, "Language, Truth, and Reason."

58. Fraser, *Unruly Practices,* p. 182.

59. Ibid.

60. Ibid., p. 181.

61. Ibid., p. 187 (italics added).

62. See Rorty, "Feminism and Pragmatism," p. 126.

63. See Fraser and Nicholson, "Social Criticism Without Philosophy."

64. Fraser, "From Irony to Prophecy to Politics," p. 157 (italics in original).

65. Fraser, *Unruly Practices,* p. 108.

66. Ibid., p. 183.

67. In fact, it is probably fair to say that Fraser does not regard the charge of totalism as in itself negative; however, Fraser's position has altered slightly since she promoted that the practices of "feminisms" (plural) in her article with Linda Nicholson, "Social Criticism Without Philosophy," and more recently in "Pragmatism, Feminism, and the Linguistic Turn," she has taken to criticizing other feminists (in this particular instance Judith Butler—see pp.163–164) for not providing the theoretical equipment necessary to "conceptualise the social totality." And Fraser now also makes the further claim that what she currently labels her neopragmatist approach can "encompass the full range of processes by which the sociocultural meanings of gender are constructed and contested" (p. 158). Once again, however, she also reveals exactly why feminism needs such an all-encompassing theory, for "it would maximize our ability to contest the current gender hegemony and to build a feminist counter hegemony" (p. 158). Clearly, Fraser's neopragmatism still

requires a Gramscian conception of the political to provide the foundations for her feminist "politics." As such, Fraser's approach remains pragmatic only in an every-day sense, one that determines her reading of other feminist theorists insofar as she approaches each text already knowing what it is that feminists need. In this respect I would firmly support Butler's call "For a Careful Reading."

68. Fraser is in some ways very upfront about her Marxist roots; see *Unruly Practices*, p. 2.

69. See Rorty's "Movements and Campaigns," in *Dissent* (winter 1995), pp. 55–60; and his later dispute with Steven Lukes in the following issue (spring 1995), pp. 263–265, for a good discussion of why the left wing feels a "political" require-ment for movements rather than campaigns.

70. See Fraser, *Unruly Practices,* especially footnote 26, p. 160, for how Fraser's "JAT," a juridical-administrative-therapeutic state apparatus, relates to an Althusserian Ideological State Apparatus (ISA) and how all this sociological struc-turalism relates to a particular reading of Foucault, one that Rorty explicitly con-tests in "Moral Identity and Private Autonomy: The Case of Foucault" in his *Essays on Heidegger and Others.* See especially p. 198 for reference to Fraser.

71. See Rorty, "The End of Leninism and History as a Comic Frame," p. 225. This idea is what Rorty considers to be Stanley Fish's antifoundationalist theory hope, the very position with which he has labeled Nancy Fraser in the past; see Rorty, "Pragmatism and Feminism," notes 15 and 17, pp. 142–143; and Fish, *Doing What Comes Naturally,* pp. 322–323.

72. Rorty, "Feminism and Pragmatism," p. 146.

73. Ibid., p. 139.

74. Ibid.

75. Ibid., p. 128.

76. Ibid.

77. Ibid.

78. Sellars, "Empiricism and the Philosophy of Mind," p. 170 in Sellars, *Science, Perception, and Reality.*

79. Hacking, "Five Parables," p. 109. I would like to thank Quentin Skinner for directing me toward this particular article; naturally, however, the fruits or fail-ings of its subsequent interpretation are my own responsibility. For a similar use of Hacking's insights for the discipline of anthropology, see Rabinow, "Representa-tions Are Social Facts," p. 237.

80. For an excellent introduction to the political role of histories of the present, upon which my own perspective is based, see Burchell, Gordon, and Miller, *The Foucault Effect;* and Barry, Osborne, and Rose, *Foucault and Political Reason.*

81. See Hacking, *The Emergence of Probability* and *The Taming of Chance.*

82. Hacking, "How Should We Do the History of Statistics?" p. 194.

83. Hacking, "Five Parables," p. 122.

84. See footnote 22 on p. 144 of Rorty's "Feminism and Pragmatism"; and Rorty's "The Contingency of Selfhood" in *Contingency, Irony, and Solidarity,* as examples of this tension.

85. Cardinal, *The Words to Say It.*

86. Cardinal, *In Other Words,* p. 41.

87. See Rose, *The Psychological Complex: Psychology, Politics, and Society in England 1869–1939;* Rose, *Governing the Soul: The Shaping of the Private Self;* and Rose, *Inventing Ourselves: Psychology, Power, and Personhood.* For a clear example of Hacking's similar methodological approach as well as a revealing over-

lap in their research interests, see Hacking, *Rewriting the Soul: Multiple Personality and the Sciences of Memory.*

88. In this regard, while Cardinal may represent the "positivity" within the freedom of "psy," we would do well to remember the negativity that such sciences also create. See Kate Millett's moving account of her experience of psychiatric treatment—treatment that, possibly unlike in America or France, is still very much an unpleasant reality within British medical institutions. See *The Loony Bin Trip.* The facts that Millett was a high-profile feminist before she was put into psychiatric care (see Millett's best seller, *Sexual Politics*), and that Cardinal only became a feminist after her literary treatment of psychoanalysis may also remind readers of the manner in which feminists are very much situated within the relations of power that our contemporary practices of freedom entail—thus the need to try and conceptualize such freedom in a more politically sophisticated manner.

89. Rose, "Assembling the Modern Self," pp. 241–242.

90. Rose, "Towards a Critical Sociology of Freedom," p. 3.

91. As an example of the type of conflict to which I refer, consider the struggle of Mexico's Mayan Indians as they confront the internationally sanctioned neoliberal reform of the PRI government. In this regard, see Higgins, "Lessons from the Indigenous."

92. See Escobar, *The Making and Unmaking of the Third World;* and Higgins, "Non-governmental Organisations."

93. Sylvester, *Feminist Theory and International Relations in a Postmodern Era.*

94. Nietzsche, *Untimely Meditations.*

95. Rorty, "Feminism and Pragmatism," p. 129.

8

Typologies Toward an Unchained Medley: Against the Gentrification of Discourse in International Relations

Stephen Chan

FIRST, A STORY

We have lost storytelling. Georges Bataille used stories, with a *récit*, to discuss the pathologies of fetish and death—and sex—long before Michel Foucault came to prominence.[1] The possibility of confessional fiction and art criticism as philosophy was offered by Walter Benjamin.[2] The aphoristic koan-like writings of Émile Cioran suggest also that continental philosophy still has much to teach us about narratives of truth.[3] In this first paragraph, however, I cite the example of M. Horkheimer and T. Adorno's retelling of the tale of Odysseus and their contention that, in the history of western literature, he was the first to realize his subjectivity.[4] For many years, inspired by this, I have sought to write about the earlier, nonwestern but Judaic figure Job and the temptations of subjectivity that came his way before he recanted the effort and God reestablished, in a great poetics of His Own Justification, His sole occupancy of subjectivity. If Job came close—was tempted by Satan to come close—but failed, how clearly or easily did Odysseus do it? Was the first subjectivity a bare breath away from the contingencies of the Olympian gods? I wonder if I might tell this tale in my own way, because I differ somewhat with Horkheimer and Adorno's reading; but I do agree with its conclusion. This is not in itself a story. It is, at least, *about* a story.

First, however, a note on stories as they are found. In the Odyssey, women have a found quality; that is, they differ not at all from the women of Greek life. Not only have they no subjectivity in the story, but they had no emancipation in life. This is not meant to validate that. Even under such conditions, however, it did not mean that men as a certain universal archetype—in a hierarchical universe under the gods—had subjectivity either. Odysseus was certainly an ideal type. That anybody, man or woman, could achieve uncontingent subjectivity was an ideal. This ideal, as I try to relate later, may be no less contingent in the third world of othernesses today. It is against an interpretation of *them* through the lenses only of our modernity and comfort that this chapter protests.

When the Greek myths and legends come down to us, they are full of subjectivities we comprehend—that is, they come to us in interpretation. Thus, when Hamlet muses, "What is Hecuba to us?" he is not reflecting on the power of Hecuba's grief and capacity for grief but on the Player King's interpretation of Hecuba. It is this that inspires Hamlet to pose his own self-interrogating questions about whether *he* should *be*, or not. And, of course, *what* he should be. This is Hamlet coming to himself as subject. Similarly, it is Ted Hughes's amazing rewriting of Medea that finally allows us to understand her full subjectivity of rage and revenge. Jason may have avoided death at the skeletal hands of the dragon's-teeth-warriors, but his captured bride, Medea, ensured he did not avoid desolation afterwards. But Hughes does what Euripides and Sophocles could not do. In their original dramas, the heroes and heroines did not have anything but a highly contingent subjectivity. They could not, for instance, ask Hamlet's question. Why could they not?

They could not because of the extraordinary, and only sometimes balancing, presence of moral self-direction and luck. You had to be lucky to live your own moral life because you could be structured by the gods to do otherwise.[5] Your agency was contingent. The Greeks used the term *harmatia* to depict the tragic flaw of the hero who unknowingly, and often with the best intentions, commits the crime that will lead to his eventual and terrible downfall—even if he has otherwise lived his life in full justice and love. Thus, Oedipus married his own mother and was sent blind into the slaughterhouse of the gods.

This is not fair. We feel it is only fair that we should be allowed a clean run with our subjectivity. Agency has, even if bounded by communitarian concerns, a normative value. What, however, could you do in the face of the gods measuring out luck? Other cultures that have similar senses of luck tell militating stories of rivalries among the gods. Thus, in the Viking or Norse mythology, Loki injects an ingredient that acts against determinism, and that is trickery. In west African religions, the role of the trickster, very like Loki, is of great importance.[6] In Greek mythology, it was not so much trickery as plain deceit. Thus, Hera often sought to deceive her husband, Zeus, in order to favor her preferred heroes on earth. But this meant that those heroes had merely multiplied upon them the contingencies of their free subjectivity—not merely Another's determination, but the arbitration of that determination by Still Another's deceit.

This is what makes the retelling of Odysseus so interesting. If he achieves his subjectivity, he does so against odds that *we* can scarcely imagine but that were certainly imagined long ago. He didn't just sail a lot of sea.

All this is certainly not technological, rational, secular, or in keeping with the received tradition of the Enlightenment. However, luck is a key ingredient in almost all pretechnological-era fables and tales. For us, we have constructed via technology a countervailing power to the gods—an instrumentality for own subjectivities. Before, you were lucky or not. There was another key ingredient in those earlier fables and tales: that of desire. "I wish" stands as a defiance of "you are fated." However, and this is where *harmatia* returns, you could not be sure of wishing, of desiring, in full knowledge of the consequences. Oedipus desired a woman but did not know she was his mother.

This was what, importantly, separated humanity from the gods. One of the powers of the gods was their ability to see consequence in advance and to desire in the knowledge of consequence. Zeus, in the guise of a swan (and you do not need Yeats's poem to recognize the full subjectivity of Zeus here), rapes Leda, who gives birth to Helen, who in her youthful beauty occasions without her foreknowledge the sack of Troy. And in Troy, all the resplendent works of architects and artists, and the recital stands and podiums for poets, were brought crashing down. The high-towered city saved them not at all. But Zeus knew when he impregnated Leda, and no unconscious tragic irony redounded upon him.

It is in the face of all this that Odysseus commences his odyssey. This is, if we use the term, the first intellectual odyssey. Not that Odysseus was an intellectual—Homer describes him merely as cunning. But what he accomplishes allows us our sense of intellectual freedom. But he had to work and sweat for it. This is explicit in the prologue to the book: "Tell us about the man who labored to bring home his storm-lashed ships." Even so, his own men unwittingly offend the sungod and, despite all the efforts of their captain, never reach home with him. He is left ashore—alone, an individual.

When Odysseus finally comes into his own kingdom—that is, when he realizes (in this order) himself at home, his son, his wife, his home itself, his kingdom—he has gathered together all of the constituents of himself as a returned person and king. But he is different from when he left twenty years earlier. Even his own son, Telemachus, does not recognize him at first; nor does his wife, Penelope. Was it just his artful disguise? Or had he changed from a determined being to a free being?

By his suffering he redeemed his key role in the sack of Troy. He also redeemed himself as a subject. We hope, at the end of the book, he lives happily ever after. We are even happy Job lives happily ever after, even though he finally forsook the chance to be a subject. To be happy on his own terms, just plain happy, at home—not gifted by luck, not determined anymore by the gods, not paying off debts incurred by his part in somebody else's dream of the future—this was the subjectivity he achieved. It took a lot to be a freely chosen domestic person. We might remember this when we freely speak of agency and individual freedom. This casual assumption of its possibility was once almost unspeakable, and this is what makes Homer great: that he did speak it.

What does this mean for us—this use of the style of Bataille, giving the story before the *récit*? It means that in Other stories, the transactions of contingency are important. Not everyone has been able to escape it. Certainly in poverty and premodernity, not everyone has the technology to contemplate escape; and, as in the case related later by Partha Dasgupta, even if gifted with technology the price of acceptance may mean in fact a severe diminution of subjectivity. Second, it means that the stories of the transactions of contingency are not well known to us. We barely know our own. How many readers had to scramble for their copies of Greek myths? Third, it means the stories may have as their premises—never mind within the developing story lines—assumptions, imaginations, and reasonings that are unknown to us or that cannot be negotiated by our technologies or by technology and modernity alone.

They can be *interpreted* by us, just as they were to Hamlet or are by Hughes. But just what is Hecuba to us if she becomes so different to what she was? What, more precisely, is for us today the equivalent of the Trojan women—those who are dispossessed, whose families are slaughtered, whose homeland is burned, and who are about to end their lives in slavery? In the Odyssey, Helen is restored to Menalaeus after the fall of Troy. When Odysseus's son, Telemachus, comes to visit them, seeking news of his father, Helen has rewritten her history so that she might be favorably inter-preted by Telemachus and the court of Menalaeus. But this was not Helen any more than that simulacrum and succubus Helen that Mephistopheles brought to Faustus. No, there is some importance in seeing things as they are, without the mediations of *our* subjectivities and interpretations. It is not we who should pretend to be the gods of the world.

But, here, a final word. For many years, Odysseus was imprisoned on the island of the goddess Calypso. Surrounded by sea, he could not escape. More to the point, the god of the sea, Poseidon, had fought for the Trojans and hated Odysseus for his part in the downfall of his favorite people and city. He was determined that Odysseus should never escape. But one day, Poseidon accepts an invitation to a banquet hosted by the Ethiopians. While he is away, in Ethiopia, Odysseus escapes. In the rest of the story, we forget the Ethiopians. Yet they really permitted the whole thing. Let us not forget the thought of those who—by their minerals, reductions to slavery, elaborations into our empires, and provision of their marketplaces and their treasuries for the profits of our banks—permit our modernity, the luxury in armchairs of our discourse. Let us not forget the thoughtful Ethiopians.

WHO NEEDS NAVIES AND
GUN EMPLACEMENTS ANYMORE?
THE EMPIRE OF ARMCHAIRS AND WORD PROCESSORS

J'accuse

It has all become very middle-class: the leafy campus, cocktails at one more conference, and—despite the bureaucratic paraphernalia of regulated universities—the joyful work of theorizing the international in rooms of our own. The production of texts and the reduction of the world to an intertextuality have even led to the cloistered arrogance that a philosophical statement may in itself be emancipatory. We mistake idealisms—in the (translated, summarized, from the) German sense—as labor in the fields of the poor, as redressing the naked refugee, as abolishing the boundaries of the state.

This is not, of course, to shirk the idea of the *Word* and its power, but merely to say that the word is not the world and that in the highly complex relationship between the two, first, there are many renditions of the word and, second, not all these renditions exist within the same discourse. Within the discourses of the world and, in this case, the world of international relations and its theory, there is a hegemonic discourse, and the metaphor of colonialism may be at least loosely applied to its outreach and attempts at settlement. Some renditions of the word are still beyond reach or have complex enough methodologies of construction and expression to be beyond easy appropriation. In an armchair discipline, "easy" had better do it—so the Indians of the Forest may be safe, though marginalized.

There have been conscious, indeed self-conscious, attempts to bring them within. Ironically, attempts to widen the IR conference circuit and the range of its habitués have resulted in the domestication of the new recruits. The Indians of the Forest learn to wear clothes; they adopt the hegemonic theoretical styles. After all, they are invited to come to the conferences of a discipline established on (for them) entirely Other—and seemingly majoritanian Other terms. The point is: They come to us and are socialized; we do not go to them; we do not live and think in the Forest.

We have forgotten stories. Stories are part of the methodologies of those we call Other. (But can it be said in an academic statement—perhaps with the vocabulary that marks our own socialization?) Here, then, is the reason for stories. It is at least a polemic. It may be a hypothesis. It is too grand to be merely a problematique. It is a point of departure. The emancipatory project of contemporary critical theory has its own telos, being both justified by and further propagating a particular philosophical discourse. I am fully conscious here of unfairness to the significant extent that there is in the vast production and histories of texts a diversity of approaches to freedom and its problematization. That to which I am referring is the selective borrowing from these texts that constitutes what might be called a "vulgar" critical theory employed in, for instance, a standardized debate between two convenient oppositional dyads: cosmopolitanism and communitarianism. The mainstream of international relations has not gone much beyond this. In this discourse, room is permitted for an Other but because the philosophy of the Other is an unknown, it is rendered as a presence that is undifferentiated and essentially unchallenging of the western academy's notions of what emancipation involves and assumes. This is a hegemony of defaults, and the default is accomplished by the permission of the other and the simultaneous silence imposed upon it. When attempts are made to render the other as a speaker in terms of discourse it is by means of typecastings, control of the academic media and publication, and assumptions that epistemologies and languages are compatible in their ontological origins. The aim of the chapter is to contest such assumptions and to reveal a telos, perpetuated from armchairs and word processors rather than gun emplacements, but that subjugates rather than emancipates.

The telos and its perpetuation have not been as conscious as all that. Nevertheless, to summarize a starting position for this chapter, we might say that: to problematize, for instance, freedom is to free nobody; to problematize in terms of western schools of thought is not to understand everybody. This constitutes a grand ambivalence for anyone coming to the study of international relations. Having said that, there may be said to be several constituent ambiguities in the intellectual history of international relations (and not just three paradigms or three great debates). To its credit, the discipline has constructed or borrowed debates that deal adequately with the first three. These center around, first, the extent international relations is a social science (a claim most rooted in the behaviorism of both realism and pluralism in the 1960s and 1970s)[7] or a humanity (in the historical conditionality of the English school and in current interests in philosophy). Second, the extent to which international relations is a science in the pure academic sense of *wissenschaft,* or pure knowledge, and the extent to which it is scientific in its applied, particularly predictive[8] sense and policy[9] sense; and, third, the extent to which international relations should be positivistically based, in the realm of the senses and their sense of evidence, and to what extent it should admit to the fragmentation of knowledge, the unreliability of evidence, and that knowledge can only success-fully (and momentarily) deconstruct the real.[10]

These ambiguities have been dealt with by giving their various antago-nisms *methodological* space. Each may therefore contain various method-ologies and these make statements and coexist. The coexistence provides the discipline with its equilibrium, which is simultaneously its politesse. There are three interrelated ambiguities, however, that have only tentative space within the discipline. These are, first, the extent to which knowledge can be truly epistemologically based, or whether ontologies construct mul-tiple epistemologies;[11] second, the extent to which multiple epistemologies and multiple ontologies are reflected in a West versus the rest divide, so that the discipline in its global appreciation is only partial rather than uni-versal—but is nevertheless hegemonic;[12] and third, the extent to which the discipline itself must be seen in terms of a structure-agency problematic[13] in which the structure is more multifaceted than before because the agents are revolting, are bringing great cloves of garlic and clashing spices to all the layers of the English stew, and are seeking to stir themselves into the ingredients at the stew's bottom while the response of the existing ingredi-ents is, at least in part, to turn into stodge. You can have too many method-ologies but, above all, you should not have foreign methodologies—so here's stodge for you all!

The debate and, in particular, methodologies that have been used to settle (not resolve) difficulties represented by the first three ambiguities—and to declare a discipline in their name—are also the socializing agents for those entering the discipline. Those from an Outside, the generalized Other, the inhabitants of the Forest, must forsake the borderlines represented by the last three in order to achieve socialization, status, fame within whatever has been created by the first three.

In this chapter I want to say a few things about how thought in the Forest, short of being socialized, short of being taken into a profession with its variegated but not truly universal discipline, has confronted that brave new enlightened/technologized world that, because it is enlightened and technologized, considers itself the only image of the world (and in which postmodern thinkers deconstruct only the images *their* world has first invented and broadcast; the Gulf War may never have taken place, but hunger and poverty take place). In the process of socialization, the question proposed by western scholars has consistently been lopsided: "How much of ours has been adopted by them?" rather than "How much of theirs has been adopted by us?" The imbalance is global; socialization has been mis-taken as an acceptable normative foundation in international relations.

Is it the development of a series of walled gardens, with ramparts, over which seeds drift but grow in different soils and where plants are pruned into different shapes? Is some of this related to Samuel Huntington's clashing civilizations?[14] Must we, like the ancient Argonauts, pass through these clashing cliffs, striving to be intact, to reach the golden fleece in the land of Colchis and, even then, battle with the Hydra-dragon and her teeth-sown warrior-children? (And what is this Other in the western heritage that pre-existed the Enlightenment? Why does international relations not know Jason?) We resist and repudiate incorporations beyond our disciplinary sense of tolerance.

The outreach of a western/enlightened/technological world has taken place in both space and time. Space we know about from simple maps of who colonized what and what has since gained independence. Time is more problematic in international relations. The retreat from map-based, empirically drawn strategic studies has not led to a sense of time in critical theory. Individuals in international relations who have supposed times and timings remain individuals—able, like R. B. J. Walker, to be singled out from the discipline as a whole. Outside critical theory, Modelski's cycles, even Fred Halliday's more recent feedback loops, do not establish a new paradigm or corrective to paradigms past.[15] We have a simple proposition: Hegemonic ideas do not colonize just like that; and, furthermore, they seek to expand into other geographical and intellectual spaces. This, however, takes time, and over time occur resistances, incorporations, applications, syncretisms, repudiations and attempted repudiations, and contingent amalgamations.

What these constitute are in fact the ingredients for a kind of "hyper-dialectic," in which various and simultaneous theses and antitheses compete with, condition, and compromise one another; and their syntheses are then fed back into an endless process contingent only upon, but not in the first instant determined by, the need for a practical association with and in the world. If merely a practical association with the world arose from this, then there is still a mediating device at least. As Dasgupta argued, what is rational can only be made rational where customs are instrumental or made instrumental for the purpose of rationality.[16] (Sometimes, of course, different rationalities are made.)

Dasgupta gives an example of a priorization of instrumentalities that explained a clash of rationalities:

> There was a village in India from which the women had to walk several miles each day to collect water from the nearest stream. A visiting aid agency saw in this the perfect location for its well-drilling project and established a well within the village itself, thinking it had thus saved the women the vast consumption of time that walking took and the vast labor that carrying water entailed.
>
> The women were very unhappy, and the aid agency was at a loss to comprehend where its rationality had failed and where its grander ambition to make the lives of Third World women easier had failed to find its echo in the satisfaction of these particular village women. The instrumen-

tal application of technology was meant to do this. Finally, the women explained to the agency what was to them, and would have been to anyone living as they lived, perfectly obvious.

First, even though not walking meant more time, it was not more free time. Their menfolk just asked for many other tasks to be performed. In this way, their sense of oppression had been increased, not decreased. Second, in the absence of any agency project being able, by itself, to change the nature of gender hierarchy, what was most important for these women was the space and time to be women (i.e., free, even if briefly, from men), to be in company and solidarity with other women, and to be able to complain together and in perfect, uninterrupted harmony reduce the image of men. The long walk to the river had given them free space and time. The shared labor had given them solidarity. And, even more, this was all they had as social life, as fun. And the aid agency had, at one rational, technologized stroke, removed their tiny and contingent but treasured freedom, discourse, solidarity, and fun—their sense of (temporary) escape, and their sense of sisterhood and social network of confidantes. For all this, labor was a small price to pay. For the agency, the labor was oppressing them. Thus, well-meaning people from a world that no longer labors saw labor as evil, set about reducing this evil, and in so doing ruined the lives of many women *as women*.

What was misunderstood was that in a world of contingencies, not only do contingencies differ from location to location but they are transacted differently.

Nevertheless, there is a project to socialize the complexities of Other thought, disregarding the transactions it makes, as suggested above; and the discipline of international relations is as guilty as any. Here, the project escapes the complexity of methodology, still less methodologies, by a mere insistence upon what is only a reductionism. The discipline needs (to change earlier metaphors) new additions to the wardrobe preshrunk to fit. Here there is, above all, the absence of empathy; to apply the last list to western history we see immediately a Europe where, over a period of two hundred years and still counting, constitutionally codified democracies and sureties of individual rights are resisted by various forms of monarchy and dictatorship. Here there have been clashes of thought—ideologies, to put it simply, but grounded in philosophical or theological systems all the same. What is finally incorporated may be as hybrid as Britain's unwritten constitutional democracy, which is simultaneously an unwritten constitutional monarchy, which has simultaneously an unwritten constitutional exercise of power by the aristocracy. This, meanwhile, with its simultaneously antique and twentieth-century judiciary, must relate, feed into, and be directed by a European Court that assumes that a foundation for rights can be established within written charters. Now, if all this seems seamless now, there have been in Europe, in this century, two world wars and one cold war, an array of neutral powers, and a state-blessed array of money-laundering banks in

Switzerland; there has been one failed League of Nations (based in the same Switzerland) that would not prevent rapine in Other countries such as China and Ethiopia and that could not in the end prevent the quarrel among Enlightenment-descended states within Europe itself that produced, among other things, a holocaust of technological killing of millions.

This is to put it at the level of states. If there were a history of psychological states of mind, then the Freudian and Lacanian separations and mixtures of forebodings, resistances, repudiations, transgressions, and compromises would be more starkly expressed and more readily understood. This is a world, exactly, that is complex and illustrates the complexity that ought to be found in international relations. Still, at the great socializing conferences of the discipline, the Other is assiduously courted to ensure the conversions necessary to propagate a universal discipline with its need for a universal core.

Within the discipline of international relations itself, despite the project of socializing the emergents from the Forest, there is only so much that socialization can accomplish immediately. Scholars are not autonomous from their domestic societies any more than they are no longer autonomous from international societies. If they can be socialized by the latter, they certainly have been by the former. The international relations of Home is perhaps often a little different from the international relations of Away. How may this be at least suggested? In the United Kingdom, there has been a largely unreflective importation of continental critical methodologies and postmodernisms. These methodologies have aided reflectivities but have not themselves often been reflected upon critically. Jürgen Habermas is a touchstone of debate; he may be found incomplete in the debates that center on him, but he is indispensable in debate. This cannot be the case in the Forestlands for a number of illustrative reasons. A postmodernity is ridiculous within premodernities and selective modernities. A Gramscian struggle within culture exists only within the precondition of technologized means by which to permeate culture. A Habermasian condition of ideal speech is possible only after the idea of speech at all is made possible by promoting literacy and taking steps toward the democratic possibility of speaking. The Lacanian formula/injunction that *jouissance* is possible only by first transgressing—breaking the Law and progressing beyond God and Freud—is possible only if, in the mind, the Law is not so embedded as to prevent transgression. It is perhaps impossible in some forms of Islamic discourse. The mind that memorized the Koran by the age of seven will forget neither the feat nor what was memorized.

This becomes a story of exceptionalities against any single universalizing discourse. What it means, however, for international relations is the existence of an internal sociology for international relations as a whole. I have indicated at least four main types for what might, residually, be noted as a discipline.[17]

What I mean here is *not* that this is an international relations that expresses different cultural or Other foundations, but that this is the result of the outreach or project of socialization achieved by the discipline thus far. It is uneven and conditional. What I want to say by this, however, is that there is often in the international relations of Home great unawareness that it has not fully socialized all academics. It has propagated a sociology of conditionalities.

Type A is an IR that, even while written in another language, emulates the mainstream of western IR and political science. It is conscious of its social scientific origins. However, it operates in the context of definite (if not always scrutable) restraining intellectual factors. These factors are derived from indigenous senses of epistemology—which are consciously recognized as deriving from a nonwestern experiential base. Japan is an example of this type.

Type B is an IR that is published by small groupings and that is consciously western in both its theory and methodology. It seeks to present to the West an image of both modernity and intellectual normality. It seeks, however, to disguise (if not conceal) the fact of alternative and challenging systems of thought that, although not having an IR component as such, nevertheless view the global context as being (though not in any reductionist or simplistic manner) theological and eschatological. A sophisticated rendition of western thought thus takes place at least in part because there is not yet a means of rendering indigenous thought in a manner to which western IR might find itself receptive. Iran is an example of this type.

Type C is an IR concerned with its strategic utility. It arises from a large IR community that, with conspicuous individual exceptions, either has no western IR theoretical culture or sees no need for a theoretical culture at all, concerned as it is with strategic and area studies. It contains within itself, however, a normative seed—a wish one day to clarify and properly articulate aspects of a received ethos in national character and international stance as well as to overcome the contradiction between that wider international stance and its immediate regional behavior. India is an example of this type, and for the moment Pakistan and Bangladesh may be seen as variations of it.

Type D is an IR that is aware of western thought and wishes to understand and incorporate it into indigenous academic discourse, but it is unable to abandon or substantially repudiate intellectual traditions and practices that, despite having been refurbished from time to time, have governed scholarship for centuries before either the European Renaissance or Enlightenment. China is an example of this type.

Western IR has had an impact everywhere but not as a total, received discipline. It influences and is influenced by indigenous disciplines and epistemologies. It would be tempting, as shorthand, to label the above types as the 80 percent, the 60 percent, the 40 percent, and the 20 percent types, according to how much western IR was actually made visible. Under the surface, however, the interplay between western and indigenous thought systems is much more conditional, subtle, and shifting than that.

This is to pitch it generously. There are vast areas of the world, and their academies, where there has been no outreach at all and where, for instance, normative thought is, by our standards, extraordinary and arcane. Here, we are still in a form of typology that is vastly generalized and still working out of a realism in that it assumes nations that affiliate to themselves cultures—if not states that affiliate to themselves what they would certainly like to know as culture-bearing nations. There are well-worn lines of justification here; but, here at least, in the following list of international normalities—considerably beyond Kant and Hegel and Frankfurt—are glimpses of if not a magical realism (however dilute) for international relations, then syncretic realisms. There are again several "worlds" of thought here, even if for the moment it is state-bound thought. One world is where historical and philosophical "stories" are generalized, if not re-created, to underpin regimes that are to an extent authoritarian but at the same time beneficent: countries like Kaunda's Zambia.[18] We might, on the other hand, consider the world of text-based normativities—which may be given interpretation on literal and exegetic grounds: various Islamic countries.[19] Other possibilities include the world that is text-based but given interpretation on a sectarian, even minor sectarian, basis: countries like Libya with its almost comprehensively unremarked Sanusi inheritance.[20]

We move away from realisms, not in the sense that the western discipline sought to do this—fixated on legal pluralisms and institutions and forms of liberalism—but in the sense that, since a great many nonwestern states are not democratic, illegal organizations have normative agendas as at least part of their projects. Thus, many Triad groups volunteered to smuggle dissidents out of China in the post-Tienanmen months and did so both successfully and without charge. Although this moves away from the project of this essay, it illustrates how much international relations must lose—not only of its claims to instant universality but also of its gentrification.

There are, within Other thoughts, dissidents. If the Forest is an outland to the West, there are outlaws within the Forest itself. Bandit kings and bandit queens interrogate the discourse of the wardens at knifepoint. There is violence and mayhem in the Forest. Each outlaw, like Toshiro Mifune's in *Roshamon*, has a different version of events, a different ethic, a different normative vision.

What then is to be done? The first thing is that we must not declare an emancipatory theory as if we had a telos. Who emancipates whom? We have a lot to learn about struggles toward freedom by those who continue to fight. The second is not to view the struggles of others as if they were Others but to link their work and thought to our own—without the mere subsuming of their work into the categories of our discourse, with its socializations and gentrifications. Time, yes, to suspend the intertextual song and dance of abstracted voyeurs (how must we seem to *their* anthropologists?). Without beads and trinkets and condescensions, it is time to go into the Forest. For many years our songs and theirs may not chime easily. But why not suspend this wretched Germanic neatness? Who said history was neat to the point of fastidiousness? Around a latetime fire, those who find that their Other is just another are sitting, clearing their throats for world music—an unchained medley.

NOTES

Much of this chapter has been an effort to give a running order, a heuristic coherence to lists and distinctions that were in part assembled without coherence in *Towards a Multicultural Roshamon Paradigm in International Relations* (Tampere, Finland: Tampere Peace Research Institute, 1996); and to others that have been produced since then. The latter will almost certainly (exasperatingly) be collected into a second *Roshamon* volume.

1. It was Susan Sontag, *Styles of Radical Will,* who, in the early 1960s in a paper entitled "The Pornographic Imagination," identified not only the uses of story by Bataille but the possibilities of very unusual stories indeed.

2. See "One-Way Street," in Benjamin, *Selected Writings.*

3. See Sontag, *Styles of Radical Will,* on Cioran. Unfortunately, some recent translations of his work do not do full justice to his literary style.

4. We have lost storytelling in late-twentieth-century critical theory. For an example of how it was done, see Horkheimer and Adorno, *Dialectic of Enlightenment,* where they retell the tale of Odysseus and how difficult it was for him to realize his subjectivity.

5. The finest study for this is Nussbaum, *The Fragility of Goodness.*

6. Pelton, *The Trickster in West Africa.*

7. The social scientific impulse is still with a large segment of international relations. See Webb, *An Introduction to Problems in the Philosophy of Social Sciences.*

8. Even though he now posits this as useful rather than definitive, see Nicholson, *Rationality and the Analysis of International Conflict.*

9. This was always true of strategic studies but remains so with a great deal of work on mediation and peace and conflict studies. See, for example, the final chapters in Higgott and Richardson, *International Relations.*

10. The latest outing here is Smith, Booth, and Zalewski, *International Theory: Positivism and Beyond.*

11. Here we are in minority territory; but see Der Derian, "The Value of Security."

12. And here the output is *very* small. For a suggestive cameo, see Alker, Biersteker, and Inoguchi, "From Imperial Power Balancing to People's Wars." For a largely unsuccessful effort, see Mazrui, *Cultural Forces in World Politics.*

13. This is, of course, a play on Jabri's concerns in *Discourses on Violence.* I apply the problematic to the discipline; Jabri applies it very persuasively to its study of war.

14. For an exchange, "splenetic" according to Huntington, between Huntingdon and myself, see Huntington, "The Clash of Civilizations."

15. Modelski's work is well known. I have, however, given a temporal as well as spatial reading to Halliday's "feedback loop," in his work on revolutions in the international system: *Rethinking International Relations,* chapter 6.

16. Dasgupta, *An Inquiry into Well-Being and Destitution.*

17. This list repeats a conclusion from my article (Chan, "Cultural and Linguistic Reductionism"), reprinted in *Roshamon,* but it relies upon a collaborative research with seven scholars from China, Japan, Iran, Pakistan, and Bangladesh. For their names, see *Roshamon,* p. 141.

18. For a deconstruction of Kaunda's "historically derived" philosophy, see Chan, *Kaunda and Southern Africa,* especially chapter 5.

19. An excellent but largely unremarked collection is the special *Islam and Politics* issue of *Third World Quarterly* 10, no. 2 (1988). For a brief though illuminating note on Islamic scriptural method, see Goddard, *Christians and Muslims,* pp. 40–44. For an example of this in action, see Sherif, *A Guide to the Contents of the Qur'an.*

20. For a most sensitive treatment, see Davis, *Libyan Politics,* especially chapters 4 and 5.

9

Conclusion

Vivienne Jabri & Eleanor O'Gorman

The chapters in this book concentrate on the implications of difference and the construction of subjectivity for feminist theory and praxis. We see here an engagement with and reflections on the tensions that arise in any discourse with normative and praxiological content that seeks to take difference into account. The challenge of difference, and specifically cultural difference, brings into sharp focus the universalizing assumptions of modernist thought and its exclusionist implications. It could be said that nowhere are these implications more blatantly apparent than in the discipline of international relations, where a number of constructed universalisms have denied difference a space within the discipline's conceptual schema. Whether such difference is based on culture, class, gender, sexuality, or any other mode of identification, the discipline has by and large ignored consideration of these, concentrating instead on foundations that seek to universalize and simplify and, with the dominance of neorealism, to reduce the complexity of human interaction to the assumed imperatives of the anarchic international system.

Dominant approaches in international relations owe their hegemony of the discipline to a claim for systematic and systemic explanations of global politics, largely defined as relations between states. Such claims are premised upon a certain assertion of inclusiveness where this is defined in terms of the unquestioned globalization of the Westphalian legacy and its attendant constructs, namely, sovereignty and territoriality. Questions of difference do not emerge here, and if they do, then the point of departure is differential power and its ramifications for balances and the emergence of hegemonic orders that determine state interaction. Where difference is differently defined—where we bring into the remit of the discipline such complexities as subjectivity, moral agency, gender, sexuality, race, and that most troublesome of constructs, culture—then such concerns are by and large challenged as belonging elsewhere, as being the purview of disciplines more concerned with domestic politics than with that special realm, international politics.

We have the option of, as Roland Bleiker suggests, "forgetting IR theory,"[1] simply disengaging from discourses that so seek to reduce the human condition to interstate balances. Such a strategy would imply a movement away from a continual effort at deconstructions of discipline-defining texts—those paragons of realism and its latter-day progenies, including neorealism and neoinstitutionalism. As Bleiker points out, "By articulating critique in relation to arguments advanced by orthodox IR theory, the impact of critical voices remains confined within the larger discursive boundaries that were established through the initial framing of debates."[2] A move out of such confinement would entail a process of "forgetting the object of critique," thereby enabling readings of global politics from a number of hitherto unconsidered or little-considered genres and perspectives.

A book devoted to feminism and the challenge of difference may easily be located in the ghetto, relegated to an increasingly widening margin, both included and excluded at one and the same time. The gesture fulfilled, ideas contained here remain on the outside of any core engagements in the discipline—the core being constituted around those reified concerns with state, the interstate, the sovereign, the international institution, the rules and norms of diplomatic behavior. These are the givens, the unquestioned elements of a baseline upon which the discipline's identity is built. These are the givens impugned whenever attempts are made to incorporate into the hallowed space that is the core of the discipline—those elements that are at the core of the human condition, such as identity, gendered social relations, discrimination based on race or sexuality, or the multitude of other exclusionary practices faced by individuals and communities alike. Rather than being acknowledged as constitutive of and emergent through the discursive and institutional continuities that are the state, sovereignty, and global relations, these elements are deemed to be added extras, included in edited texts as the odd (and often last) chapter or in theory courses as the odd (and again last) lecture.

We may therefore adopt a strategy of "forgetting" orthodoxy in IR theory and simply pursue our interest in expanding the agenda of the discipline, for this alone highlights its exclusions. There is no attempt implicated in such a strategy for seeking converts or for constructing another reified discourse. This is rather a reflexive attitude that occupies a form of interstitial space, one that recognizes its emergence from the discursive practices of the discipline but that is also highly aware of its alterity, its moment of difference. The ideas contained in a text such as this are not solely of interest to feminists or critical social theorists, but they touch at what we see to be of core importance in international relations, with inquiry into such themes as the constitution of moral agency, the move beyond easy dichotomies exemplified by cosmopolitanism and communitarianism, the implications of care as an ethical moment, inquiry into the notion of everyday resistance, the construction of identity and the aesthetic ethics of self-understanding, the consequences of development practices that pitch the general against the local, and, finally, how we in the affluent West construct the other through negation. These are themes that are related by a shared interest in difference, specifically cultural difference, its constitution, and its implications for the normative and praxiological content of international relations thought in general and feminist approaches in particular.[3]

This book is an engagement with feminism and the challenge of cultural difference. There is an explicit normative content in a discourse that takes as given that ethics, gender, and culture matter in international relations and the texts we produce about the international. These categories or constructs are in themselves not taken as given, however, but are recognized as being framed around ontological complexities that may not be reduced to rarefied or even reified simplifications. There is also the related assumption that political identity, or the question of how we think "the political," may not be confined to the state or global politics to the interstate. The discourse of sovereignty has so limited the political imagination that to think of the multiple sites of political presence, as the chapters in this collection do, is clearly to challenge the naturalization of the state as the only site of political affiliation, identity, or moral obligation.

The achievement of critical thought in international relations is that we may no longer take the state, sovereignty, or bounded community for granted. Nor can we base our theories of the international on an orthodoxy built upon dualisms of the domestic versus the international, the private as opposed to the public sphere, the universal versus the particular, the inside pitched against an alien other. The greatest challenge of critical thought, however, is also one that stems from precisely such reflection on the givens of social and political life, for, if the juxtaposition of sovereignty and political identity is questioned, the immediate imperative seems to call for alternative forms of political expression, a form of transformation of the notion of political community that transcends exclusionist practices and the institutions from which such practices emerge. But there are no blueprints contained here, nor is there a universal emancipatory project. What there is, however, is reflection on the challenge of difference in a discourse such as feminism that has a historically self-declared normative content. As Andrew Linklater has recently pointed out, "Questions about the relationship between moral universals and cultural difference have a central place in contemporary debates in international relations theory."[4] But how do we think of or conceptualize difference; how is difference manifest in the situated lived experience of the individual; and how do our discourses on difference constitute the exclusionist practices we seek to transform?

These are questions that have manifest importance in the theories of international relations and the practices of inclusion and exclusion that take place in global politics. While orthodox approaches in the discipline have ignored questions of cultural difference, the linguistic turn in the broader social sciences and humanities, as well as critical international relations, have recognized the place of language and interpretation in social interaction and the epistemologies and ontologies that underpin social and political thought. The linguistic turn also marked a move away from positivism and its core assumptions, primary among which are the correspondence theory of truth and the dualism of fact and value. We could no longer conceive of theory and the language contained therein as an unproblematic "mirror of nature," to use Rorty's term, nor could we utilize linguistic categories as somehow representational of a pregiven reality. Just as gender could not be conceived in essentialist or biological terms but as social construct, so too the term *culture* or *cultural difference* could not be reduced to any firm boundaries or authentic origins.

With the globalization of all aspects of social relations comes a sharpened focus on culture and cultural difference. There is, however, a sense in which culture, like the state, is taken as ontologically unproblematic, a form of primitive bounded community aspiring toward the greater heights of abstract statehood/sovereignty. One consequence of this is a discourse that utilizes culture in terms that have predominated thought in international relations, namely, the inevitability of confrontation and the assertion of the requirement for balances and hegemonic systems. This form of reductionism is evident in Samuel Huntington's recent evocation of a "clash of civilisations,"[5] where "civilisation" is defined in monolithic and essentialist terms, where any differences that exist within each category are denied a presence in a system of confrontation that is reminiscent of a neorealist conception of the interstate system. Those deemed "other" in civilizational terms come to constitute a threat against a monolithic West, itself conceived as coherent, and certain of its boundaries and achievements. This form of exclusionist discourse is also present in the triumphalist terms in which Francis Fukuyama proclaims the "end of history" as the moment when the liberal West comes to constitute the model according to which others may be judged.[6]

What the chapters in this collection show is that culture, like gender, matters in international relations but that both are constructs that defy easy reductions and stable definitions. The exclusionist discourses presented by Huntington and Fukuyama are replicated in the empiricist literature, which treats both gender and culture as "independent variables." These remain unproblematized, given categories that contain an essential core, such as biological difference, or clearly ascribed cultural markers, such as color, dress code, religious affiliation, or geographic origin. Such representations again assume a norm, usually inscribed as western man, against whom all others may be judged. If there are no easy reductions and definitions, how then do we justify the use of constructs such as "women" and "culture" in a collection of essays that is precisely geared to unravel and reflect upon the impact of difference on the theory and politics of feminist international relations?

As the chapters here make all too clear, there is no assumption of a singular category named "woman," predefined or transcendent. The use of the plural term immediately points to the view that gender is socially constructed and is implicated in the identification of individuals in different social settings. The various modes of identification are, however, manifested differently across time and space, and it is this difference that distinguishes and determines the lived experiences of women in contingent social matrices. Practices and modes of signification that construct gender are in themselves interlaced with complex systems of meaning that define and constitute particular societies. This is the challenge that has for long faced feminist discourse as a normative project.

The challenge of difference, and specifically cultural difference, brings into sharp focus the universalizing assumptions of modernist thought and their exclusionist implications. Feminism as a political project emerges from the modernist tradition and in so doing comes into direct confrontation with questions related to subjectivity and difference. Rooted in eighteenth-century Enlightenment thought, the modernist vision of ethics and political transformation assumes a universal ontology based on reason and autonomy, where the agent of social change is the individual unencumbered by group membership and capable of deliberative reasoning on social norms and institutions. It is precisely this vision that early feminist thought, from Mary Wollstonecraft through the suffrage movement and the women's movement of the 1960s, adopted as its aspiration. The critique of social forces that subjugate women—that confine them within oppressive, unequal, and exploitative relations—is here combined with the political aim of emancipation based on equality between women and men. That "one is not born a woman, but, rather, becomes one,"[7] as Simone de Beauvoir so elegantly phrased the emergence of gendered relations, underpins the cry for equality, for the transformation of social relations toward justice, equality, and free participation within the public sphere. If femininity and masculinity are societal constructs, a transformative agenda would encompass the delegitimation of such constructs to build equality between the sexes.

The main focus here is gender difference, and the aim of a feminist transformative project is the elimination of such difference. As Nancy Fraser
points out:

> The political task was thus clear: the goal of feminism was to throw off
> the shackles of "difference" and establish equality, bringing women and
> men under common measure. To be sure liberal feminists, radical femi-
> nists, and socialist feminists might dispute how best to achieve this goal,
> but they nevertheless shared a common vision of gender equity, which
> involved minimising gender difference.[8]

Contained within this distinctly modernist vision is the view that women
across the signifying divides of culture and society share a common
agenda, irrespective of differences that define the lived experience of
women. The aspiration of this vision is global in orientation, the implication being that we could form judgments of the lived experience of women
elsewhere and campaign toward intervention in order to achieve equality
where oppressive social and cultural practices are apparent. There is here a
certain cosmopolitanism based on a discourse of universal rights, of the
right to intervention where such rights are violated, and a political mobilization process that is truly global in scope and whose targets are not only
governments and international institutions but women themselves.

As Kimberly Hutchings shows in her chapter, this powerful feminist
vision has come under increasing scrutiny and reflection within the domain
of feminist ethics. Seyla Benhabib's critique of the Kantian project precisely seeks to move the frame from the "generalized other," which is the
basis of the cosmopolitan project in feminism, to the so-called concrete
other, where self and other come to be recognized in their situatedness in
time and place. The form of situatedness that has preoccupied feminist
ethics is predominantly related to gender difference and the celebration of
such difference in place of its denial. Rooted in early-twentieth-century
campaigns against war, this version of feminism found its place within
feminist discourse in the late 1970s with the writings of Mary Daly and
Adrienne Rich.[9] What has come to be known as "cultural feminism" has a
clear epistemological, ontological, and ethical message that is at one and
the same time a wholesale critique of what is seen as the masculinist discourse of Enlightenment reason and a celebration of attributes associated
with women. The ontology that underpins this approach is homogeneous,
unproblematized, and ahistorical woman; and it is this ontology that frames
the epistemology of "standpoint feminism," which takes the view that
knowledge must be grounded in women's lived experience.[10] The ethical
position related to this is a belief in woman's peaceful nature emergent
from her role as nurturer, a position prominent among women peace
activists in the 1980s and underlying the "care perspective" advocated by

Carol Gilligan.[11] The autonomous self of Kantian reason is here replaced with the "relational self."

In seeking to develop a nonexclusionist mode of ethics in an international context, Benhabib's efforts at concretizing Habermasian discourse ethics through taking account of the situated self comes under interrogation in Hutchings's chapter. What emerges from this interrogation is a critique of the search for moral certitude based on foundations that remain problematic in any discourse that seeks to move beyond exclusionist assumptions. What Hutchings seeks, through her use of Rortian phenomenology, is a move away from the epistemological grounding of moral claims, a grounding that must remain insecure since "there are no guarantees of the validity of moral judgments that are discoverable."

Rather than asking how a universalist ethical project can be reconciled with difference, the view that emerges from Hutchings's chapter is that we must look to how different social settings produce and come to constitute difference in moral expression. It is crucial, however, that we do not essentialize culture but see culture as a site upon which a plurality of subjectivities emerge through the self-understanding of the creative self. This is a position in Vivienne Jabri's chapter that highlights the implications for normative discourses in international relations, including feminism, of the view that to account for the complexities of subjectivity is to recognize "the multiple narratives that constitute the self." Arguing for a feminism of dissent, Jabri posits creativity and critique as the sites through which the self, as ethical subject, engages with a performative transformation and refiguration of the self's relations to an established social order and its constitutive structures of signification/domination.

International relations theory, because of the contributions of feminist and other critical perspectives, is having to reflect on its situatedness in time and place. There is a tendency, as indicated above, to see the West as the baseline of all epistemologies and ontologies and to inscribe culture as a signifier applicable to the so-called nonwestern. A move out of such easy dichotomies requires precisely a problematization of subjectivity, so that both self and other are equally rendered sites of inscription and signification. Such a move allows for a recognition of difference as constituted around dominant modes of representation of the "other," but as also being the site through which creativity emerges and dissent is made manifest.[12]

The problematization of subjectivity and its implications for a feminist praxis is also a theme that is taken up by Nalini Persram and Eleanor O'Gorman. A number of issues emerge from both chapters that have direct bearing not only for international relations generally but for feminism's account of epistemology. Where Persram points to the complexities of subjectivity through her interrogation of Spivak's critique of subaltern studies,

O'Gorman highlights the complexities of the resistant or revolutionary subject. A reading through Persram's chapter points to a highly important, but little-developed, question in international relations thought, which is the question of how the excluded come to acquire voice and how our efforts to construct discourses around the marginalized come to constitute the very exclusionist practices we wish to transform.

O'Gorman's chapter similarly opens out an agenda for international relations thought centered on the question of the revolutionary subject. Unlike orthodox approaches to this theme, exemplified in international relations by the dominant voice of theorists such as Theda Skocpol, O'Gorman points to the possibility of local and everyday forms of resistance. Traditionally in international relations thought, the idea of change and resistence is related to the state as agent, or to class and state, if more sociological approaches considered in the literature of the discipline are taken into account. What is significant in O'Gorman's reading of resistance, specifically for international relations, is not only a questioning of what constitutes the revolutionary subject but also the idea that such subjectivity is tied into and constituted by the everyday and the local—locations that remain undertheorized in international relations.

The critical turn in international relations has been focused primarily on epistemological and ontological questions. There is, as Neufeld suggests, a concern with reflexivity, with how our theories and our understandings of the world construct the world that we know and that we make the remit of our discipline.[13] Theory is implicated, but the realm of practice stretches beyond the hallowed portals of academic international relations. Sarah White's reflections on development policy are not only of relevance in highlighting the essentializing implications of development policies but point to the importance for international relations of reflecting on the relationship between theoretical discourse and the practices that emerge from established official and nonofficial institutions.

That the western conception of freedom and subjectivity cannot be taken as the paradigmatic model upon which other societies may build is a theme that is strongly reflected upon in the last two chapters of this collection. Where Nicholas Higgins concentrates on the challenge to western liberalism from feminist discourse as the West's internal other, Stephen Chan provides a critique of the form of cultural triumphalism discussed above. Higgins's "Supposing Truth to Be a Woman" directly explores the epistemological consequences for international relations of the inclusion of a multiplicity of meanings and inscriptions associated with the feminist critique, arguing for a philosophical pragmatism that is both reflexive and inclusive. Through an intricately explored dialogue between the liberal pragmatism of Richard Rorty's and Nancy Fraser's self-proclaimed socialist pragmatism, Higgins provides a dialogical narrative that problematizes the subject of western thought; but it is in itself a critique of epistemologies—including those within feminism—that assume singular hegemonic representations.

Chan has long been a prominant voice in the discipline, calling for the inclusion of other voices. In this collection, he points to the problems associated with mere gestures. Inclusion for Chan does not mean simply the addition of an "other" named nonwestern but rather a wholesale reflection on the epistemologies and ontologies that dominate the discipline, including some of its critical voices. As Chan indicates in his chapter, there is no singular voice named "other" that we may include or add to our discipline or our emancipatory projects—just as there is no epistemology that does not at the same time reflect a dominant ontology.

Chan's concerns are reflected throughout *Women, Culture, and International Relations.* We have moved beyond the coherent subject of Cartesian thought and any view of a singular category named "woman" or even feminism. In so doing, we have reflected on the implications of such a move for feminist international relations, and our reflections are certainly not confined to readings in the discipline but move beyond its confines in a bid to move the debate forward—not just for feminist international relations but for the discipline of IR as a whole.

This collection of essays articulates what may be called a second-generation agenda for feminist international relations. The challenge to the feminist project as praxis relates to how we may incorporate difference in our attempts to reconceptualize politics and feminism's historical concern with freedom from oppression and exploitation. The ontological challenge to feminism is that we could no longer adopt an essentialist category "woman" as the defining baseline of theory and praxis. If woman is made, and if she is made differently according to the contingent cultural matrices that surround her, the practical imperative is to recognize both gender oppression and the axes of power that contextualize such oppression in the particular societies in which women and/or feminists engage with the political.

We may therefore ask whither emancipation when the resisting subject and external liberator are questioned. The capitulation of the essential subject of feminism does not herald the death of dissent but opens out a multiplicity of creative possibilities emancipated from the limits of confined significations. Engaging with difference through the problematization of subjectivity does not have to threaten moments of collectivity across issues and cultures but must unmask an assumed sameness as a partial expression of solidarity, empathy, and unity. The implication, finally, is that the homogenizing effects of rhetorical globalizing pretensions must be countered through the effects of the personal and local struggles that create relations international.

NOTES

1. Bleiker, "Forget IR Theory."
2. Ibid., p. 58.
3. Linklater, "The Question of the Next Stage in International Relations Theory."
4. Linklater, *The Transformation of Political Community*, p. 56.
5. Huntington, *The Clash of Civilizations*. See Chan's critique of Huntington in Chan, "Too Neat and Under-thought a World Order."
6. Fukuyama, *The End of History and the Last Man*.
7. de Beauvoir, *The Second Sex*, p. 301.
8. Fraser, in *Justice Interruptus*, p. 176. Fraser provides a useful account of the trajectory of feminist thought on the question of difference. See pp. 173–188 of *Justice Interruptus*.
9. See Daly, *Gyn/Ecology;* and Rich, *Of Woman Born*.
10. See Harding, *The Science Question in Feminism*.
11. Gilligan, *In a Different Voice*.
12. See Jabri, "Textualising the Self."
13. Neufeld, *The Restructuring of International Relations Theory*.

Bibliography

Agarwal, Bina. "Gender, Resistance, and Land: Interlinked Struggles over Resources and Meanings in South Asia," *Journal of Peasant Studies* 22, no. 1 (1994): 81–125.

Alcoff, L. "Cultural Feminism Versus Post-Structuralism," in N. Tuana and R. Tong, eds., *Feminism and Philosophy: Essential Readings in Theory, Reinterpretation, and Application.* Boulder: Westview Press, 1995.

Alexander, M. J., and C. T. Mohanty, eds. *Feminist Genealogies, Colonial Legacies, Democratic Futures.* London: Routledge, 1997.

Alker, Hayward R., Jr., Thomas J. Biersteker, and Takashi Inoguchi, "From Imperial Power Balancing to People's Wars," in J. Der Derian and M. J. Shapiro, eds., *International/Intertextual Relations.* New York: Lexington Books, 1989.

Allen, W. *Without Feathers.* London: Sphere Books, 1978.

Araki, M. "Women's Clubs, Associations, and Other Relations in Southern Zambia: Interactions Between Development Interventions and People's Own Strategies." Ph.D. diss., University of East Anglia, 1997.

Archer, Michael, Guy Brett, and Catherine de Zegher, *Mona Hatoum* (London: Phaidon Press, 1997).

Arendt, Hannah. *The Human Condition.* Chicago: University of Chicago Press, 1968.

———. *On Violence.* London: Penguin, 1970.

———. "Thinking and Moral Considerations," *Social Research*, Fiftieth Anniversary Issue (spring/summer, 1984): 7–37.

Barry, Andrew, Thomas Osborne, and Nikolas Rose, eds. *Foucault and Political Reason: Liberalism, Neo-Liberalism, and Rationalities of Government.* London: UCL Press, 1996.

Beall, Jo, Shireen Hassim, and Alison Todes. "'A Bit on the Side'? Gender Struggles in the Politics of Transformation in South Africa," *Feminist Review* 33 (autumn 1989).

Benhabib, Seyla. *Critique, Norm, and Utopia.* New York: Columbia University Press, 1986.

———. *The Reluctant Modernism of Hannah Arendt.* Thousand Oaks, Calif.: Sage, 1996.

———. *Situating the Self: Gender, Community, and Postmodernism in Contemporary Ethics.* Cambridge: Polity Press, 1992.

189

Benhabib, Seyla, and Fred Dallmyr, eds. *The Communicative Ethics Controversy.* Cambridge: MIT Press, 1990.

Benjamin, Walter. *Selected Writings: Vol. 1, 1913–1926,* edited by Marcus P. Bullock and Michael W. Jennings. Cambridge, Mass.: Belknap Press, 1996.

Bennett, Olivia, Jo Bexley, and Kitty Warnock, eds. *Arms to Fight, Arms to Protect: Women Speak Out About Conflict.* London: Panos, 1995.

Bhabha, Homi K. "Culture's In-Between," in S. Hall, and P. du Gay, eds., *Questions of Cultural Identity.* London: Sage, 1996.

———. *The Location of Culture.* London: Routledge, 1994.

Bleiker, Roland. "Forget IR Theory," *Alternatives* 22, no. 1 (1997): 57–86.

Brown, Chris. *International Relations Theory: New Normative Approaches.* London: Harvester Wheatsheaf, 1992.

Brownmiller, Susan. *Against Our Will: Men, Women, and Rape.* New York: Bantam, 1976.

Bubeck, Diemut. *Care, Gender, and Justice.* Oxford: Clarendon Press, 1995.

Burchell, Graham, Colin Gordon, and Peter Miller, eds. *The Foucault Effect: Studies in Governmentality.* London: Harvester Wheatsheaf, 1991.

Burguieres, Mary. "Feminist Approaches to Peace: Another Step for Peace Studies," *Millennium* 19, no. 1 (1990): 1–18.

Butler, Judith. "Contingent Foundations: Feminism and the Question of 'Postmodernism,'" in S. Benhabib, J. Butler, D. Cornell, and N. Fraser, *Feminist Contentions,* with an introduction by L. Nicholson. London: Routledge, 1995.

———. "For a Careful Reading," in S. Benhabib, J. Butler, D. Cornell, and N. Fraser, *Feminist Contentions,* with an introduction by L. Nicholson. London: Routledge, 1995.

———. *Gender Trouble: Feminism and the Subversion of Identity.* London: Routledge, 1990.

Campbell, David, and Michael Dillon. *The Political Subject of Violence.* Manchester: Manchester University Press, 1993.

Cardinal, Marie. *In Other Words,* trans. Amy Cooper. London: Women's Press, 1996.

———. *The Words to Say It.* London: Women's Press, 1993.

Chan, Stephen. "Cultural and Linguistic Reductionism and a New Historical Sociology for International Relations," *Millennium* 22, no. 3 (1993): 423–442.

———. *Kaunda and Southern Africa: Image and Reality in Foreign Policy.* London: I. B. Tauris, 1992.

———. "Too Neat and Under-thought a World Order: Huntington and Civilisations," *Millennium* 26, no. 1 (1997): 137–140.

Cixous, Hélène. "The Laugh of the Medusa," in Robyn R. Warhol and Diane Price Herndl, eds., *Feminisms: An Anthology of Literary Theory and Criticism.* New Brunswick, N.J.: Rutgers University Press, 1991.

Cohn, Carol. "Sex and Death in the Rational World of Defense Intellectuals," in M. Malson et al., eds., *Feminist Theory in Practice and Process.* Chicago: University of Chicago Press, 1989, 107–138.

Connell, R. W. *Masculinities.* Los Angeles: University of California Press, 1995.

Coppola, Francis Ford. *Apocalypse Now.* Columbia-MEI-Warner, 1979.

Daly, M. *Gyn/Ecology.* Boston: Beacon, 1978.

Dasgupta, Partha. *An Inquiry into Well-Being and Destitution.* Oxford: Clarendon Press, 1993.

Davidson, A. "Ethics as Ascetics: Foucault, the History of Ethics, and Ancient

Thought," in G. Gutting, ed., *The Cambridge Companion to Foucault.* Cambridge: Cambridge University Press, 1994.

Davis, John. *Libyan Politics: Tribe and Revolution—An Account of the Zuwaya and Their Government.* London: I. B. Tauris, 1987.

de Beauvoir, Simone. *The Second Sex,* trans. E. M. Parshley. New York: Vintage, 1973.

Deleuze, Gilles, and Felix Guattari. *Anti-Oedipus: Capitalism and Schizophrenia,* trans. Richard Hurley et al. New York: Viking Press, 1977.

Der Derian, James. "A Reinterpretation of Realism: Genealogy, semiology, dromology," in Der Derian, ed., *International Theory: Critical Investigations.* London: Macmillan, 1995.

———. "The Value of Security: Hobbes, Nietzsche, and Baudrillard," in D. Campbell and M. Dillon, eds., *The Political Subject of Violence.* Manchester: Manchester University Press, 1993.

Derrida, Jacques. *Spurs: Nietzsche's Styles.* London: University of Chicago Press, 1979.

Diamond, Irene, and Lee Quinby, eds. *Feminism and Foucault: Reflections in Resistance.* Boston: Northeastern University Press, 1988.

Donzelot, Jacques. *The Policing of Families,* translated from the French by Robert Hurley. London: Hutchinson, 1980.

Duby, G., and M. Perot, eds. *A History of Women,* 5 vols. London: Belknap Press, 1993.

Elshtain, Jean Bethke. *Women and War.* Chicago: University of Chicago Press, 1995.

Elson, D. "Male Bias in Macroeconomics: The Case of Structural Adjustment," in Elson, ed., *Male Bias in the Development Process.* Manchester: Manchester University Press, 1991.

Enloe, Cynthia. *Bananas, Beaches, and Bases in Making Feminist Sense of International Politics.* London: Pandora Press, 1989.

———. *Does Khaki Become You? The Militarization of Women's Lives,* 2d ed. London: Pandora Press, 1988.

Escobar, Arturo. *The Making and Unmaking of the Third World.* Princeton: Princeton University Press, 1995.

Fish, Stanley. *Doing What Comes Naturally.* Durham: Duke University Press, 1989.

———. "What Makes an Interpretation Acceptable?" in R. B. Goodman, ed., *Pragmatism: A Contemporary Reader.* London: Routledge, 1995.

Foucault, Michel. "Afterword: The Subject and Power," in Hubert L. Dreyfus and Paul Rabinow, *Michel Foucault: Beyond Structuralism and Hermeneutics.* Hemel Hempstead: Harvester Press, 1982.

———. *The Care of the Self.* Harmondsworth: Penguin, 1988.

———. *The History of Sexuality: An Introduction,* trans. R. Hurley. Harmondsworth: Penguin, 1978.

———. "Introduction" to *Herculin Barbin: Being the Recently Discovered Memoirs of a Nineteenth Century French Hermaphrodite.* New York: Pantheon, 1980.

———. *Language, Counter-Memory, Practice: Selected Essays and Interviews,* trans. Donald F. Bouchard and Sherry Simon. Ithaca: Cornell University Press, 1977.

———. "Nietzsche, Genealogy, History," in Paul Rabinow, ed., *The Foucault Reader.* London: Penguin, 1984.

———. *Power/Knowledge: Selected Interviews and Other Writings 1972–1977,* ed. Colin Gordon. Hemel Hempstead: Harvester Wheatsheaf, 1980.

————. "Practicing Criticism," in Lawrence Kritzman, ed., *Michel Foucault: Politics, Philosophy, Culture—Interviews and Other Writings 1977–1984.* London: Routledge, 1988.

————. *The Use of Pleasure.* Harmondsworth: Penguin, 1987.

————. "What Is Enlightenment?" in Paul Rabinow, ed., *The Foucault Reader.* London: Penguin, 1984.

Frankenberg, Ruth. *White Women, Race Matters: The Social Construction of Whiteness.* Minneapolis: University of Minnesota Press, 1993.

Fraser, Nancy. "From Irony to Prophecy to Politics: A Response to Richard Rorty," in R. B. Goodman, ed., *Pragmatism: A Contemporary Reader.* London: Routledge, 1995.

————. *Justice Interruptus: Critical Reflections on the "Postsocialist" Condition.* London: Routledge, 1997.

————. "Pragmatism, Feminism, and the Linguistic Turn," in S. Benhabib, J. Butler, D. Cornell, and N. Fraser, *Feminist Contentions*, with an introduction by L. Nicholson. London: Routledge, 1995.

————. *Unruly Practices: Power, Discourse, and Gender in Contemporary Social Theory.* Oxford: Polity Press, 1989.

Fraser, Nancy, and Linda Gordon. "A Genealogy of Dependency: Tracing a Keyword of the Welfare State," in P. James, ed., *Critical Politics.* Melbourne: Arena, 1994.

Fraser, Nancy, and Linda Nicholson. "Social Criticism Without Philosophy: An Encounter Between Feminism and Postmodernism," *Theory, Culture, and Society* 5 (1988): 373–394.

Frye, Marilyn. *The Politics of Reality: Essays in Feminist Theory.* Freedom, Calif.: Crossing Press, 1983.

Fukuyama, Francis. *The End of History and the Last Man.* London: Hamish Hamilton, 1992.

Giddens, Anthony. *Central Problems in Social Theory.* London: Macmillan, 1979.

————. *The Constitution of Society.* Cambridge: Polity Press, 1984.

————. *Modernity and Self-Identity: Self and Society in the Late Modern Age.* Cambridge: Polity Press, 1991.

Gilligan, Carol. *In a Different Voice: Psychological Theory and Women's Development.* Cambridge: Harvard University Press, 1982.

Goddard, Hugh. *Christians and Muslims.* Richmond: Curzon Press, 1995.

Goetz, Anne-Marie. "Feminism and the Claim to Know: Contradictions in Feminist Approaches to Women in Development," in Rebecca Grant and Kathleen Newland, eds., *Gender and International Relations.* Milton Keynes: Open University Press, 1991.

————. "Local Heroes: Patterns of Field Worker Discretion in Implementing GAD Policy in Bangladesh." Discussion Paper no. 358 IDS (Institute of Development Studies), 1996.

————. "The Politics of Integrating Gender to State Development Processes: Trends, Opportunities, and Constraints in Bangladesh, Chile, Jamaica, Mali, Morocco, and Uganda." Occasional Paper no. 2, UNRISD (United Nations Research Institute for Social Development), 1995.

Grant, Rebecca, and Kathleen Newland, eds. *Gender and International Relations.* Milton Keynes: Open University Press, 1991.

Gunew, Sneja, ed. *A Reader in Feminist Knowledge.* London: Routledge, 1991.

Habermas, Jürgen. "Discourse Ethics: Notes on a Program of Philosophical Justification," in Seyla Benhabib and Fred Dallmyr, eds., *The Communicative Ethics Controversy.* Cambridge: MIT Press, 1990, 60–110.

Hacking, Ian. *The Emergence of Probability.* Cambridge: Cambridge University Press, 1975.

———. "Five Parables," in R. Rorty, J. B. Schneewind, and Q. Skinner, eds., *Philosophy in History.* Cambridge: Cambridge University Press, 1984.

———. "How Should We Do the History of Statistics?" in G. Burchell, C. Gordon, and P. Miller, eds., *The Foucault Effect: Studies in Governmentality.* Hemel Hempstead: Harvester Wheatsheaf, 1991.

———. "Language, Truth, and Reason," in M. Hollis and S. Lukes, eds., *Rationality and Relativism.* Oxford: Blackwell, 1982.

———. *Rewriting the Soul: Multiple Personality and the Sciences of Memory.* Princeton: Princeton University Press, 1995.

———. *The Taming of Chance.* Cambridge: Cambridge Unversity Press, 1991.

Hall, S. "Introduction: Who Needs Identity?" in S. Hall and P. du Gay, eds., *Questions of Cultural Identity.* London: Sage, 1996.

Halliday, Fred. *Rethinking International Relations.* London: Macmillan, 1994.

Harasym, Sarah, ed. *The Postcolonial Critic.* New York: Routledge, 1990.

Harding, Sandra. *Feminism and Methodology.* Bloomington: Indiana University Press, 1987.

———. *The Science Question in Feminism.* Ithaca: Cornell University Press, 1986.

Harris, Adrienne, and Ynestra King. *Rocking the Ship of State: Towards a Feminist Peace Politics.* Boulder: Westview Press, 1989.

Hartsock, Nancy. "The Feminist Standpoint: Developing the Ground for a Specifically Feminist Historical Materialism," in S. Harding, ed., *Feminism and Methodology.* Milton Keynes: Open University Press, 1987, 157–180.

———. "Foucault on Power: A Theory for Women?" in Linda J. Nicholson, ed., *Feminism/Postmodernism.* New York: Routledge, 1990.

Hearn, Jeff, and David H. J. Morgan, eds. *Man, Masculinities, and Social Theory.* London: Unwin Hyman, 1990.

Heckman, Susan. *Moral Voices Moral Selves.* Cambridge: Polity Press, 1995.

Higgins, Nicholas. "Lessons from the Indigenous: Zapatista Rebellion and the Transcendence of the Locale." *Millennium,* 1999.

———. "Non-governmental Organisations and the Politics of Complex Humanitarian Emergencies," in H. Smith, ed., *New Thinking in International Relations.* University of Kent: Kent Papers in Politics and International Relations, 1996.

———. "A Question of Style: The Politics and Ethics of Cultural Conversation in Rorty and Connolly," *Global Society* 10, no. 1 (1996): 25–42.

Higgott, Richard, and J. L. Richardson, eds. *International Relations: Global and Australian Perspectives on an Evolving Discipline.* Canberra: Australian National University, 1991.

Hirsch, Marianne, and Evelyn Fox-Keller, eds. *Conflicts in Feminism.* New York: Routledge, 1990.

Holmes, Robert. *On War and Morality.* Princeton: Princeton University Press, 1989.

Horkheimer, M., and T. Adorno. *Dialectic of Enlightenment.* New York: Herder and Herder, 1972.

Howard, Rhoda. *Human Rights and the Search for Community.* Boulder: Westview Press, 1995.

Hoy, D. C., ed. *Foucault: A Critical Reader.* Oxford: Blackwell, 1986.

Huntington, Samuel P. *The Clash of Civilizations and the Remaking of World Order.* New York: Simon and Schuster, 1996.

———. "The Clash of Civilizations: A Response," *Millennium* 26, no. 1 (1997): 141–142.

Hurley, Susan. *Natural Resources.* Oxford: Oxford University Press, 1989.

Hutchings, Kimberly. "Foucault and International Relations Theory," in Moya Lloyd and Andrew Thacker, eds., *The Impact of Michel Foucault on the Social Sciences and Humanities.* Basingstoke: Macmillan, 1997.

———. *Kant, Critique, and Politics.* London: Routledge, 1996.

Isaksson, Eva, ed. *Women and the Military System.* London: Harvester Wheatsheaf, 1988.

Jaar, Alfredo, "Two or Three Things I Imagine About Them," Lower, Upper, and New Galleries, February 14–March 29, 1992, Whitechapel, London.

Jabri, Vivienne. *Discourses on Violence.* Manchester: Manchester University Press, 1996.

———. "Restyling the Subject of Responsibility in International Relations," *Millennium* 27, no. 1 (1998): 591–612.

———. "Textualising the Self: Moral Agency in Inter-Cultural Discourse," *Global Society: Journal of Interdisciplinary International Relations* 10, no. 1 (1996): 57–68.

Jaggar, A. "Feminist Ethics: Some Issues for the Ninetees," *Journal of Social Philosophy* 20 (1989): 91–107.

Kandiyoti, D. "Bargaining with Patriarchy," *Feminist Studies* 2 (1988): 274–290.

Kriger, Norma J. *Zimbabwe's Liberation War: Peasant Voices.* Cambridge: Cambridge University Press, 1992.

Lan, David. *Guns and Rain: Guerrillas and Spirit Mediums in Zimbabwe.* London: James Currey, 1985.

Landry, Donna, and Gerald Maclean, eds. *The Spivak Reader.* London: Routledge, 1996.

Larrabee, Mary, ed. *An Ethic of Care.* New York: Routledge, 1993.

Linklater, Andrew. *Men and Citizens in the Theory of International Relations.* London: Macmillan, 1990.

———. "The Question of the Next Stage in International Relations Theory: A Critical-Theoretical Point of View," *Millennium* 21, no. 1 (1992): 77–98.

———. *The Transformation of Political Community.* Cambridge: Polity Press, 1998.

Lukes, Stephen. *Power: A Radical View.* London: Macmillan, 1974.

Macdonald, Sharon. "Drawing the Lines—Gender, Peace, and War: An Introduction," in Macdonald, Pat Holden, and Shirley Ardener, eds., *Images of Women in Peace and War: Cross-Cultural and Historical Perspectives.* London: Macmillan, 1987.

Macdonald, Sharon, Pat Holden, and Shirley Ardener, eds. *Images of Women in Peace and War: Cross-Cultural and Historical Perspectives.* London: Macmillan, 1987.

MacIntyre, A. *After Virtue: A Study in Moral Theory.* London: Duckworth, 1981.

MacKinnon, Catherine. *Feminism Unmodified: Discourses on Life and Law.* Cambridge: Harvard University Press, 1987.

Mandaville, Peter G. "Reimagining the Umma: Translocal Space and the Changing Boundaries of Muslim Political Community." Ph.D. diss., University of Kent, 1999.

Mani, Lata. "Contentious Traditions: The Debate on *Sati* in Colonial India," in Kumkum Sangari and Vaid Sudesh, eds., *Recasting Women: Essays in Indian Colonial History.* India: Kali for Women, 1989; New Brunswick, N.J.: Rutgers University Press, 1990.

Marchand, Marianne, and Jane Parpart, eds. *Feminism/Postmodernism/ Development.* London: Routledge, 1995.

Martin, Biddy. "Feminism, Criticism, and Foucault," in Irene Diamond and Lee Quinby, eds., *Feminism and Foucault: Reflections on Resistance.* Boston: Northeastern University Press, 1988.

Mazrui, Ali. *Cultural Forces in World Politics.* London: James Currey, 1990.

McCarthy, F. "The Target Group: Women in Rural Bangladesh," in E. Clay and B. Schaffer, eds., *Room for Manoeuvre.* London: Heinemann, 1984.

Mies, M., and V. Shiva. *Ecofeminism.* London: Zed Books, 1990.

Millett, Kate. *The Loony Bin Trip.* London: Virago Press, 1991.

———. *Sexual Politics.* London: Virago Press, 1970.

Mohanty, Chandra. "Feminist Encounters: Locating the Politics of Experience," in Linda Nicholson and Steven Seidman, eds., *Social Postmodernism: Beyond Identity Politics.* Cambridge: Cambridge University Press, 1995.

———. "Under Western Eyes: Feminist Scholarship and Colonial Discourses," *Feminist Review* 30 (autumn 1988): 61–88.

Mohanty, Chandra, Ann Russo, and Lourdes Torres, eds. *Third World Women and the Politics of Feminism.* Bloomington: Indiana University Press, 1991.

Molyneux, M. "Mobilization Without Emancipation: Women's Interests, the State, and Revolution in Nicaragua," *Feminist Studies* 11, no. 2 (1985).

Moore, Henrietta L. *A Passion for Difference: Essays in Anthropology.* Cambridge: Polity Press, 1994.

Morgan, S., and F. Morris. *Rites of Passage: Art for the End of the Century.* London: Tate Gallery Publications, 1995.

Morris, John N. *Versions of the Self: Studies in English Autobiography from John Bunyan to Stuart Mill.* New York: Basic Books, 1966.

Morriss, M. "Values as an Obstacle to Economic Growth in South Asia: An Historical Survey," *Journal of Economic History* 27, no. 4 (December 1967).

Moser, C. "Gender Planning in the Third World: Meeting Practical and Strategic Gender Needs," *World Development* 17, no. 11 (1989).

Mouffe, C., ed., *Deconstruction and Pragmatism.* London: Routledge, 1996.

Nardin, Terry, and David Mapel, eds. *Traditions of International Ethics.* Cambridge: Cambridge University Press, 1992.

Neufeld, Mark A. *The Restructuring of International Relations Theory.* Cambridge: Cambridge University Press, 1995.

Nicholson, Linda, ed. *Feminism/Postmodernism.* New York and London: Routledge, 1990.

Nicholson, Michael. *Rationality and the Analysis of International Conflict.* Cambridge: Cambridge University Press, 1992.

Nietzsche, Friedrich. *Beyond Good and Evil.* London: Penguin, 1990 [1886].

———. *Untimely Meditations,* trans. R. J. Hollingdale. Cambridge: Cambridge University Press, 1983.

Nussbaum, Martha C. *The Fragility of Goodness: Luck and Ethics in Greek Tragedy and Philosophy.* Cambridge: Cambridge University Press, 1986.

Okin, Susan Moller. *Justice, Gender, and the Family.* New York: Basic Books, 1989.

O'Neill, Onora. "Transnational Justice," in D. Held, ed., *Political Theory Today.* Cambridge: Polity Press, 1991, 276–304.

Parpart, Jane, and Kathleen Staudt, eds. *Women and the State in Africa.* Boulder: Lynne Rienner, 1989.

Parry, Benita. "Overlapping Territories and Intertwined Histories: Edward Said's Postcolonial Cosmopolitanism," in M. Sprinker, ed., *Edward Said: A Critical Reader.* Oxford: Blackwell, 1992.

———. "Problems in Current Theories of Colonial Discourse," in Bill Ashcroft, Gareth Griffiths, and Helen Tiffin, eds., *The Postcolonial Studies Reader.* London: Routledge, 1995.

Pelton, Robert D. *The Trickster in West Africa: A Study of Mythic Irony and Sacred Delight.* Berkeley: University of California Press, 1980.

Peterson, V. Spike, and Anne Sisson Runyan. *Global Gender Issues.* Boulder: Westview Press, 1993.

Pettman, Jan Jindy. *Worlding Women: A Feminist International Politics.* London: Routledge, 1996.

Pierson, Ruth Roach. "'Did Your Mother Wear Army Boots?' Feminist Theory and Women's Relation to War, Peace, and Revolution," in Sharon Macdonald, Pat Holden, and Shirley Ardener, eds., *Images of Women in Peace and War: Cross-Cultural and Historical Perspectives.* London: Macmillan, 1987.

Prakash, Gyan. "Subaltern Studies as Postcolonial Criticism," *American Historical Review* 99, no. 4 (1994): 1475–1490.

Rabinow, Paul, ed. *The Foucault Reader.* London: Penguin, 1984.

———. "Representations Are Social Facts: Modernity and Post-modernity in Anthropology," in J. Clifford and G. E. Marcus, eds., *Writing Culture: The Poetics and Politics of Ethnography.* London: University of California Press, 1986.

Rajan, Rajeswari Sunder. *Real and Imagined Women.* London: Routledge, 1994.

Ranger, Terence. *Peasant Consciousness and the Guerrilla War in Zimbabwe.* London: James Currey, 1985.

Rawls, J. *A Theory of Justice.* Oxford: Oxford University Press, 1971.

Renteln, Alison. *International Human Rights: Universalism Versus Relativism.* London: Sage, 1990.

Rich, Adrienne. *Of Woman Born.* New York: Bantam, 1977.

———. *On Lies, Secrets, and Silence: Selected Prose 1966–1978.* London: Norton, 1979.

Ridd, Rosemary, and Helen Callaway, eds. *Caught Up in Conflict: Women's Responses to Political Strife.* London: Macmillan, 1986.

Riley, Denise. *Am I That Name? Feminism and the Category of Women in History.* London: Macmillan, 1988.

Robbins, Bruce. "The East Is a Career: Edward Said and the Logics of Professionalism," in Michael Sprinker, ed., *Edward Said: A Critical Reader.* Oxford: Blackwell, 1992.

Robinson, F. "Globalizing Care: Ethics, Feminist Theory, and International Relations," *Alternatives* 22 (1997): 113–134.

Rogers, B. *The Domestication of Women.* London: Kogan Page, 1980.

Rorty, Richard. *Consequences of Pragmatism.* Minneapolis: University of Minnesota Press, 1982.

———. *Contingency, Irony, and Solidarity.* Cambridge: Cambridge University Press, 1989.

———. "Does Academic Freedom Have Philosophical Presuppositions?" *Academe* 80, no. 6 (1994): 52–63.

———. "The End of Leninism and History as a Comic Frame," in A. M. Melzer, J.

Weinberger, and M. R. Zinman, eds., *History and the Idea of Progress.* London: Cornell University Press, 1995.

———. *Essays on Heidegger and Others.* Cambridge: Cambridge University Press, 1991.

———. "Feminism and Pragmatism," in R. B. Goodman, ed., *Pragmatism: A Contemporary Reader.* London: Routledge, 1995.

———. "Human Rights, Rationality, and Sentimentality," in S. Shute and S. Hurley, eds., *On Human Rights: The Oxford Amnesty Lectures 1993.* New York: Basic Books, 1993, 111–134.

———."Movements and Campaigns," *Dissent* (winter 1995).

———. *Objectivity, Relativism, and Truth.* Cambridge: Cambridge University Press, 1991.

———. "Two Cheers for the Cultural Left," *South Atlantic Quarterly* 89 (1990): 227–234.

Rose, Nickolas. "Assembling the Modern Self," in R. Porter, ed., *Rewriting the Self: Histories from the Renaissance to the Present.* London: Routledge, 1997.

———. *Governing the Soul: The Shaping of the Private Self.* London: Routledge, 1990.

———. *Inventing Ourselves: Psychology, Power, and Personhood.* Cambridge: Cambridge University Press, 1996.

———. *The Psychological Complex: Psychology, Politics, and Society in England 1869–1939.* London: Routledge, 1985.

———. "Towards a Critical Sociology of Freedom," Inaugural Lecture delivered May 5, 1992 at Goldsmith's College. London: University of London, Goldsmith's College, 1993.

Ruddick, Sarah. *Maternal Thinking: Towards a Politics of Peace.* London: Women's Press, 1990.

Said, Edward W. *Orientalism.* Harmondsworth: Penguin, 1985.

———. *Representations of the Intellectual: The 1993 Reith Lectures.* London: Vintage, 1994.

Sandel, M. *Liberalism and the Limits of Justice.* Cambridge: Cambridge University Press, 1982.

Sarkar, T. "Nationalist Iconography: Images of Women in Nineteenth Century Bengali Literature," *Economic and Political Weekly* 22, no. 47 (1987).

Sawicki, Jana. *Disciplining Foucault: Feminism, Power, and the Body.* New York: Routledge, 1991.

———. "Foucault, Feminism, and Questions of Identity," in Gary Gutting, ed., *The Cambridge Companion to Foucault.* Cambridge: Cambridge University Press, 1994.

Scott, James C. *Weapons of the Weak: Everyday Forms of Peasant Resistance.* New Haven: Yale University Press, 1985.

Scott, Joan Wallach. "The Evidence of Experience," in Terrence J. McDonald, ed., *The Historic Turn in the Human Sciences.* Ann Arbor: University of Michigan Press, 1996.

Scott, Leda. "Women and the Armed Struggle for Independence in Zimbabwe (1964–1979)." Occasional Paper no. 25, Edinburgh University, Centre for African Studies, 1990.

Seidman, Gay W. "Women in Zimbabwe: Postindependence Struggles," *Feminist Studies* 10, no. 3 (1984): 419–440.

Sellars, Wilfred. *Science, Perception, and Reality.* London: Routledge and Kegan Paul, 1963.

Seung, T. K. *Structuralism and Hermeneutics.* New York: Columbia University Press, 1986.

Sharma, U. *Women's Work, Class, and the Urban Household.* London: Tavistock, 1985.

Sherif, F. *A Guide to the Contents of the Qur'an.* London: Ithaca Press, 1985.

Singer, Peter. "Famine, Affluence, and Morality," in C. Beitz et al., eds., *International Ethics.* Princeton: Princeton University Press, 1985.

Skinner, Q. "Meaning and Understanding in the History of Ideas," *History and Theory* 8 (1969): 3–53.

———. "Reply to My Critics," in J. Tully, ed., *Meaning and Context.* Oxford: Polity Press, 1988.

Smith, Steve, Ken Booth, and Marysia Zalewski, eds. *International Theory: Positivism and Beyond.* Cambridge: Cambridge University Press, 1996.

Sontag, Susan. *Styles of Radical Will.* London: Vintage, 1994.

Spivak, Gayatri C. "Can the Subaltern Speak?" in Cary Nelson and Lawrence Grossberg, eds., *Marxism and the Interpretation of Culture.* London: Macmillan, 1988.

———. *In Other Worlds: Essays in Cultural Politics.* London: Routledge, 1988.

———. *Outside in the Teaching Machine.* New York: Routledge, 1993.

———. "Teaching for the Times," in Jan Nederveen Peiterse and Bhikhu Parekh, eds., *The Decolonization of Imagination: Culture, Knowledge, and Power.* London: Zed Books, 1995.

———. "Three Women's Texts and a Critique of Imperialism," in Henry Louis Gates Jr., ed., *"Race," Writing, and Difference.* Chicago: University of Chicago Press, 1985, 1986.

Steans, Jill. *Gender and International Relations: An Introduction.* Cambridge: Polity Press, 1998.

Stiehm, Judith Hicks. "The Effect of Myths About Military Women on the Waging of War," in Eva Isaksson, ed., *Women and the Military System.* London: Harvester Wheatsheaf, 1988.

Sylvester, Christine. *Feminist Theory and International Relations in a Postmodern Era.* Cambridge: Cambridge University Press, 1994.

———. "Some Dangers in Merging Feminist and Peace Projects," *Alternatives* 12 (1987): 493–509.

———. *Zimbabwe: The Terrain of Contradictory Development.* Boulder: Westview Press, 1991.

Tampere Peace Research Institute. *Towards a Multicultural Roshamon Paradigm in International Relations.* Tampere, Finland: Tampere Peace Research Institute, 1996.

Thacker, Andrew. "Foucault and the Writing of History," in Moya Lloyd and Andrew Thacker, eds., *The Impact of Michel Foucault on the Social Sciences and Humanities.* Basingstoke: Macmillan, 1997.

Trainspotting. 1995. Polygram and Noel Gay Motion Picture Company, after a novel by Irvine Welsh.

Tronto, Joan. *Moral Boundaries: A Political Argument for an Ethic of Care.* New York: Routledge, 1993.

———. "Women's Morality: Beyond Gender Differences to a Theory of Care," *Signs* 12 (1987): 644–663.

Venn, C. "Beyond Enlightenment? After the Subject of Foucault, Who Comes?" *Theory, Culture, and Society* 14, no. 3 (1997): 1–28.

Virilio, Paul. *War and Cinema: The Logistics of Perception,* trans. Patrick Camiller. London: Verso, 1989.

Walker, R. B. J. *Inside/Outside: International Relations as Political Theory.* Cambridge: Cambridge University Press, 1993.

Walzer, Michael. *Just and Unjust Wars,* 2d ed. New York: Basic Books, 1992.

———. *Spheres of Justice: A Defence of Pluralism and Equality.* Oxford: Blackwell, 1985.

Warren, Karen, and Duane Cady, eds. *Hypatia Special Issue: Feminism and Peace* 9, no. 2 (1994).

Webb, Keith. *An Introduction to Problems in the Philosophy of Social Sciences.* London: Pinter, 1995.

White, S. C. *Arguing with the Crocodile: Gender and Class in Bangladesh.* London: Zed Books, 1992.

———. "Men, Masculinities, and the Politics of Development," *Gender and Development* 5, no. 2 (1997).

Whitehead, A. "'I'm Hungry, Mum': The Politics of Domestic Budgeting," in K. Young et al., eds., *Of Marriage and the Market: Women's Subordination Internationally and Its Lessons.* London: Routledge and Kegan Paul, 1984.

Wood, G., ed. *Labelling in Development Policy.* London: Sage, 1985.

Young, Robert. *White Mythologies: Writing History and the West.* London: Routledge, 1990.

Zalewski, Marysia, and Jane L. Parpart, eds. *The 'Man' Question in International Relations.* Boulder: Westview Press, 1997.

The Contributors

Vivienne Jabri is senior lecturer in international relations and director of the University of Kent's London Centre of International Relations. She is author of *Discourses on Violence* and *Mediating Conflict,* and coeditor (with Stephen Chan) of *Mediation in Southern Africa.* She is currently writing a book on constructions of self and normative theory in international relations.

Eleanor O'Gorman, based at the University of Cambridge, completed a Ph.D. on gender, resistance, and Zimbabwe's liberation struggle in 1999. She previously lectured in politics and development at the School of Development Studies, University of East Anglia. Her primary research interests include feminist theory in international relations, conflict studies, and development.

Stephen Chan is dean of the Faculty of Humanities and professor of international relations and ethics at the Nottingham Trent University. He has published a wide range of works on Southern Africa, including *Kaunda and Southern Africa: Image and Reality in Foreign Policy* and *Exporting Apartheid: Foreign Policies in Southern Africa.* Among his publications on culture and international theory is *Towards a Multicultural Roshamon Paradigm in International Relations.* His poetry collections include *Crimson Rain.*

Nicholas Higgins, a Leverhulme research fellow, is currently completing his Ph.D. at the University of Kent at Canterbury; his thesis topic is "The Subject of Conflict: Mayan Indians and the Modern Mexican State." His publications include "A Question of Style: The Politics and Ethics of Cultural Conversation in Rorty and Connolly" and "Mexico's Mayan Conflict: The Zapatista Uprising and the Poetics of Cultural Resistance."

Kimberly Hutchings is senior lecturer in politics at the University of Edinburgh. She has published a range of work on normative international theory and feminist philosophy and is the author of *Kant, Critique, and Politics.* She is currently working on a book on normative international theory and one on Hegel and feminist philosophy.

Nalini Persram is lecturer in politics at Trinity College, Dublin. She is currently working on a comparative study of immigration policy and colonial ideology in France, Britain, and the Netherlands with respect to political culture, gender, "race," and the Guianese community in Europe. She has published in the areas of feminist theory, Caribbean nationalist identity and politics, and postcolonial subjectivity and is coeditor, with Jenny Edkins and Veronique Pin-Fat, of *Sovereignty and Subjectivity.*

Sarah C. White is lecturer in development studies at the University of East Anglia. Her main writings reflect on gender and class in rural Bangladesh, the nongovernmental sector in Bangladesh, the significance of masculinities for gender and development, and the connections between theology and development. She is author of *Arguing with the Crocodile: Gender and Class in Bangladesh* and coauthor, with Romy Tiongco, of *Doing Theology and Development: Meeting the Challenge of Poverty.* She is currently writing a book on gender, race, and development.

Index

About the Book

This book expands the agenda of feminist IR by considering the heterogeneity of women's voices in the realm of world politics, as well as the challenges that this diversity poses.

The authors develop a theoretical discourse that incorporates the combined notions of difference and emancipation in a discussion of the agency of women and their transformative capacity. They use a normative approach to understanding the multiple subjectivities of women and the plurality of their experiences.